Careers in
Human Services

Careers in
Human Services

Editor
Michael Shally-Jensen, Ph.D.

SALEM PRESS
A Division of EBSCO Information Services, Inc.
Ipswich, Massachusetts

GREY HOUSE PUBLISHING

Publisher's Cataloging-In-Publication Data
(Prepared by The Donohue Group, Inc.)

Careers in human services / editor, Michael Shally-Jensen, Ph.D. --
  [First edition].

   pages : illustrations ; cm. -- (Careers in--)

   Edition statement supplied by publisher.
   Includes bibliographical references and index.
   ISBN: 978-1-61925-778-8 (hardcover)

   1. Human services--Vocational guidance--United States. 2. Allied health personnel--
Vocational guidance--United States. I. Shally-Jensen, Michael.

HV10.5 .C375 2015
361/.0023/73

First Printing

PRINTED IN THE UNITED STATES OF AMERICA

CONTENTS

PUBLISHER'S NOTE

Careers in Human Services contains twenty-five alphabetically arranged chapters describing specific fields of interest in this broad industry segment. Merging scholarship with occupational development, this single comprehensive guidebook provides human services students with the necessary insight into potential careers, and provides instruction on what job seekers can expect in terms of training, advancement, earnings, job prospects, working conditions, relevant associations, and more. *Careers in Human Services* is specifically designed for a high school and undergraduate audience and is edited to align with secondary or high school curriculum standards.

Scope of Coverage

Understanding the wide net of jobs in human services is important for anyone preparing for a career within them. *Careers in Human Services* comprises twenty-five lengthy chapters on a broad range of occupations including traditional and long-established jobs such as Elementary School Teacher and Social Worker, as well as in-demand jobs like Employment Specialist, Rehabilitation Counselor, and Art Therapist. This excellent reference also presents possible career paths and high-growth and emerging occupations within this field.

Careers in Human Services is enhanced with numerous charts and tables, including projections from the US Bureau of Labor Statistics, and median annual salaries or wages for those occupations profiled. Each chapter also notes those skills that can be applied across broad occupation categories. Interesting enhancements, like **Fun Facts**, **Famous Firsts**, and dozens of photos, add depth to the discussion. A highlight of each chapter is **Conversation With** – a two-page interview with a professional working in a related job. The respondents share their personal career paths, detail potential for career advancement, offer advice for students, and include a "try this" for those interested in embarking on a career in their profession.

Essay Length and Format

Each chapter ranges in length from 3,500 to 4,500 words and begins with a Snapshot of the occupation that includes career clusters, interests, earnings and employment outlook. This is followed by these major categories:

- **Overview** includes detailed discussions on: Sphere of Work; Work Environment; Occupation Interest; A Day in the Life. Also included here is a Profile that outlines working conditions, educational needs, and physical abilities. You will also find the occupation's Holland Interest Score, which matches up character and personality traits with specific jobs.

- **Occupational Specialties** lists specific jobs that are related in some way, like Health Information Technician and Library Technician, and Career & Technical Education Teacher and Vocational Rehabilitation Counselor. Duties and Responsibilities are also included.

- **Work Environment** details the physical, human, and technological environment of the occupation profiled.

- **Education, Training, and Advancement** outlines how to prepare for this field while in high school, and what college courses to take, including licenses and certifications needed. A section is devoted to the Adult Job Seeker, and there is a list of skills and abilities needed to succeed in the job profiled.

- **Earnings and Advancements** offers specific salary ranges, and includes a chart of metropolitan areas that have the highest concentration of the profession.

- **Employment and Outlook** discusses employment trends, and projects growth to 2020. This section also lists related occupations.

- **Selected Schools** list those prominent learning institutions that offer specific courses in the profiled occupations.

- **More Information** includes associations that the reader can contact for more information.

Special Features

Several features continue to distinguish this reference series from other career-oriented reference works. The back matter includes:
- Appendix A: Guide to Holland Code. This discusses John Holland's theory that people and work environments can be classified into six different groups: Realistic; Investigative; Artistic; Social; Enterprising; and Conventional. See if the job you want is right for you!
- Appendix B: General Bibliography. This is a collection of suggested readings, organized into major categories.
- Subject Index: Includes people, concepts, technologies, terms, principles, and all specific occupations discussed in the occupational profile chapters.

Acknowledgments

Special mention is made of editor Michael Shally-Jensen, who played a principal role in shaping this work with current, comprehensive, and valuable material. Thanks are due to Allison Blake, who took the lead in developing "Conversations With," with help from Vanessa Parks, and to the professionals who communicated their work experience through interview questionnaires. Their frank and honest responses provide immeasurable value to *Careers in Human Services*. The contributions of all are gratefully acknowledged.

EDITOR'S INTRODUCTION

An Overview

The human services professions, also known as community and social services, are for people who have a strong desire to help support and improve other people's lives. Careers in human services appeal to persons with a keen interest in making life easier and more fulfilling for those in need. Workers in this field usually are good listeners/communicators and enjoy interacting with others. They provide their constituents with vital services, such as social support, healthcare assistance, child and family services, training and education, employment assistance, food and housing assistance, mental health services, occupational and rehabilitative counseling, and much more. Excluding schools and hospitals, the human services field provides about 5 million workers with employment, making it one of the main service industries in the U.S. economy.

Working in Human Services

Human services provide a direct, applied approach to supporting positive human development, both individually and within communities. People with an interest in helping individuals access needed resources or helping to foster healthy families and communities by providing an environment in which all can learn and grow, will be attracted to human services work. Positions in this field can be "hands-on," as in the case of social work and therapeutic services, or they can involve more in the way of planning, organizing, and disseminating information.

Human service workers assist a diverse population of clients, people of every age with a broad range of issues. Often, clients are living with more than one problem and therefore may fall into more than one client population—for example, a veteran with a mental condition may also have a problem with substance abuse. In general, however, there are a few key populations served by human services workers.

Children and families. Human service workers ensure that children live in safe homes and have their basic needs met. Services provided might include assisting parents with applications for food stamps or affordable housing and locating reliable childcare.

In some cases, such as those involving physical abuse or domestic violence, human service workers might recommend that children be removed from their parents' home and placed in foster care or a group home. Such removal may be temporary or permanent; the goal is to work with parents toward improving the situation so that children can return home. If a return to parental custody is not possible, human service workers try to find permanent homes and adoptive parents for the children.

The elderly. Human service workers who assist older clients help them to live independently in their own homes or in assisted-living facilities. This might mean coordinating the delivery of prepared meals to the home or the placement of personal care aides to help with daily living activities.

For older clients who are unable to live alone, human service workers help with their placement in residential care facilities, including nursing homes. For clients nearing the end of their lives, human service workers may coordinate the provision of hospice care.

People with disabilities. In working with people who have disabilities, human service workers often focus on helping clients to live independently. Types of assistance include finding rehabilitation services to allow clients to adapt to the disability, working with employers on establishing positions that may be filled by clients with disabilities, and referring clients to personal care services that can help with daily living activities.

For people with disabilities who cannot live independently, human service workers help locate suitable residential care facilities.

People with mental illnesses. Human service workers strive to help clients who have mental conditions to access appropriate resources, such as self-help and support groups. In addition, they help clients with severe mental illness to become self-sufficient and receive proper care. Human service workers refer clients to providers of personal care services, group housing, or residential care facilities.

People with addictions. Human service workers assist people who are struggling with various types of addiction, including to alcohol or gambling. They evaluate clients' needs and direct clients to the appropriate rehabilitation facilities, including both inpatient and outpatient treatment centers. They also refer clients to groups or programs that help clients get support outside of treatment. Some human service workers might work with families of addicts, helping family members understand the nature of addiction and referring them to support programs for families.

People with criminal records. People who have been imprisoned face challenges in re-entering society, such as adjusting to normal conditions and overcoming the stigma of their criminal record. Human service workers help these clients integrate back into society by matching them with job opportunities or training programs, helping them find housing, and directing them to support programs aimed at preventing a return to crime.

Immigrants. Immigrants often need help adjusting to life in a new country. Human service workers help them find housing, jobs, and other resources, such as programs for learning English. In some cases, human service workers also refer clients to legal aid services to assist immigrants with paperwork and other administrative issues.

The homeless. Human service workers help people who are homeless to meet basic needs. They may refer clients to a variety of providers, such as temporary or permanent housing facilities, organizations that serve meals, and job centers that can assist the clients in finding jobs or learning new skills. Some clients might need guidance in finding treatment to address an underlying cause of their homelessness (such as drug dependency).

Veterans. Adjusting to civilian life after military service, especially combat service, can be difficult. Human service workers assist veterans in a variety of ways: by finding housing, by applying skills gained in the military to civilian jobs, and by navigating through the extensive network of veteran services available.

Combat veterans often face other challenges, such as adapting to physical or mental disability. Human service workers direct veterans with disabilities to services that provide appropriate assistance.

Types of Human Service Organizations

Human service agencies are often managed by state or local governments. There is also a large number of nonprofit—and some for-profit—human service organizations. Some organizations focus on working with a particular population or alleviating a specific type of problem. Others work with a wide range of populations and issues.

Employment agencies provide clients with the assistance necessary to find and keep jobs. Employment agencies include job placement agencies and vocational rehabilitation services for people with disabilities.

Food and nutrition agencies help clients get healthy meals or learn the skills necessary to prepare nutritious meals themselves. Food delivery programs and food banks are common services.

Housing and shelter organizations help clients find appropriate temporary or permanent housing. Organizations include senior housing facilities, homeless shelters, and transitional housing.

Legal and victims assistance organizations assist people who have been victims of crime. These organizations also provide information to educate the public about crime prevention, and they help rehabilitate people who have been convicted of crimes. Examples include abuse prevention programs, juvenile justice organizations, and prisoner rehabilitation programs.

Multipurpose human service organizations provide multiple services that help clients improve their situation. Among these organizations are senior citizen centers, foster care and adoption agencies, and women's shelters.

Public safety and disaster relief organizations help people prepare for and recover from disasters. Examples include disaster relief and search-and-rescue organizations.

Youth development organizations provide recreational and social programs for children and teenagers. Among these are Big Brothers/Big Sisters, Boys & Girls Clubs, and after school programs.

xii Careers in Human Services

Education and Training

There has been a shift in recent years away from large institutions and centralized control to more community-based settings and localized control. This has given workers new challenges and new opportunities. Workers must know how to work with clients and families to tie together a vast array of community resources, specialized assistance, and personal supports to promote well-being, empowerment, and community participation. Workers require training in the latest frameworks and skill sets to understand and adapt to changes currently shaping the field.

The education level and experience needed by human services workers varies by occupation. Taking part in volunteer work and helping to provide community services are valuable ways in which to establish community support and social networks. Many employers prefer human service assistants with some related work experience or college courses in human services, such as social work, multiculturalism, or one of the social or behavioral sciences. Other employers prefer an associate's degree or a bachelor's degree in human services or social work. A number of employers provide in-service training, such as seminars and workshops. For most professional jobs, a college degree is required for entry level positions. A master's degree is widely recommended, but not always required, for a variety of professional positions in the human services.

Conclusion

Human service work is both rewarding and challenging. Like most careers, the suitability of workers for these jobs varies by individual. Most human service workers build relationships with their clients out of concern and a desire to help, aware that clients do not always express their gratitude. Human service workers help clients improve their lives, and it can be satisfying to see results over time. These results are often dramatic and show how much people can accomplish when they receive professional assistance.

As the U.S. population grows, so too will the demand for the kinds of help that human service agencies provide. The financial resources available to these organizations, however, generally do not grow as quickly as the demand for services, thus increasing competition among agencies seeking funds from the same donors. (Much of a human service organization's budget is based on highly unpredictable charitable donations.) Human service workers are often asked to provide additional services without being offered additional income. Some workers find the resulting stress hard to manage.

Few human service workers pursue these careers solely for the income, however. Workers cite a passion for the field, noting that human service jobs provide opportunities to help people in need and to find solutions to community problems. In that respect, the job is its own satisfaction.

Sources

Burger, William E. *Human Services in Contemporary America.* Belmont, CA: Brooks/Cole, 2013.

Cousins, Linwood H., ed. *Encyclopedia of Human Services and Diversity.* Los Angeles: SAGE, 2014.

Moffat, Colleen Teixeira. *Helping Those in Need: Human Services Workers.* Washington, DC: Bureau of Labor Statistics, 2011.

Social Welfare History Project. http://www.socialwelfarehistory.org/

—M. Shally-Jensen, Ph.D.

Activities Therapist

Snapshot

Career Cluster: Health Care; Human Services

Interests: Patient rehabilitation, therapeutic programs and services, special needs services, teaching/leading activities, social work

Earnings (Yearly Average): $41,775

Employment & Outlook: Average Growth Expected

OVERVIEW

Sphere of Work

Activities therapists provide creative therapeutic services and treatments aimed at helping their patients improve their emotional and mental well-being, gain independence, improve self-expression, build new skills, and develop self-confidence. They develop and implement medically approved therapies and programs to meet the needs, abilities, and interests of patients with mental and physical illnesses or disabilities. The range of therapies used by activities therapists during rehabilitation or treatment is wide and includes art therapy, music therapy, dance therapy, recreational therapy, horticultural

or nature therapy, sports therapy, religious therapy, social therapy, and manual arts therapy.

Work Environment

Activities therapists work in medical settings that include psychiatric facilities, hospitals, and substance abuse facilities, as well as community and institutional settings, such as schools, prisons, and retirement facilities. In medical environments, activities therapists generally partner with medical and social service professionals, such as doctors and social workers, to increase a patient's confidence, skill set, and mood or outlook. In community and institutional settings, activities therapists partner with educational and therapeutic professionals, such as teachers, special education coordinators, and recreational therapists, to meet students' or patients' therapeutic needs.

Profile

Working Conditions: Work Indoors
Physical Strength: Light to Medium Work
Education Needs: Bachelor's Degree, Master's Degree
Licensure/Certification: Recommended
Physical Abilities Not Required: No Heavy Labor
Opportunities For Experience: Internship, Volunteer Work, Part-Time Work
Holland Interest Score*: SEI

* See Appendix A

Occupation Interest

Individuals attracted to the field of activities therapy tend to be physically strong and energetic people who people who have the ability to teach and lead a variety of activities. They exhibit traits such as imagination, problem solving, desire to help, patience, sense of humor, and caring. Activities therapists must be able to work as part of a team of therapy professionals to meet patient needs.

A Day in the Life—Duties and Responsibilities

The daily occupational duties and responsibilities of activities therapists will be determined by the individual's area of job specialization and work environment. Areas of activities therapy job specialization include art therapy, music therapy, dance therapy, recreational therapy, sports therapy, religious therapy, social therapy, horticultural or nature therapy, and manual arts therapy. Activities therapists encourage their patients to make more frequent use of available resources, build on existing but overlooked skills, and try new activities.

In general, activities therapists should be prepared to greet patients as they arrive for therapeutic activities. Activities therapists interact with patients throughout the day in a friendly and supportive manner and conduct patient assessments so that they can record the needs, interests, and abilities of patients. As they monitor patients' symptoms, reactions, and progress through the assessments, activities therapists constantly revise patient treatment plans and implement treatment through activities, therapy sessions, and workshops. Examples of group activities include arts and crafts, nature-oriented activities such as gardening, and performing arts activities, as well as personal hygiene and self-care instruction and individual and small group community integration exercises such as bus riding practice and restaurant ordering.

In addition to patient interaction, activities therapists are often required to meet with patient treatment teams, physicians, or patient families and describe patient progress in therapeutic activities. This occupation includes supervising and scheduling tasks such as supervising therapeutic staff and volunteers, preparing therapeutic materials and equipment, and overseeing the safety, upkeep, and maintenance of therapeutic equipment and facilities. Activities therapists schedule therapeutic program events such as nature studies, recreational sports leagues, dances, adapted team sports, and classes.

Duties and Responsibilities

- **Conferring with a patient's physician and rehabilitation team**
- **Planning the rehabilitation program and instructing the patient in the performance of specific activities**
- **Revising activity programs based on an evaluation of patient's progress**
- **Preparing reports describing patient's reactions and symptoms**

OCCUPATION SPECIALTIES

Horticultural Therapists

Horticultural Therapists plan, coordinate and conduct therapeutic gardening programs to facilitate the rehabilitation of physically and mentally handicapped patients. They conduct gardening sessions and revise the programs to conform and grow with the progress of the patients.

Art Therapists

Art Therapists plan and direct activities that help mentally ill and physically disabled patients use art for nonverbal expression and communication.

Music Therapists

Music Therapists plan, organize and direct instrumental and vocal music activities and experiences to help patients with communication, social, daily living or problem solving skills.

Dance Therapists

Dance Therapists plan, organize and lead dance and body movement activities to improve patients' mental outlook and physical well-being.

Manual-Arts Therapists

Manual-Arts Therapists plan and organize woodworking, photography, metalworking, agriculture, electricity and graphic arts activities in collaboration with a rehabilitation team and prepare reports that show development of patient work tolerance, emotional and social development and ability to meet physical and mental demands of employment.

WORK ENVIRONMENT

Physical Environment

Activities therapists work in rehabilitation facilities, hospitals, nursing homes, therapy clinics, and schools. Therapeutic office settings used by activities therapists may be shared with other therapeutic professionals, including recreational, physical, occupational, or speech and language therapists.

Relevant Skills and Abilities

Communication Skills
- Persuading others
- Speaking effectively
- Writing concisely

Interpersonal/Social Skills
- Being patient
- Being sensitive to others
- Cooperating with others
- Providing support to others
- Working as a member of a team

Organization & Management Skills
- Coordinating tasks
- Making decisions
- Managing people/groups
- Performing duties that change frequently

Research & Planning Skills
- Creating ideas
- Developing evaluation strategies
- Using logical reasoning

Human Environment

Activities therapists interact with a wide variety of people and should be comfortable providing therapeutic services to those with physical, mental, and emotional illnesses and special needs. Activities therapists usually work as part of a patient treatment team, which includes patient families, social workers, teachers, doctors, and additional therapists. As a member of a treatment team, activities therapists participate in frequent team meetings and are responsible for communicating patient progress to fellow team members.

Technological Environment

Activities therapists use a wide range of technology and equipment in their work, including telecommunication tools, word processing software, and computer applications such as spreadsheets. Equipment used by activities therapists during therapy sessions may include musical instruments, sports equipment, art supplies, and adaptive technology such as wheelchairs and pool lifts.

EDUCATION, TRAINING, AND ADVANCEMENT

High School/Secondary

High school students interested in pursuing the profession of activities therapist should develop good study habits. High school courses in the arts, physical education, psychology, anatomy, and sociology will prepare students for collegiate studies. Students interested in the activities therapy field will benefit from seeking internships or part-time work in therapeutic programs or with people with mental and physical special needs.

Suggested High School Subjects
- Arts
- Child Growth & Development
- College Preparatory
- Crafts
- English
- Health Science Technology
- Instrumental & Vocal Music
- Metals Technology
- Ornamental Horticulture
- Photography
- Physical Education
- Physiology
- Pottery
- Psychology
- Social Studies
- Sociology
- Theatre & Drama
- Woodshop

Famous First

Susan E. Tracy, considered the first occupational therapist, served as the director of the Training School for Nurses at the Adams Nervine Asylum in Boston, pictured here. In 1906 Tracy set up the first training course in activities therapy to prepare students for teaching patient activities. She advised that variety in activity choices was key in order to match individual patient interests and therapeutic goals.

College/Postsecondary

Postsecondary students interested in pursuing training in activities therapy should complete coursework in their preferred specialization (i.e. art therapy, music therapy, dance therapy, recreational therapy, horticultural or nature therapy, or manual arts therapy), as well as courses on counseling, physical education and therapy, special education, abnormal psychology, ethics, anatomy, physiology, and assistive technology. Postsecondary students interested in attending graduate school will benefit from seeking internships or work in therapeutic programs or with people with mental or physical special needs. Membership in the American Therapeutic Recreation Association (ATRA) may provide networking opportunities and connections. Prior to graduating, college students interested in joining the activities therapy profession should apply to graduate school in their preferred therapeutic specialization or secure related work such as therapy assistant or special education assistant.

Related College Majors
- Art Therapy
- Dance Therapy
- Music Therapy
- Occupational Therapy

Adult Job Seekers

Adult job seekers in the activities therapy field have generally completed bachelor's- or master's-level training in art therapy, music therapy, dance therapy, recreational therapy, or occupational therapy from an accredited university, as well as earned necessary professional certification. Activities therapists seeking employment will benefit from the networking opportunities, career workshops, and job lists offered by professional therapy associations such as the ATRA.

Professional Certification and Licensure

Some states regulate activities therapists by requiring specified education and experience for certification to practice. Those who meet the requirements can qualify for certification by the professional association representing their area of specialization. Requirements usually entail either a bachelor's or a master's degree in the area of specialization, a written examination and an internship of at least 480 hours. Attendance and participation in professional conferences and workshops is common in order to enhance efficiency and knowledge in the field.

Additional Requirements

Individuals who find satisfaction, success, and job security as activities therapists will be knowledgeable about the profession's requirements, responsibilities, and opportunities. Successful activities therapists engage in ongoing professional development and find satisfaction from working as collaborative members of interdisciplinary teams devoted to improving the health and well-being of patients. Because individuals in this profession work with emotionally or physically vulnerable people and have access to personal patient information, they must strive to maintain high ethical and professional standards. Membership in professional therapy associations is encouraged among all types of activities therapists as a means of building status within the professional community and networking.

EARNINGS AND ADVANCEMENT

Salaries of activities therapists vary according to the type and size of employer, educational background, work experience, professional registration and region of the country. Median annual earnings of activities therapists were $41,775 in 2013. The lowest ten percent earned less than $26,118, and the highest ten percent earned more than $66,430.

Activities therapists may receive paid vacations, holidays and sick days; life and health insurance; and retirement benefits. These are usually paid by the employer.

Metropolitan Areas with the Highest Employment Level in this Occupation

Metropolitan area	Employment [1]	Employment per thousand jobs	Hourly mean wage
New York-White Plains-Wayne, NY-NJ	980	0.19	$25.67
Philadelphia, PA	580	0.32	$21.61
Chicago-Joliet-Naperville, IL	560	0.15	$21.94
Boston-Cambridge-Quincy, MA	510	0.29	$18.60
Nassau-Suffolk, NY	380	0.31	$23.94
Los Angeles-Long Beach-Glendale, CA	340	0.09	$30.24
Atlanta-Sandy Springs-Marietta, GA	320	0.14	$19.87
Washington-Arlington-Alexandria, DC-VA-MD-WV	300	0.13	$23.55
Warren-Troy-Farmington Hills, MI	260	0.23	$24.54
St. Louis, MO-IL	230	0.18	$20.05

[1]Does not include self-employed. Source: Bureau of Labor Statistics

EMPLOYMENT AND OUTLOOK

There were about 20,000 recreational therapists, of which activities therapists are a part, employed nationally in 2012. About two-thirds worked in nursing care facilities and hospitals. The remainder worked in residential facilities, community mental health centers, adult day care programs, correctional facilities, community programs for people with disabilities, and substance abuse centers.

Employment of activities therapists is expected to grow about as fast as the average for all occupations through the year 2022, which means employment is projected to increase 10 percent to 15 percent. In nursing care facilities, employment will grow slightly faster than the occupation as a whole as the number of older adults continues to grow. Employment is expected to slow, however, in hospitals as services shift to outpatient settings and employers try to contain costs.

Employment Trend, Projected 2010–20

Health Diagnosing and Treating Practitioners: 20%

Activities Therapists: 13%

Total, All Occupations: 11%

Note: "All Occupations" includes all occupations in the U.S. Economy. Source: U.S. Bureau of Labor Statistics, Employment Projections Program

Related Occupations
- Art Therapist
- Music Therapist
- Occupational Therapist
- Physical Therapist
- Recreational Therapist

Conversation With . . .
ANTHONY F. VICARI

Certified Alzheimer's Disease and Dementia Care
Trainer, Activity Therapist/Director of Activities
8 years, Las Vegas, NV

1. What was your individual career path in terms of education/training, entry-level job, or other significant opportunity?

I went to the University of Buffalo and earned bachelor degrees in music performance and music education, then started as a school teacher in music. I went on to earn a master's in administration and an education specialist degree in curriculum and instruction. This is a degree above the master's degree that enabled me to specialize in language arts and mathematics. I worked in all aspects of private and public education for 27 years and retired as an elementary school principal at an early age. I couldn't sit home, so I volunteered at a skilled nursing home by starting a book club for the elders. The home's administrator came to me and said, "You're still young; I want you to be part of our team." One thing led to another, and I got my Activity Director Certification from the National Certification Council of Activity Professionals (NCCAP). I was an activity professional and led programming for all the elders, and was specifically assigned to work with ventilator patients. I then went into administration and was Director of Residential Living for a continuous care retirement community. I supervised all the activity directors in our independent, assisted and skilled nursing communities. My last job was at a behavioral health/psychiatric hospital as an Activity Therapist working with patients who suffered from manic depression, schizophrenia, bipolar disorder, or had major or manic depression. This past month, I retired from full-time work as an Activity Therapist to start my own education training service teaching health care professionals skills and strategies for working with dementia patients. I view this as a natural extension of my Activity Therapy work because it's so important to understand these patients and help them lead the best lives possible.

I am certified with two Activity Professional organizations and hold a Certified Alzheimer's Disease and Dementia Care Trainer certification with the National Certification Council of Dementia Practitioners.

2. What are the most important skills and/or qualities for someone in your profession?

First, you must have a servant's heart. Second, someone who is going into this field needs to know that it's not lucrative. You also need to be a good conversationalist, ready to talk – but primarily listen. Really, that's what this person you are serving in a nursing home or hospital wants. In this field, the focus is not you anymore. It's that person you are serving.

The activity therapist works from the side of recreational leisure to enhance a patient's quality of life, so it's also important to be creative. For instance, I developed a great writing program for my psychiatric patients where I read different poems about anger, depression, or feeling overwhelmed. We discussed them as a group and how they related to their futures. Then I added photographs, and we wrote about our feelings through the photographs. It was wonderful how these patients expressed themselves through writing, and helped themselves feel better.

3. What do you wish you had known going into this profession?

I wish I had known more about patient behaviors. When someone moves into a long term care facility, there's a lot of "giving up" of personal things. Many of these people are angry, frustrated, lonely, and bored. You might think they are attacking you. They're not attacking you. You must have a lot of empathy and good working strategies and skills to help these people retain their dignity.

4. Are there many job opportunities in your profession? In what specific areas?

Yes! Entry-level positions are called activity assistants. Here is Las Vegas, employers are always looking for help in areas including skilled nursing, adult day services, memory care programs and independent/assisted living. Once someone has that experience and continues learning and gains national certification, the good ones get promoted to director positions.

5. How do you see your profession changing in the next five years, what role will technology play in those changes, and what skills will be required?

Everything is computer-based: all reports, treatment plans, or patient care plans, which is a planned and orchestrated program for an individual based on an initial assessment. An activity professional needs to network and become part of national organizations such as the National Association of Activities Professionals, which holds annual conferences that are vital for professional growth and provide the required continuing education hours for re-certification.

6. What do you enjoy most about your job? What do you enjoy least about your job?

Bringing joy to someone else's life — seeing that smile or receiving a note of appreciation — those are the things that meant the most to me.

The paperwork was definitely the least enjoyable but it's critical. Everything is documented.

7. Can you suggest a valuable "try this" for students considering a career in your profession?

Absolutely volunteer in the community. Do that in high school. If one wants to do this work, it's very worthy and full of dignity and respect.

SELECTED SCHOOLS

Many colleges and universities have bachelor's degree programs in recreational therapy or related subjects. The student may also gain an initial grounding at a technical or community college. Consult with your school guidance counselor or research post-secondary programs in your area. The online Therapeutic Recreation Directory (see below) contains a listing of accredited schools and programs.

MORE INFORMATION

American Art Therapy Association
225 North Fairfax Street
Alexandria, VA 22314-1574
888.290.0878
www.arttherapy.org

American Dance Therapy Association
10632 Little Patuxent Parkway
Suite 108
Columbia, MD 21044-3263
410.997.4040
www.adta.org

American Music Therapy Association
8455 Colesville Road, Suite 1000
Silver Spring, MD 20910
301.589.3300
www.musictherapy.org

National Center on Physical Activity and Disability
1640 W. Roosevelt Road
Chicago, IL 60608-6904
800.900.8086
www.ncpad.org

National Council for Therapeutic Recreation Certification
7 Elmwood Drive
New City, NY 10956
845.639.1439
www.nctrc.org

Therapeutic Recreation Directory
www.recreationtherapy.com

Simone Isadora Flynn/Editor

Art Therapist

Snapshot

Career Cluster: Health Care; Human Services

Interests: Art, creative thinking, encouraging others to express themselves

Earnings (Yearly Average): $41,775

Employment & Outlook: Average Growth Expected

OVERVIEW

Sphere of Work

An art therapist is a recreational therapist who specializes in the use of art in conjunction with psychotherapy to help treat a variety of psychological, physical, and emotional issues. Most art therapists have a background in art or are art enthusiasts who take satisfaction in helping people (or are trained caregivers). They believe in the value of painting, drawing, sculpture, and other artistic activities to alleviate pain and stress, aid in the recovery of a mental illness or trauma, or otherwise help people lead more fulfilling lives.

Work Environment

Art therapists work in offices or treatment/therapy rooms in a variety of medical and mental health institutions. They also work in counseling centers at schools, recreational rooms in prisons, senior citizen centers, domestic violence shelters, and other locations where therapeutic services are rendered or required. They interact mostly with patients or clients, and may also collaborate regularly with other therapists and health care professionals, as well as social workers or teachers. Most therapists work during regular daytime hours, although evenings and weekends may be part of their schedules, based on client needs.

Profile

Working Conditions: Work Inside
Physical Strength: Light Work
Education Needs: Bachelor's Degree
Licensure/Certification:
   Recommended
Physical Abilities Not Required: No
   Heavy Labor
Opportunities For Experience:
   Volunteer Work, Part-Time Work
Holland Interest Score*: ESI

* See Appendix A

Occupation Interest

Art therapists must be passionate about helping people and comfortable around those with special needs. They need to be creative and imaginative thinkers to apply their knowledge and skills to specific cases. While a high level of artistic ability is valued, it is not necessary. More importantly, the therapist needs to be able to encourage others to be expressive and believe deeply in the importance of art in healing and personal growth. Other necessary qualities include patience, empathy, and excellent communication skills.

A Day in the Life—Duties and Responsibilities

Art therapists work with individuals by appointment or with groups of patients in regularly scheduled workshops or sessions. A mental health organization might offer an art class every day or once a week that is attended by a select group of patients. An art therapist may also arrange to meet with patients individually in his or her office or studio. They may specialize in the needs of a targeted population, such as children, the elderly, or the terminally ill, or those with emotional or mental health concerns.

Art therapists are not art teachers, although in some situations they do work on developing artistic skills and techniques; rather, they are more concerned with the process of creativity and their patients' ability to express themselves. Some of their projects may require little artistic prowess beyond the ability to scribble or cut and paste.

The art therapist's first task is to assess the needs of the patient and devise a treatment program. In many cases, an art therapist receives patients by referral and is provided with a relevant diagnosis and set of goals to use as a springboard. He or she then selects activities that work towards fulfilling those treatment goals. For example, to treat depression, an art therapist might have a patient draw or paint about events that are deeply seeded in the unconscious. Similarly, an art therapist might arrange for children who have been traumatized by war to make paper dolls to help lessen their fear, or guide a group of teenagers with low self-esteem as they collaborate on a quilt or mural.

As the treatment unfolds, the art therapist observes behavior, analyzes the work, evaluates the progress being made, and prepares reports to share with other therapists or doctors. The therapist also maintains supplies and tools and makes purchases when necessary. Some therapists also do their own billing and other paperwork.

Duties and Responsibilities

- Providing art supplies to patients
- Helping patients express their feelings through art
- Counseling patients

WORK ENVIRONMENT

Physical Environment

Art therapists work in a variety of settings, including hospitals, mental health facilities, rehabilitation centers, prisons, senior citizen centers, and schools. Art therapists mostly use non-toxic materials that do not pose a health hazard, although they may work occasionally with a ventilation system. They also select tools and equipment with the safety of patients in mind.

Relevant Skills and Abilities

Creative/Artistic Skills
- Being skilled in art, music or dance

Interpersonal/Social Skills
- Being able to remain calm
- Being sensitive to others
- Cooperating with others
- Providing support to others
- Teaching others
- Working as a member of a team

Organization & Management Skills
- Coordinating tasks
- Demonstrating leadership
- Making decisions
- Managing people/groups
- Meeting goals and deadlines
- Paying attention to and handling details
- Performing duties that change frequently

Research & Planning Skills
- Creating ideas

Human Environment

Art therapy requires strong interpersonal and collaboration skills. A therapist must be able to work one-on-one and with a group of patients. If on a team of professionals, which is often the case, the therapist communicates regularly with doctors, psychologists, teachers, recreation leaders, or other staff. Most report directly to a supervisor and may be responsible for assistants or part-time employees.

Technological Environment

Art therapists use computer technology for many different applications, including projects with their patients. Art tools and media are dependent on projects, but could include a sewing machine, pottery wheel, woodworking tools, or a dry mounting press and printer for photography. Standard office equipment is also used.

EDUCATION, TRAINING, AND ADVANCEMENT

High School/Secondary

A college preparatory program supplemented with art courses and psychology will provide the best foundation for postsecondary studies. Other courses that develop the imagination, such as music, theatre, or creative writing, can be useful as well. Also important are extracurricular activities and volunteer work in the arts or with people with special needs.

Suggested High School Subjects
- Arts
- Child Care
- Child Growth & Development
- Crafts
- English
- Graphic Communications
- Health Science Technology
- Humanities
- Photography
- Pottery
- Psychology
- Sociology

Famous First

The first art therapist to receive a Fulbright Award for her work in the field was Frances E. Anderson. One of the founders of the American Art Therapy Association in 1969, Anderson is a researcher, professor, and practitioner who has influenced a number of key areas, including work with victims of trauma. One organization she has worked with is Communities Healing through Art, or CHART, which assists persons living in areas affected by natural disasters and other crises.

College/Postsecondary

A bachelor's degree in therapeutic recreation is the minimum requirement for state licensing. Coursework may include the arts, psychology, research methods, human development, theories of therapy, assessment and evaluation, therapeutic techniques, and ethics. An undergraduate internship or practicum provides the necessary clinical experience for licensure.

Graduate degrees in art therapy can be helpful for career development. A master's degree in art therapy or a similar program is required for certification as a Registered Art Therapist (ATR). Most professional positions require the certification. In most cases, a doctorate or several years of experience is necessary for advancement. Often, advancement can result in more creative freedom and teaching opportunities, or the ability to move into a supervisory position or private practice.

Related College Majors
- Art Therapy

Adult Job Seekers

Counselors, social workers, and others in related occupations with a master's degree or higher can obtain certification after completion of a one-year postgraduate art therapy program. Many artists also find that art therapy is the next logical step in their careers. Scholarships and night classes can make the transition easier for those with jobs or other responsibilities. Membership in a professional art therapy association can provide additional networking and job finding opportunities for adult job seekers.

Professional Certification and Licensure

Of the states that license art therapists, designations include Licensed Professional Art Therapist (LPAT) and Licensed Creative Arts Therapist (LCAT), while others classify them as recreational therapists, mental health counselors, or other related occupations. Requirements vary widely. Prospective art therapists should check the licensure requirements of their home state.

Certifications are available from professional art therapy organizations, such as the American Art Therapy Association and National Council for Therapeutic Recreation Certification. The American Art Therapy Association offers three levels of credentials

Registered Art Therapist (ATR), for those who have met educational requirements and postgraduate clinical experience; Registered Art Therapist-Board Certified (ATR-BC), for those with the ATR who have passed the national exam; and Art Therapy Certified Supervisor (ATCS), for those who are certified and also have received specific training and skills in supervision. The National Council for Therapeutic Recreation Certification (NCTRC) offers certification for Certified Therapeutic Recreation Specialist (CTRS), for those with a related bachelor's degree and internship experience. Certification renewal usually requires continuing education.

Additional Requirements

Art therapists must maintain patient confidentiality. Certified art therapists must adhere to a code of ethics set forth by the credentialing organization.

Fun Fact

The client may determine the media used in art therapy. For instance, since it takes longer to cover a large surface using oil pastels than paint, clients have more time to discuss their feelings as they create.

Source: http://www.allpsychologycareers.com/topics/art-therapy-techniques.html

EARNINGS AND ADVANCEMENT

Opportunities for advancement are limited. In larger institutions, an art therapist might be promoted to supervise other art therapists or a therapy team, but such positions are difficult to find. Median annual earnings of art therapists were $41,775 in 2012. The lowest ten percent earned less than $26,118, and the highest ten percent earned more than $66,430. Those who work in large institutions or who have more experience are likely to earn more. Art therapists in private practice earn amounts that vary according to the number of people they see.

Art therapists may receive paid vacations, holidays, and sick days; life and health insurance; and retirement benefits. These are usually paid by the employer.

Metropolitan Areas with the Highest Employment Level in this Occupation

Metropolitan area	Employment [1]	Employment per thousand jobs	Hourly mean wage
New York-White Plains-Wayne, NY-NJ	980	0.19	$25.67
Philadelphia, PA	580	0.32	$21.61
Chicago-Joliet-Naperville, IL	560	0.15	$21.94
Boston-Cambridge-Quincy, MA	510	0.29	$18.60
Nassau-Suffolk, NY	380	0.31	$23.94
Los Angeles-Long Beach-Glendale, CA	340	0.09	$30.24
Atlanta-Sandy Springs-Marietta, GA	320	0.14	$19.87
Washington-Arlington-Alexandria, DC-VA-MD-WV	300	0.13	$23.55
Warren-Troy-Farmington Hills, MI	260	0.23	$24.54
St. Louis, MO-IL	230	0.18	$20.05

[1]Does not include self-employ ed. Source: Bureau of Labor Statistics

EMPLOYMENT AND OUTLOOK

Recreational therapists, of which art therapists are a part, held about 20,000 jobs nationally in 2012. Most worked in nursing care facilities, hospitals, residential care facilities, community mental health centers, adult day care programs, correctional facilities, community programs for people with disabilities, substance abuse centers and state and local government agencies.

Employment of art therapists is expected to grow about as fast as the average for all occupations through the year 2022, which means employment is projected to increase 10 percent to 15 percent. This is mostly the result of a growing elderly population having more recreational therapy needs. Art therapy is a relatively new and growing field and there are an increasing number of positions available, especially for graduates who can creatively develop new opportunities for this specialty.

Employment Trend, Projected 2010–20

Health Diagnosing and Treating Practitioners: 20%

Art Therapists: 13%

Total, All Occupations: 11%

Note: "All Occupations" includes all occupations in the U.S. Economy. Source: U.S. Bureau of Labor Statistics, Employment Projections Program

Related Occupations
- Music Therapist
- Occupational Therapist

Conversation With . . .
DONNA BETTS

Professor of Art Therapy
George Washington University, Washington, DC
President of the American Art Therapy Association
Art Therapist, 20 years

1. What was your individual career path in terms of education/training, entry-level job, or other significant opportunity?

I did a lot of art in high school and it helped my growth and development. I got my Bachelor of Fine Arts from the Nova Scotia College of Art and Design University.

I found out about art therapy after I graduated and became really excited because I could combine all of my interests: helping other people; psychology; and art. I thought, "This is it!" I went back to school to complete my prerequisites in psychology so I could go on and get my master's, which is required to enter our field. I earned the degree at The George Washington University, then worked at a school for children and adults with multiple disabilities for four years. However, I wanted to conduct research so I went to Florida State University for my doctorate. There, I established myself as a scholar, more or less the go-to person for art therapy assessments. It took two years to complete my doctorate. I remained in Tallahassee for seven years because I also worked at an eating disorders clinic. I loved working with that population and appreciated the challenge. It inspired me to work harder.

I then returned to GWU where I am a research faculty member and also teach two classes each semester. Right now I am working with a company to help veterans with PTSD (post-traumatic stress disorder). We are in the preliminary stages of a research study that will employ a graphic novel authoring tool — a software program — that will enable clients to re-tell their trauma through narrative and visual format on a computer.

2. What are the most important skills and/or qualities for someone in your profession?

Compassion, good interpersonal skills, solid understanding of psychological theory and practice, and an ability to create artwork and to understand the way different art materials work. Also, an appreciation for the effects of art-making on neurobiological functions. For example, when you express yourself through art materials, you use a nonverbal part of your brain. That's where traumatic memories are stored, and that's why art therapy can be really successful. For instance, when people with PTSD make art, it's easier to deal with traumatic memories, which brings them to a point where they can start to talk about what happened to them.

3. What do you wish you had known going into this profession?

Between my timing — which, like so many things, is often luck — and my contacts, I've been very fortunate. Each career step forward has built upon the last one. I can't say there is anything I wish I'd known in advance.

4. Are there many job opportunities in your profession? In what specific areas?

Job opportunities tend to be in metro areas where there's an awareness of the benefits of art therapy, particularly cities where universities offer art therapy programs. The jobs can be anywhere you'd find mental health practitioners: Veteran's Administration services, psychiatric facilities, hospitals, schools, or private practices. Some therapists go back to their rural hometowns and start their own programs, and those people are pioneers who are creating jobs.

5. How do you see your profession changing in the next five years, what role will technology play in those changes, and what skills will be required?

The American Art Therapy Association is working hard to establish state licenses for art therapists to protect the public through enforcement of standards that restrict practice to qualified professionals. So far, eight states license art therapists, and 27 are taking steps in this direction.

In addition, telehealth is also a hot topic now. Say a patient has psychiatric issues and lives in a remote place with no access to a therapist. Under the telehealth movement, some therapists will Skype, or government entities may back the creation of internet-based tools that enable doing therapy from home. This raises ethical concerns for all mental health practitioners. In art therapy, we face a tech-related dilemma – if you create a drawing on an iPad, is it art therapy? Making art with paint or clay is a different experience than drawing on an iPad. I believe art therapists can successfully offer their clients a choice of traditional media as well as digital options.

6. What do you enjoy most about your job? What do you enjoy least about your job?

It was rewarding to see how art therapy contributed to the recovery of my clients with anorexia. When you see how your work and dedication is helping someone — that is why I went to work every day. The paperwork is the least enjoyable part, but that's true for any job.

7. **Can you suggest a valuable "try this" for students considering a career in your profession?**

When I evaluate master's program applicants now, a strong candidate is someone who has volunteered in some capacity helping others. Ideally, they would volunteer in a setting where they are able to facilitate the use of art, under the guidance of an art therapy supervisor.

SELECTED SCHOOLS

Many colleges and universities have bachelor's degree programs in recreational therapy or related subjects; some offer a focus on art therapy. The student may also gain an initial grounding at a technical or community college. Consult with your school guidance counselor or research post-secondary programs in your area. The online Therapeutic Recreation Directory (see below) contains a listing of accredited schools and programs; and the web site of the American Art Therapy Association (see below) has a list of approved graduate schools.

MORE INFORMATION

American Art Therapy Association
225 North Fairfax Street
Alexandria, VA 22314
888.290.0878
www.arttherapy.org

International Art Therapy Organization (IATO)
info@theiato.org
www.internationalarttherapy.org

National Council for Therapeutic Recreation Certification (NCTRC)
7 Elmwood Drive
New City, NY 10956
845.639.1439
www.nctrc.org

Sally Driscoll/Editor

Career & Technical Education Teacher

Snapshot

Career Cluster: Education & Training; Human Services
Interests: Teaching, working with students, public speaking
Earnings (Yearly Average): $55,120
Employment & Outlook: Average Growth Expected

OVERVIEW

Sphere of Work

Career and technical education teachers teach career-related technical skills to middle and high school students. They also provide education to college-aged students or adults at vocational and technical schools. Career and technical instructors teach courses in a wide variety of fields, including automotive repair, computer science, and the culinary arts. The work of these teachers focuses on specific real-world skills, as opposed to broader theories. Their job is to equip students with practical, hands-on, career-related skills to be used in the field.

Work Environment

Career and technical education teachers work in schools. As many schools are closed in the summer months, many teachers do not work during this period. However, some teachers may work year round. In addition to classroom work, career and technical education instructors spend a significant amount of time working outside of the classroom, preparing lesson plans, grading assignments, and carrying out various administrative tasks.

Profile

Working Conditions: Work Indoors
Physical Strength: Light Work
Education Needs: Junior/Technical/Community College, Bachelor's Degree
Licensure/Certification: Required
Physical Abilities Not Required: No Heavy Labor
Opportunities For Experience: Internship, Military Service, Part-Time Work
Holland Interest Score*: SEC

* See Appendix A

Occupation Interest

Career and technical education teachers must have the patience and desire to impart knowledge to students. Individuals who are interested in entering the field must be willing to work with both adults and students. Many career and technical educators transition to the role after working in fields closely related to the subjects they teach.

A Day in the Life—Duties and Responsibilities

The workday of a career and technical education teacher begins each morning at school, but his or her work begins long before that. Like other teachers, career and technical education teachers prepare lesson plans for their classes, which vary in length, frequency, and format based on the employing institution. Class planning takes up a large portion of an instructor's time.

In addition to preparing lesson plans, instructors must make time to advise students outside of class and grade assignments. Teachers of younger students may also meet regularly with parents. Career and technical courses are designed to be hands on, and instructors must spend time organizing their classrooms or workshops to ensure they are safe and accessible for students. Teachers must also establish rules or guidelines for the use of equipment, machinery, or technology and enforce those rules in class. During free periods, instructors may reorganize their classrooms, meet with students, retool lesson plans, or grade assignments.

The workday of a career and technical teacher typically extends beyond regular school hours. Some teachers may teach classes during the summer months or in the evenings. Additionally, career and technical teachers may attend conferences or other professional-development events and work with other teachers to construct or improve lesson plans.

Duties and Responsibilities

- Developing practical and technical programs of study
- Presenting information and demonstrating skills in a classroom setting
- Testing and evaluating students
- Working with advisory committees from business and industry
- Recruiting participants

WORK ENVIRONMENT

Physical Environment

The physical environment in which career and technical education teachers work varies based on each particular instructor's specialty. A teacher specializing in automotive repair will likely work in a garage-like environment, while an instructor specializing in information technology (IT) will typically work in a computer lab.

Human Environment

Career and technical education teachers interact regularly with students and are responsible for running their classrooms and guiding students through hands-on instruction. They must be aware of their students' safety at all times. Teachers communicate on a regular basis with colleagues and school administrators and may also hold conferences with parents.

Relevant Skills and Abilities

Communication Skills
- Speaking effectively
- Writing concisely

Interpersonal/Social Skills
- Cooperating with others
- Motivating others
- Teaching others
- Working as a member of a team

Organization & Management Skills
- Coordinating tasks
- Managing people/groups
- Paying attention to and handling details

Research & Planning Skills
- Creating ideas
- Developing evaluation strategies

Technological Environment

The technological environment of career and technical education teachers is dependent on the courses they teach. An IT class will rely heavily on computer technology, while a culinary arts or automotive repair class will rely on machine technology, hand tools, and appliances. It is important for teachers to issue specific instructions regarding the proper use of classroom equipment.

EDUCATION, TRAINING, AND ADVANCEMENT

High School/Secondary

Most technical careers require a solid understanding of mathematics and science, and aspiring career and technical education teachers are encouraged to explore coursework in both areas. Decisions regarding course specialization are field dependent. For example, a chef uses principles of chemistry, as do those who work in health and medicine. A mechanic uses principles of physics and engineering, as do those who work in robotics. Individuals interested in teaching should also develop their verbal and written communication skills.

Suggested High School Subjects
- Agricultural Education
- Applied Communication
- Applied Math
- Applied Physics
- Arts
- Building Trades & Carpentry
- Business
- Business & Computer Technology
- Child Growth & Development
- College Preparatory
- Composition
- English
- Family & Consumer Sciences
- First Aid Training
- Health Science Technology
- Industrial Arts
- Literature
- Mathematics
- Psychology
- Science
- Speech
- Trade/Industrial Education

Famous First

The first vocational high school for girls was the Trade School for Girls, opened in Boston in 1904. Subjects taught were sewing, advanced sewing, dressmaking, millinery (hatmaking), costume design, domestic science, and machine operation. The school was racially mixed and, besides providing day classes for fulltime students, offered evening classes for adults. The building used was previously owned by a Catholic diocese, and when the property was purchased by the school the chapel was converted to a gymnasium.

College/Postsecondary

Postsecondary training for most career and technical education teachers is tailored to their respective fields. An aspiring culinary arts instructor will typically study the culinary arts but also take courses in education, while an aspiring automotive repair instructor will learn the trade as well as how to communicate his or her understanding of the trade in a classroom setting. Regardless of specialization, an associate's or bachelor's degree is required for most positions, though some teachers may instead accumulate knowledge and experience through hands-on work in the field.

Related College Majors
- Agricultural Teacher Education
- Bilingual/Bicultural Education
- Business Teacher Education (Vocational)
- Education Administration & Supervision, General
- Elementary/Pre-Elementary/Early Childhood/Kindergarten Education
- Family & Consumer Science Education
- Health Teacher Education
- Marketing Operations Teacher Education (Vocational)
- Secondary/Jr. High/Middle School Teacher Education
- Technology Teacher Education/Industrial Arts Teacher Education
- Trade & Industrial Teacher Education (Vocational)
- Vocational Education Teacher

Adult Job Seekers

The field of career and technical education may be a good fit for adults who have already spent time learning and practicing a trade or skill and would like to pass their knowledge on to students. Many adults who aspire to become career and technical education teachers later in life already have significant training and practical experience, which may make them capable teachers.

Professional Certification and Licensure

Certification and licensure are required for career and technical education teachers, although the specific requirements vary from state to state. Some states require every teacher to hold a bachelor's degree, while others require a number of years of experience followed by a period of supervised student teaching. Organizations such as the National Center for Alternative Certification provide helpful tools for those who lack training in education but have technical skills suited to the field of career and technical education.

Additional Requirements

Career and technical education teachers must be patient with their students and capable of communicating assignments and instructions in a manner easy for students to follow. They must be able to plan detailed lessons but also improvise when students do not understand.

Fun Fact

It used to be known as voke ed and, in some schools, had a separate track that was not academically rigorous. Now it's known as Career & Technical Education, and its students are on the fast track to success. According to the Georgetown University Center on Education and the Workforce, 43 percent of of young workers with this certification earn more than those with an associate degree and 27 percent earn more than those with a bachelor's degree!

Source: www.cte.osceola.k12.fl.us/cte_facts.shtml

EARNINGS AND ADVANCEMENT

Earnings depend on the individual's education, experience, and specialty area, and the type, size, and geographic location of the employer. Career and technical education teachers have lower salaries in rural areas. Advancement into administrative positions in departments of education, colleges and universities and corporate training departments is possible, though such positions may require advanced degrees.

Median annual earnings of career and technical education teachers were $55,120 in 2013. The lowest ten percent earned less than $38,560, and the highest ten percent earned more than $81,680.

Career and technical education teachers may receive paid vacations, holidays, and sick days; life and health insurance; and retirement benefits. These are usually paid by the employer.

Metropolitan Areas with the Highest Employment Level in this Occupation

Metropolitan area	Employment	Employment per thousand jobs	Hourly mean wage
Houston-Sugar Land-Baytown, TX	1,860	0.67	$55,570
Dallas-Plano-Irving, TX	1,700	0.79	$52,420
New York-White Plains-Wayne, NY-NJ	1,370	0.26	$82,800
Charlotte-Gastonia-Rock Hill, NC-SC	1,310	1.50	$49,990
Richmond, VA	1,100	1.81	$58,170
Philadelphia, PA	1,080	0.59	$69,650
Miami-Miami Beach-Kendall, FL	1,010	0.99	$54,540
Washington-Arlington-Alexandria, DC-VA-MD-WV	1,010	0.43	$72,320
Los Angeles-Long Beach-Glendale, CA	990	0.25	$79,510
Atlanta-Sandy Springs-Marietta, GA	880	0.38	$55,990

Source: Bureau of Labor Statistics

EMPLOYMENT AND OUTLOOK

There were approximately 240,000 career and technical education teachers employed nationally in 2012. Employment is expected to grow about as fast as the average for all occupations through the year 2022, which means employment is projected to increase 5 percent to 12 percent. Job growth due to increasing student enrollments will be tempered by more of a focus on traditional academic subjects.

Employment Trend, Projected 2010–20

Vocational Education Teachers, Postsecondary: 12%

Total, All Occupations: 11%

Career/Technical Education Teachers: 9%

Career/Technical Education Teachers, Middle school: 5%

Career/Technical Education Teachers, Secondary School: 5%

Note: "All Occupations" includes all occupations in the U.S. Economy. Source: U.S. Bureau of Labor Statistics, Employment Projections Program

Related Occupations
- College Faculty Member
- Farm & Home Management Advisor
- Secondary & Middle School Teacher
- Special Education Teacher
- Vocational Rehabilitation Counselor

Related Military Occupations
- Personnel Specialist
- Training Specialist & Instructor

Conversation With . . .
CHARLOTTE GRAY

Career & Tech Lead Teacher, Family & Consumer Sciences
Holt High School, Wentzville, Missouri
Teacher, 27 years

1. What was your individual career path in terms of education/training, entry-level job, or other significant opportunity?

After high school, I attended Patricia Stevens Career College in St. Louis and graduated with a diploma in fashion merchandising and a minor in public relations. Back then, it was known as a finishing school for girls. Today, I would compare the program to Career and Technical Education (CTE). During college, I worked in retail sales, shipping, and bookkeeping for a small family-owned business and found it was not exactly what I wanted to do for the rest of my life. I enrolled at the University of Missouri and somehow found my way to the Home Economics Education program. I really enjoyed the course work and had a great advisor who saw the potential in me to be a teacher. After graduating, I got a teaching position and worked for several years. I became involved with the Association for Career and Technical Education (ACTE) and during a national conference, a professor from The Ohio State University asked me if I'd be interested in attending their master's program as a graduate assistant. I said yes. So, I quit my teaching job and went back to college. I finished my master's and returned to teaching and never looked back. I currently teach courses in child development and culinary arts in a high school. The goal of Family and Consumer Science (FACS) courses is to equip students to survive and thrive in daily life and to show them how to apply their knowledge and skills in real-world situations.

2. What are the most important skills and/or qualities for someone in your profession?

Leadership is important. You must be organized, flexible, patient, and good at multi-tasking. You have to enjoy hands-on, project-based teaching. You have to be creative, dependable, self-motivated, a critical thinker, a team player, a good listener, and have strong written and verbal communication skills.

3. What do you wish you had known going into this profession?

That there would be constant changes in the education system that you have no control over. I wish I had realized the number of hours you have to spend planning and preparing lessons to be an exemplary teacher. And in a small school, you might teach six or seven different classes, all of which you have to prep for daily. Finally, I wish I had known how to motivate the unmotivated.

4. Are there many job opportunities in your profession? In what specific areas?

The need for FACS teachers continues to grow nationwide, and this specialty is on most states' critical needs list. Many teachers are retiring, so jobs are becoming available yearly. A FACS education major has many opportunities outside of teaching because of the wide variety of course work required: child development, family living, consumer economics, foods and nutrition, clothing and textiles, living environments, interpersonal relationships, human sexuality, parenting, family financial management, consumer purchasing, and resource management. Some of the fields FACS majors could end up in include culinary arts, dietetics, interior design, youth services, apparel design and community health services.

5. How do you see your profession changing in the next five years? What role will technology play in those changes, and what skills will be required?

Schools are more career-focused than ever. It's hard to know what technological advances are coming, particularly in the classes covered by Careers in Technical Education and FACS, but the challenge for teachers and schools will be to keep up with the technology.

6. What do you enjoy most about your job? What do you enjoy least about your job?

I am passionate about what I teach and worry about children who have relied heavily on convenience in their lives. The best part of my job is seeing students use what they have learned in my classroom in their everyday lives, from realizing the importance of nutrition to learning to get the desired response from a preschooler using positive statements.

I don't enjoy the politics behind education today, and disagree with the emphasis placed on everyone going to a four-year college. There's not enough emphasis on how to live a healthy life, financially and nutritionally, nor on healthy relationships. Some days I just want to spend time exploring ideas with students, but there never seems to be time because of all the mandates and testing.

7. Can you suggest a valuable "try this" for students considering a career in your profession?

Work as an aide for the FACS teachers in your school. Take as many FACS or CTE classes as will fit in your schedule. Get involved with Family, Career and Community Leaders of America (fccla.com). Take a class working with young children where you actually get to assist with teaching. Offer to help at after-school programs.

SELECTED SCHOOLS

Many colleges and universities have bachelor's degree programs in education and related subjects; some offer a focus on career/technical education. The student may also gain initial grounding in the field at a technical or community college. Consult with your school guidance counselor or research post-secondary programs in your area. The web site of the Association for Career and Technical Education (see below) has a section on "Postsecondary Education Resources" and other tools and resources.

MORE INFORMATION

American Association for Adult and Continuing Education
10111 Martin Luther King Jr. Hwy.
Suite 200C
Bowie, MD 20720
301.459.6261
www.aaace.org

American Association for Employment in Education
3040 Riverside Drive, Suite 125
Columbus, OH 43221
614.485.1111
www.aaee.org

American Association of Colleges for Teacher Education
1307 New York Avenue, NW
Suite 300
Washington, DC 20005-4701
202.293.2450
www.aacte.org

American Federation of Teachers
Public Affairs Department
555 New Jersey Avenue, NW
Washington, DC 20001
202.879.4400
www.aft.org

Association for Career and Technical Education
1410 King Street
Alexandria, VA 22314
800.826.9972
www.acteonline.org

National Association of State Directors of Career Technical Education Consortium
8484 Georgia Avenue, Suite 320
Silver Spring, MD 20910
www.careertech.org

National Education Association
1201 16th Street, NW
Washington, DC 20036-3290
202.833.4000
www.nea.org

Molly Hagan/Editor

Case Worker/Social Services Assistant

Snapshot

Career Cluster: Human Services

Interests: Sociology, counseling, psychology, assessment, communication

Earnings (Yearly Average): $29,230

Employment & Outlook: Faster Than Average Growth Expected

OVERVIEW

Sphere of Work

Case workers/social services assistants work with social workers to provide clients with much-needed social services. Case worker/social services assistant is a general job category that includes a wide range of job titles and duties, such as home health care assistant, family or patient advocate, case worker, outreach worker, adult day care worker, and mental health worker. Case workers/social services assistants help often at-risk individuals to find resources, develop new coping strategies, resolve problems and conflicts, and secure opportunities. They work with

individual clients to lessen the impact of, and in some cases resolve, unemployment, poverty, drug and alcohol dependency, homelessness, relationship problems, and domestic abuse. Case workers/social services assistants may work with individuals, families, or targeted populations such as prisoners or the elderly.

Work Environment

Case workers/social services assistants spend their workdays seeing clients in a wide variety of settings, including offices, residential facilities, homeless shelters, adult day care facilities, schools, prisons, hospitals, and substance abuse clinics. Case workers/social services assistants may have a fixed office where they receive clients or may travel to see clients. Given the diverse demands of the case worker/social services profession, case workers/social services assistants may need to work days, evenings, weekends, and on-call hours to meet client or caseload needs.

Profile

Working Conditions: Work both Indoors and Outdoors
Physical Strength: Light Work
Education Needs: Bachelor's Degree
Licensure/Certification: Usually Not Required
Physical Abilities Not Required: No Heavy Labor
Opportunities For Experience: Internship, Apprenticeship, Volunteer Work, Part-Time Work
Holland Interest Score*: SEC

* See Appendix A

Occupation Interest

Individuals drawn to the case worker/social services profession tend to be intelligent and socially conscious people who have the ability to quickly assess situations, find resources, demonstrate caring, and help solve social problems. Successful case workers/social services assistants display traits such as leadership, understanding, patience, responsibility, time management, knowledge of human behavior, initiative, and concern for individuals and society. Case workers/social services assistants should find satisfaction in spending time with a wide range of people, including those considered at-risk and those from diverse cultural and socioeconomic backgrounds.

A Day in the Life—Duties and Responsibilities

The daily occupational duties and responsibilities of case workers/social services assistants will be determined by the individual's area of job specialization, education level, and work environment. The range of possible duties and responsibilities includes assisting clients with welfare, childcare, and food stamp applications, teaching clients practical life skills such as including cooking, cleaning, and shopping, overseeing client job search efforts, and helping clients arrange transportation and housing. Case workers/social services assistants may remind patients to take and renew medications as needed, participate in client team meetings, provide client updates to supervisors and client families, complete client in-take interviews for drug rehab or residential facilities, or refer clients to community services or agencies.

They sometimes conduct workshops for clients in residential facilities, visit housebound clients, conduct home visits for foster care, adoption, and abuse allegation cases, and provide students' workshops on topics such as conflict resolution, sexual education, school attendance, and drug addiction. In addition to these many and varied responsibilities, case workers/social services assistants serve as a connection between students, teachers, and families, offer workshops to families on topics such as adoption, foster care, domestic violence, sibling rivalry, and homelessness, and work as court-ordered facilitators between families and social service agencies.

Case workers/social services assistants are also responsible for completing patient charts and required documentation on a daily basis.

Duties and Responsibilities

- Teaching communication to individuals or groups
- Using art and other therapies to promote mental health
- Interviewing and assessing the needs of clients
- Examining financial documents such as rent receipts and tax returns to determine whether the client is eligible for welfare programs
- Keeping records and writing reports
- Providing practical help and emotional support
- Transporting or accompanying clients

OCCUPATION SPECIALTIES

Group Work Program Aides

Group Work Program Aides as directed by professionals, lead informal group activities.

Case Aides

Case Aides handle simpler services in less complex cases under close tutelage and supervision.

Management Aides

Management Aides provide tenants of housing projects and apartments with information on rules and services.

Recreation Leaders

Recreation Leaders run recreation activities in voluntary agencies under close supervision of recreation supervisors.

Community Workers

Community Workers assist professionals in promoting awareness of social services to those who do not seek them.

WORK ENVIRONMENT

Physical Environment

The immediate physical environment of case workers/social services assistants varies based on the caseload and specialization of the individual. Case workers/social services assistants spend their workdays seeing clients in a wide variety of settings, including offices, outpatient facilities, nursing homes, residential facilities, homeless shelters, schools, prisons, hospitals, and substance abuse clinics.

Relevant Skills and Abilities

Communication Skills
- Listening attentively
- Speaking effectively
- Writing concisely

Interpersonal/Social Skills
- Being patient
- Cooperating with others
- Counseling others
- Providing support to others
- Representing others
- Working as a member of a team

Organization & Management Skills
- Demonstrating leadership
- Managing time
- Performing duties that change frequently

Research & Planning Skills
- Analyzing information
- Solving problems

Human Environment

Case workers/social services assistants work with a wide variety of people and should be comfortable meeting with children, people with mental illness, incarcerated people, the elderly, people with physical illnesses, homeless people, abusers and the abused, and distressed families.

Technological Environment

Case workers/social services assistants must be comfortable using computers and applicable software to access client records and file paperwork. Because they are often on the road, driving to and from client homes and different facilities, case workers/social services assistants should also be comfortable spending a large chunk of the work day on the road, if needed. The use of cell phones and other telecommunications tools is also essential to ensure availability during on-call hours.

EDUCATION, TRAINING, AND ADVANCEMENT

High School/Secondary

High school students interested in pursuing a career in the case worker/social services sector should, first and foremost, prepare themselves by developing good study habits. High school-level study of foreign languages, public safety, sociology, psychology, and education will provide a strong foundation for work as a social and services assistant or for college-level work in the field. Due to the diversity of case worker/social services specialties, high school students interested in this career path will benefit from seeking internships or part-time work that expose the students to diverse groups of people and social needs. High school students may be able to secure employment as case workers/social services assistants directly out of high school, although candidates with college degrees generally earn more and have more interesting job duties.

Suggested High School Subjects
- Applied Communication
- Composition
- English
- Government
- Political Science
- Psychology
- Sociology
- Speech

Famous First

The first social services aides to participate in a prominent program aimed at providing comprehensive aid to needy families were the aides associated with Hull House in Chicago in the 1890s. Hull House was founded by Jane Addams, pictured, and Ellen Starr, and it served immigrant families by offering social, educational, and cultural programs under a single roof. The effort proved so successful that, by the 1920s, there were over 500 so-called settlement houses modeled on Hull House.

College/Postsecondary

Postsecondary students interested in becoming case workers/social services assistants should work towards an associate's degree or bachelor's degree in social work or a related field, such as psychology, counseling, or gerontology. Coursework in education, public safety, psychology, and foreign languages may also prove useful in their future work.

Postsecondary students can gain work experience and potential advantage in their future job searches by obtaining internships or part-time employment in social service agencies or with at-risk populations such as the elderly or the homeless.

Related College Majors

- Child Care & Guidance Workers & Managers, General
- Community Health Services
- Community Organization, Resources & Services
- Social Work

Adult Job Seekers

Adults seeking employment as case workers/social services assistants should have, at a minimum, a high school diploma or associate's degree. Some social service organizations and specialties require a master's degree and second language proficiency. Adult job seekers should educate themselves about the educational and professional license requirements of their home states and the organizations where they seek employment. Adult job seekers will benefit from joining professional associations to help with networking and job searching. Professional social services associations, such as the Action Network for Social Work Education and Research (ANSWER) and the Center for Clinical Social Work, generally offer career workshops and maintain lists and forums of available jobs.

Professional Certification and Licensure

Professional certification and licensure is not required of case workers/ social services assistants. However, those individuals planning to advance in the social services profession often choose to pursue social work certification, which varies by state and specialty.

Additional Requirements

Individuals who find satisfaction, success, and job security as case workers/social services assistants will be knowledgeable about the profession's requirements, responsibilities, and opportunities. High levels of integrity and personal and professional ethics are required of case workers/social services assistants, as professionals in this role interact with vulnerable people and have access to the personal information of their clients. Membership in professional social services associations is encouraged among all case workers/social services assistants as a means of building status within the professional community and networking.

Fun Fact

The film *Beetlejuice* produced a novel concept for caseworkers and clients, with an "afterlife caseworker." In the film, the dearly departed get three meetings, during all of eternity, with their caseworker, as well as a *Handbook for the Recently Deceased.*

Source: http://beetlejuice.wikia.com/wiki/Neitherworld_Waiting_Room

EARNINGS AND ADVANCEMENT

With experience, case workers/social services assistants may advance to supervisory positions. Advanced degrees or certificates are typically necessary for advancement. Median annual earnings of case workers/ social services assistants were $29,230 in 2013. The lowest ten percent earned less than $19,620, and the highest ten percent earned more than $46,620.

Case workers/social services assistants may receive paid vacations, holidays, and sick days; life and health insurance; and retirement benefits. These are usually paid by the employer.

Metropolitan Areas with the Highest
Employment Level in this Occupation

Metropolitan area	Employment[1]	Employment per thousand jobs	Hourly mean wage
New York-White Plains-Wayne, NY-NJ	20,000	3.82	$16.89
Los Angeles-Long Beach-Glendale, CA	12,870	3.24	$16.30
Minneapolis-St. Paul-Bloomington, MN-WI	8,550	4.77	$15.66
Philadelphia, PA	6,810	3.70	$13.89
Boston-Cambridge-Quincy, MA	6,660	3.81	$18.15
Chicago-Joliet-Naperville, IL	5,750	1.55	$14.17
Seattle-Bellevue-Everett, WA	4,630	3.19	$14.54
Washington-Arlington-Alexandria, DC-VA-MD-WV	4,420	1.87	$19.64
Newark-Union, NJ-PA	4,380	4.58	$15.01
Pittsburgh, PA	4,200	3.72	$13.13

Source: Bureau of Labor Statistics

EMPLOYMENT AND OUTLOOK

Case workers/social services assistants held about 373,000 jobs nationally in 2012. About two-thirds worked in health care or social assistance industries, offering adult day care, group meals, crisis intervention, counseling and job training. About one-fourth were employed by state and local governments, primarily in public welfare agencies and facilities for mentally disabled persons. Some also supervised residents of group homes.

Employment is expected to grow faster than the average for all occupations through the year 2022, which means employment is projected to increase 20 percent to 25 percent. Job opportunities are expected to be excellent, not only because of projected rapid growth in this occupation, but because of the high need to replace persons who leave the field or retire. Turnover among case workers/social services assistants in group homes is reported to be especially high.

Employment Trend, Projected 2010–20

Case Workers/Social Services Assistants: 22%

Community and Social Service Occupations: 17%

Total, All Occupations: 11%

Note: "All Occupations" includes all occupations in the U.S. Economy. Source: U.S. Bureau of Labor Statistics, Employment Projections Program

Related Occupations
- Marriage Counselor
- Nursing Aide
- Preschool Worker
- Recreation Worker
- School Counselor
- Social Worker
- Substance Abuse Counselor

Conversation With . . .
ALISSA HEIL

Social Services Supervisor
Georgia Department of Family and
Children Services, Case Worker, 4½ years

1. What was your individual career path in terms of education/training, entry-level job, or other significant opportunity?

I started college as a biology/pre-med major, then switched to child and family devel-opment. I essentially stumbled upon it. I just fell in love with the things I was learning, in terms of family systems and emotional health. I interned in my very last year of undergrad at the Georgia Department of Family and Children Services (DFCS). I mostly did investigations with an investigator. I took a year off after graduating and ran a mentorship and after-school program for kids in low income housing in my community while working at a campus ministry. I then got my master's degree in social work at the University of Georgia and interned at DFCS. In Georgia, we have a really neat program where the cost of tuition for my master's in social work was paid for in return for committing my first two years of employment to DFCS, and I have been there ever since.

2. What are the most important skills and/or qualities for someone in your profession?

First and foremost, you have to love what you do. You have to be passionate, and feel strongly enough to advocate for your clients' needs. That gives you the energy to persevere when you have to deal with layers of barriers. You need to have 100 percent people skills to work positively with families and 100 percent administrative skills to manage the paperwork. Flexibility is important, and creativity—the ability to think outside the box. The clients we work with often have a variety of challenges that may include poverty, substance abuse, mental health issues. It's rare that we're working on just one issue to overcome.

3. What do you wish you had known going into this profession?

There's not a whole lot that can prepare you for this work, but because of my intern-ships, I felt very prepared. Before I entered the field, all I ever heard about was the high burnout rates and that it was such a "hard" job. That negativity could set you up for failure if you subscribe to it. It was helpful knowing that there are people who have done this job for a really, really long time and really love their job and are good at it.

4. **Are there many job opportunities in your profession? In what specific areas?**

There are a lot of jobs. I work in child welfare. We overlap with a number of agencies: domestic abuse shelters, homeless shelters, substance abuse and hospital settings, hospice. Working for DCFS is the emergency room equivalent, or the combat zone, of social services. In other types of work, you can really want an adult to make positive decisions for their life, but when you're working with kids, there's an obligation beyond that.

5. **How do you see your profession changing in the next five years? What role will technology play in those changes, and what skills will be required?**

We're always looking for ways to streamline documentation, for instance, with dictation services. Databases and access to information is big: knowing a family's previous interaction with agencies. Our data that tracks volume and outcomes also streamlines our reporting to the federal government, which is linked to funding.

6. **What do you enjoy most about your job? What do you enjoy least about your job?**

What I enjoy most are the relationships that you build with your families and children. Knowing at the end of the day that what I do matters. Seeing the way a child or family grows and changes over time, or how kids thrive in a different environment is very re-warding. There are successes.

I work in foster care and adoption. Every day has some combination of emails and phone calls, coordinating with other providers and communicating with the adoptive and foster families, talking to the schools about their concerns. There are home visits and a fair amount of court involvement, and working with the kids around preparing them for court and preparing them for outcomes.

What I like least is that there are so many things competing for your attention. Trying to prioritize everybody's needs can be challenging. You're dealing with people's lives. You don't want anybody to wait. Having to continually fight through barriers and systematic obstacles can become frustrating. And there are some people who, no matter what you do or provide, you can never help.

7. **Can you suggest a valuable "try this" for students considering a career in your profession?**

A lot of agencies will allow you to shadow. I think interning prepared me more than anything for interacting with people who are very different from me. Any experience where you're exposed to many kinds of people and can practice your people skills will be helpful. The same goes for a job that requires managing a lot of priorities at the same time.

SELECTED SCHOOLS

Many colleges and universities have bachelor's degree programs in subjects related to social work. The student may also gain an initial grounding at a technical or community college. Consult with your school guidance counselor or research area post-secondary programs to find the right fit for you. For a list of top schools in the field of social work, see the entry "Social Worker" in the present volume.

MORE INFORMATION

American Case Management Association
11701 West 36th Street
Little Rock, AR 72211
501.907.2262
www.acmaweb.org

Council for Standards of Human Service Education
2118 Plum Grove Road, #297
Rolling Meadows, IL 60008
www.cshse.org

National Organization for Human Services
1600 Sarno Road, Suite 16
Melbourne, FL 32935
www.nationalhumanservices.org

Simone Isadora Flynn/Editor

Childcare Worker

OVERVIEW

Sphere of Work

Childcare workers, also referred to as childcare providers and childcare givers, are responsible for the care of children in daycare settings. Childcare workers may care for young children on a full-time basis and for older children in before- and after-school programs. They be self employed or employed by public and private schools, businesses, and childcare centers. Childcare workers maintain the physical safety and socio-emotional health of children. Childcare workers may also attend to the development of pre-literacy skills, fine and gross motor skills, practical life skills, and language acquisition of children under their care.

Work Environment

Childcare workers spend their workdays in schools, childcare facilities, businesses, and homes. Childcare workers tend to work very long hours to accommodate families' work schedules. In addition, childcare workers may be required to work year round and have unpaid vacations and days off. In school settings, childcare workers work in before- and after-school daycare programs. In childcare facilities, childcare workers work in dedicated classrooms segregated by age and developmental abilities. In businesses, childcare workers work in daycare facilities established for the children of employees. Childcare workers may also work in family homes or establish daycare facilities in their own homes following state regulations about space, child-to-caregiver ratios, and cleanliness.

Profile

Working Conditions: Work Indoors
Physical Strength: Medium Work
Education Needs: On-The-Job Training, High School Diploma or G.E.D., Apprenticeship
Licensure/Certification: Required
Physical Abilities Not Required: No Heavy Labor
Opportunities For Experience: Internship, Apprenticeship, Volunteer Work, Part-Time Work
Holland Interest Score*: RES, SCR, SEC

* See Appendix A

Occupation Interest

Individuals drawn to the occupation of childcare worker tend to be responsible, nurturing, responsive, patient, observant, playful, and caring. Childcare workers should enjoy routine tasks and spending long hours with children. Childcare workers may have experience in child rearing, cooking, household management, music and games, arts and crafts, and educational theory.

A Day in the Life—Duties and Responsibilities

The daily duties and responsibilities of childcare workers vary based on the childcare specialization and employer. Potential daycare worker specializations include home-based childcare, school-based childcare, business-based childcare, and young child daycare facilities.

Childcare workers support children's learning and development by preparing daily activities. They must also supervise interactions between children and intervene as needed to promote positive play. As needed, childcare workers also discipline children in child-centered and positive ways.

Childcare workers are responsible for the health and well-being of the children in their care. Childcare workers must maintain a sanitary environment, cleaning childcare facilities and playground equipment. Those caring for very young children must also oversee toileting, bathroom activities, and hand-washing. They also provide age-appropriate rest times and naps for young children. Sometimes families may ask childcare workers to administer medications.

Family outreach is an important part of the job of the childcare worker. Each day, childcare workers greet children and families upon arrival to the childcare facility. They also regularly communicate with families through communication practices, such as an activity notebook and phone calls. In addition, all childcare workers must maintain records and satisfy state childcare rules. Childcare workers must document any medications given to children, the number and types of food fed to children, and any disciplinary incidents or accidents.

Duties and Responsibilities

- Waking, dressing and feeding children
- Directing children in eating, playing and similar activities
- Assisting disabled children to classes and treatment rooms
- Reading to children and providing experiences in art, music and outdoor play
- Disciplining children and recommending or initiating other measures to control behavior

WORK ENVIRONMENT

Physical Environment

A childcare worker's immediate physical environment is a childcare area or classroom based in their own home, an outside residential home, a school, a business, or a daycare facility or regulated institution. Childcare workers generally work forty-hour weeks or more, engaged in physically demanding activity. Childcare workers follow may follow an academic schedule or need to be available year round to meet the needs of their employers.

Human Environment

Childcare workers are in constant contact with children of all ages, their families, and other care providers and teachers. Childcare workers may be responsible for children with physical and mental disabilities, and must be comfortable working with people from a wide range of backgrounds.

Relevant Skills and Abilities

Interpersonal/Social Skills
- Being able to remain calm
- Cooperating with others
- Providing support to others
- Teaching others
- Working as a member of a team

Organization & Management Skills
- Demonstrating leadership
- Handling challenging situations
- Managing people/groups

Technological Environment

Childcare workers may use computers and telecommunication tools to perform their job and to ensure contact with children's families in case of emergency. In addition, childcare facilities increasingly include computers for student use and learning. Childcare workers should be comfortable teaching children to use educational software and games.

EDUCATION, TRAINING, AND ADVANCEMENT

High School/Secondary

High school students interested in becoming childcare workers should develop good study habits and seek out childcare experience. Interested high school students should take courses in psychology, education, child development, physical education, and the arts. Coursework in a foreign language may be helpful as well. Those interested in the field of early childhood education will benefit from seeking internships or part-time childcare work with children at camps, after-school programs, preschools, or childcare centers. High school students may be hired as childcare workers upon graduation.

Suggested High School Subjects
- Applied Communication
- Arts
- Child Care
- Child Growth & Development
- Crafts
- English
- Family & Consumer Sciences
- First Aid Training
- Foods & Nutrition
- Literature
- Physical Education
- Psychology
- Sociology

Famous First

The first childcare workers' insurance policy was issued in 1950 by the American Associated Insurance Companies of St. Louis, Missouri. The policy covered babysitters available through the Missouri State Employment Service, bonding them up to $2,500 each for fraud and dishonesty.

College/Postsecondary

College students interested in the field of early childhood education should consider majoring in education and earning initial teaching certification as part of their undergraduate education program. Those interested in early childhood education should complete coursework in psychology, education, child development, physical education, and the arts. The majority of childcare worker jobs do not require a college degree and, as a result, college students may be hired as childcare workers either during college or upon graduation.

Related College Majors
- Child Care & Guidance Workers & Management

Adult Job Seekers

Adults seeking jobs as childcare workers should research the education and certification requirements of their home states as well as of the childcare facilities or programs where they seek employment. Adult job seekers in the early childhood education field may benefit from the employment workshops and job lists maintained by professional teaching associations such as the National Association for the Education of Young Children (NAEYC).

Advancement is limited and depends on the size of the facility and the education level of the childcare worker. An experienced childcare worker may become a supervisor or may establish his or her own childcare center. More advanced positions often require bachelor's or master's degrees.

Professional Certification and Licensure

Professional certification and licensure requirements for childcare workers vary between states and schools. The range of childcare requirements is vast and includes high school education, childcare experience, the national Child Development Associate (CDA) credential, the Child Care Professional (CCP) designation, college-level education courses, associate's degree, and bachelor's degree. Some states also require first aid and CPR certification, background checks, and immunizations before beginning work in a daycare facility.

Additional Requirements

Individuals who find satisfaction, success, and job security as childcare workers will be knowledgeable about the profession's requirements, responsibilities, and opportunities. Childcare workers must have high levels of integrity and ethics as they care for young children and may have access to their families' personal information. Individuals who intend to establish in-home childcare facilities need to educate themselves about best business practices and state requirements. Childcare workers need to find satisfaction in the work itself as the compensation offered childcare workers tends to be low and opportunities for professional advancement are few.

Fun Fact

Necessity really is the mother of invention. Consider all the ways that working moms came up with to watch over their babies before day care. Native Americans strapped infants to cradle boards. Migrant laborers set up baby tents in beet fields. Workers processing shellfish let their toddlers play on the nearby docks. And the offspring of Southern dirt farmers were tied to pegs at the edges of the fields.

Source: www.socialwelfarehistory.com/programs/child-care-the-american-history/

EARNINGS AND ADVANCEMENT

Earnings depend on the experience and education of the individual worker, and the type, size, and geographic location of the child care facility. Although the pay is generally low, more education means higher earnings in some cases. In 2013, median annual earnings of childcare workers were $19,600. The lowest ten percent earned less than $16,430, and the highest ten percent earned more than $29,770.

Childcare workers may receive paid vacations, holidays, and sick days; life and health insurance; and retirement benefits. These are usually paid by the employer.

Metropolitan Areas with the Highest Employment Level in this Occupation

Metropolitan area	Employment[1]	Employment per thousand jobs	Hourly mean wage
New York-White Plains-Wayne, NY-NJ	35,310	6.73	$12.45
Houston-Sugar Land-Baytown, TX	14,670	5.32	$9.20
Los Angeles-Long Beach-Glendale, CA	14,050	3.53	$11.68
Atlanta-Sandy Springs-Marietta, GA	13,810	5.99	$10.35
Chicago-Joliet-Naperville, IL	11,140	3.01	$11.28
Philadelphia, PA	10,580	5.75	$10.16
Washington-Arlington-Alexandria, DC-VA-MD-WV	10,070	4.25	$11.49
Dallas-Plano-Irving, TX	9,760	4.54	$9.99
Nassau-Suffolk, NY	8,750	7.08	$13.22
Minneapolis-St. Paul-Bloomington, MN-WI	7,490	4.18	$10.96

[1]Does not include self-employed. Source: Bureau of Labor Statistics

EMPLOYMENT AND OUTLOOK

Childcare workers held about 1.3 million jobs nationally in 2012. About 40 percent worked part-time. Employment is expected to grow faster than the average for all occupations through the year 2022, which means employment is projected to increase 10 percent to 15 percent. The number of children enrolled in childcare or preschool programs is likely to continue to increase, creating demand for additional childcare workers.

Employment Trend, Projected 2010–20

Personal Care and Service Occupations: 21%

Childcare Workers: 14%

Total, All Occupations: 11%

Note: "All Occupations" includes all occupations in the U.S. Economy. Source: U.S. Bureau of Labor Statistics, Employment Projections Program

Related Occupations
- Home Health Aide
- Housekeeper
- Preschool Worker
- Teacher Assistant

Conversation With . . . NICOLE FERRIS

Director
Creative Kids Beekman, Hopewell Junction, NY
Childcare Worker, 7½ years

1. What was your individual career path in terms of education/training, entry-level job, or other significant opportunity?

I was a nursing major going to school full time, but only three days a week, so I got a part-time job and started as an evening floater, relieving full-time teachers at the end of the day. As my college schedule changed, I was able to work full-time as a toddler teacher. I fell in love with working with young kids. I really enjoy working with this age group, which is 6 weeks until about 5 years old. I knew this is what I really wanted to do. I didn't want to work with 7, 8, 9, 10 year olds. So I got an associate's degree in human services and I'm working on my bachelor's degree in early childhood development. I also have a New York Sate Children's Program Administrator certificate, which allows me to be a director in a New York-licensed child care center. Eventually, I'd love to open my own center, but for now, this is the perfect job. I still get to go into the classrooms and see the kids grow up and learn and play and hit milestones, but I also get to interact with staff and be a valuable resource for them.

2. What are the most important skills and/or qualities for someone in your profession?

One of the most important things I look for is someone who's nurturing, because we are working with such a young age and they do still have their tantrums and meltdowns and need that extra affection. You have to be super energetic and creative, because they're super energetic. You also have to be comfortable speaking with parents because there are days when we have to relay the bad stuff—Johnny bit somebody today or maybe we're noticing some type of developmental delay. That's not for everybody. It's not fun giving bad news.

3. What do you wish you had known going into this profession?

Although my education has gotten me to the point where I am, I would have preferred to know this is what I wanted to do before I started college, because you don't have to have a degree to work in a child care center in New York. You can have a Child Development Associate Certificate, which is much more cost effective. I work with people who have bachelor's degrees and master's degrees in education and they're thousands of dollars in debt. Day care and child care don't pay what the public schools do. I'm pursuing my bachelor's because, as a director, I realize I can benefit from the additional education.

4. Are there many job opportunities in your profession? In what specific areas?

There are. You can be the owner of a center. You can do what I'm doing, which is being a director. I oversee all the staff, the state regulations, those kinds of things. There are assistant directors who plan activities for children. There are teachers, including positions in before- and after-school programs.

5. How do you see your profession changing in the next five years? What role will technology play in those changes, and what skills will be required?

Technology is going to play a huge role in education in general, not just early childhood education. Even now, the need and want for computers, tablets and smart boards is huge. Kids in our 4-year-old/preschool program start using the computers and tablets with educational games because when they get to kindergarten, they'll have to be familiar with them. Then there are the things you wouldn't necessarily think of, like security. At most centers, you can't just walk in. Each parent types their own specific code to get in. There are cameras in the classroom. Facebook is becoming a big thing—families love to see what we're doing throughout the day.

6. What do you enjoy most about your job? What do you enjoy least about your job?

The most rewarding part is watching them grow and learning every day. We have babies who are learning to walk and talk. Children are learning to problem solve with puzzles and games, and learning to socialize. And, unlike public schools, we get to interact with the parents every single day as opposed to a few times a year. What I like least is the paperwork. The state of New York has lots of regulations, ranging from the type of classroom pet allowed to evacuation drills. It's my job to make sure every classroom and every teacher is following those regulations. It can be tedious.

7. Can you suggest a valuable "try this" for students considering a career in your profession?

I suggest a part-time job in a day care center, or even volunteering. Babysitting is great, but how often are you working with four or more children? Working as a camp counselor is better because even though the children are older, you're getting experience working with groups of children.

SELECTED SCHOOLS

A college degree is not necessary in most cases for work as a childcare worker. For those interested in taking college courses and raising their qualifications, a technical or community college is a good place to start. For supervisory positions a college degree in education can be valuable. Students are advised to consult with a school guidance counselor or research area post-secondary programs to find the right program.

MORE INFORMATION

Association for Child & Youth Care Practice
6753 State Road
Parma, OH 44134
440.843.5505
www.acycp.org

Association for Childhood Education International
17904 Georgia Avenue, Suite 215
Olney, MD 20832
800.423.3563
www.acei.org

Center for the Child Care Workforce
555 New Jersey Avenue, NW
Washington, DC 20001
202.662.8005
www.ccw.org

Council for Professional Recognition
2460 16th Street NW
Washington, DC 20009
800.424.4310
www.cdacouncil.org

National Association for the Education of Young Children
1313 L Street NW, Suite 500
Washington, DC 20005
800.424.2460
www.naeyc.org

National Association for Family Childcare
1743 W. Alexander Street
Salt Lake City, UT 84199
801-886-2322
www.nafc.org

Simone Isadora Flynn/Editor

Clergy

Snapshot

Career Cluster(s): Human Services

Interests: Theology, public speaking, listening, supporting others, communicating with others

Earnings (Yearly Average): $56,250

Employment & Outlook: Average Growth Expected

OVERVIEW

Sphere of Work

Clergy are trained spiritual leaders in a community of faith. They conduct religious rites and ceremonies such as weddings and funerals, devise and oversee religious education programs, offer comfort to those who are suffering illness or grief, and counsel people troubled by family or personal problems. Most clergy work in a house of worship. Some work in the military, medical facilities, prisons, private corporations, or social service agencies, or choose to teach in seminaries and religious schools.

Work Environment

Clergy are usually on call at all times. A member of the clergy can be called upon at any time to perform their ministerial duties. Clergy thus must be flexible and adaptable, able to work with changing situations as they arise. As the standard office schedule is usually not possible, clergy often take two days off during the week. Depending upon the size of the worship institution and its ability to provide secretarial assistance, there may be extensive administrative and financial records to maintain in addition to scholarly and caregiving duties.

Profile

Working Conditions: Work Indoors
Physical Strength: Light Work
Education Needs: Bachelor's Degree, Master's Degree
Licensure/Certification: Usually Not Required
Physical Abilities Not Required: No Heavy Labor
Opportunities For Experience: Military Service, Volunteer Work
Holland Interest Score*: SAI

* See Appendix A

Occupation Interest

Individuals interested in pursuing a career in religion should be adept at understanding the theology of their specific faith tradition and applying it in practical situations, and should also possess a strong sense of compassion. Because clergy need to be comfortable interacting with people on an individual basis, in small numbers, and in large groups, they should be both good listeners and skilled public speakers. Some background in psychology and social services is also helpful, as clergy need to be able to deal calmly with unexpected emergencies.

A Day in the Life—Duties and Responsibilities

The typical workday for members of clergy varies greatly, often depending on the size and location of the religious institution in which they are employed. Clergy in small houses of worship may find themselves as the only paid staff members, so a great deal of administrative office work must be included in the schedule, even with volunteer secretarial help that is sometimes offered. Clergy in larger institutions often have a more specific focus. They may specialize in youth ministry, visitation of the sick and bereaved, financial and administrative planning for expansion of the institution, or scholarly message preparation and delivery on a weekly basis.

All clergy study sacred texts, interpret religious laws, follow current religious and social events, provide instruction and counseling, care for the needy, lead prayer, and perform religious ceremonies as requested. Participation in local community events may also be required.

In group settings such as committee meetings, clergy must interact diplomatically with a variety of people who may hold strong opinions on sensitive subjects. On an individual basis, clergy act as trustworthy counselors who may hear extremely personal and confidential information. In rare instances, such as cases of child or spousal abuse, they may be required to contact law enforcement officials.

Duties and Responsibilities

- Waking, dressing and feeding children
- Directing children in eating, playing and similar activities
- Assisting disabled children to classes and treatment rooms
- Reading to children and providing experiences in art, music and outdoor play
- Disciplining children and recommending or initiating other measures to control behavior

WORK ENVIRONMENT

Physical Environment

Much of the work of clergy is performed in an office or study setting; however, clergy are on-call professionals who must have reliable and accessible means of transport, as they need to respond quickly when emergencies occur.

Relevant Skills and Abilities

Communication Skills
- Listening attentively
- Speaking effectively
- Writing concisely

Interpersonal/Social Skills
- Being able to remain calm
- Being patient
- Counseling others
- Providing support to others
- Teaching others
- Working as a member of a team

Organization & Management Skills
- Handling challenging situations
- Making decisions
- Managing people/groups
- Managing time
- Organizing information or materials

Research & Planning Skills
- Solving problems
- Using logical reasoning

Human Environment

In large institutions, clergy interact with other staff members and laity, requiring the use of diplomatic and administrative abilities. In smaller institutions, where clergy may be the only paid staff, a slower pace and less human interaction is common, and personal scheduling and work discipline become even more important. In hospitals, military bases, and secular colleges, chaplains should be prepared to work with people from various religions, as well as those who have no religious background.

Technological Environment

Fewer houses of worship are able to provide professional secretarial assistance, which means that clergy are increasingly required to be familiar with software programs for word processing, desktop publishing, presentations, and financial transactions (especially with regard to taxation regulations for nonprofit institutions).

EDUCATION, TRAINING, AND ADVANCEMENT

High School/Secondary

High school students who wish to become clergy can best prepare by studying English, history, languages, philosophy, and psychology. Since many public schools do not offer courses in religion, interested high school students may wish to request credit for courses taken at a local college or an independent high school of the student's faith tradition. Volunteer work with a nonprofit organization or hospital is also helpful preparation.

Suggested High School Subjects
- Business & Computer Technology
- College Preparatory
- English
- History
- Humanities
- Literature
- Philosophy
- Political Science
- Psychology
- Social Studies
- Sociology
- Speech
- Theatre & Drama

Famous First

The first congressional chaplain was the Reverend William Linn, a Presbyterian minister who served in the First Congress from May 1, 1789, to December 10, 1790.

College/Postsecondary

If possible, prospective clergy should take specific seminary preparatory courses at a college founded by the faith in which the student seeks ordination. However, counseling, psychology, and philosophy courses at universities offering no religious studies also provide a solid background. Those interested in military chaplaincy should obtain ROTC training as well, and education courses are necessary for students interested in ministry at a private school or college.

While some independent worship organizations do not require an advanced degree in theology or divinity, many do. Unlike most graduate schools, however, faith seminaries may not require a Graduate Record Exam (GRE) score. Because the requirements for a traditional divinity degree are diverse, students seeking to be a chaplain at the university level may want to consider a more focused degree in their faith's theology and history or in counseling, subjects that are more commonly available for doctoral degrees. Many universities include teaching requirements in a chaplain's job description, and thus prefer applicants who hold or are candidates for a doctoral degree.

Related College Majors
- Bible/Biblical Studies
- Biblical & Other Theological Languages & Literatures
- Pastoral Counseling & Specialized Ministries
- Religion/Religious Studies
- Religious Education
- Theology/Theological Studies

Adult Job Seekers

Life experience is a valuable asset in this field, which requires empathy for the struggles of daily life. Volunteer administrative positions in churches or other institutions of faith provide valuable background. Many seminaries offer courses and degrees online, with varying amounts of on-campus requirements. For work in hospitals, chaplains are usually required to have extensive Clinical Pastoral Education (CPE) preparation, in which candidates participate in volunteer training under the supervision of senior staff hospital chaplains. Teaching and youth counseling experience is important in religious schools and in university settings. Similarly, those seeking employment as corporate chaplains will want to be at familiar with business career activities. Adults seeking clergy positions should familiarize themselves with the requirements of the organizations where they wish to work.

Professional Certification and Licensure

Denominational ordination is usually required at some point, often after a trial period of employment, and certification by the state is necessary in order to officiate at weddings and funerals. In some states, it is possible to be ordained by the state itself, without specific religious affiliation. Chaplains may obtain certification from the Association of Professional Chaplains, National Association of Catholic Chaplains, or National Association of Jewish Chaplains.

Additional Requirements

Clergy are often called upon to provide counseling in sensitive situations; confidentiality in these cases is extremely important, as is the ability to ascertain when professional psychological help is needed, and, on rare occasions, when law enforcement should be notified. Some faiths have lifestyle requirements, such as celibacy or vows of poverty, for their clergy members.

Fun Fact

During the Middle Ages, the clergy's social rank came right behind the king, the nobles and the knights. A religious celebration was held each month, in keeping with a time when life revolved around the seasons.

Source: http://westernreservepublicmedia.org/middleages/feud_clergy.htm

EARNINGS AND ADVANCEMENT

Earnings vary greatly depending on the type of religion and can also be influenced by the experience of the clergy and the geographic location of the congregation.

Roman Catholic priests earn a salary. With further training and experience, they can rise in the ranks of administration of the Catholic Church. Diocesan priests had median annual earnings of $23,294 in 2012. Priests take a vow of poverty and are supported by their religious order. Any personal earnings are given to the order. Their vow of poverty is recognized by the Internal Revenue Service, which exempts them from paying federal income tax.

Most Protestant ministers are paid a salary, although a few are paid from the offering collections or even serve as a volunteer. Some denominations are tightly organized and have a rigid hierarchy through which one may advance, while in other denominations ministers may advance to a top position more quickly. Median annual earnings of Protestant ministers were $49,417 in 2012. In large, wealthier denominations, Protestant ministers often earned significantly higher salaries than those in smaller congregations. Rabbis earn a salary. Since there is no formal hierarchy among congregations, rabbis can advance to head rabbis of well-established congregations, serve in the military or teach in Rabbinical seminaries. Median annual earnings of rabbis were $96,038 in 2012.

Clergy usually receive a package of benefits which may include paid vacations, holidays, and sick days; life and health insurance; a car allowance; free housing; travel and education allowances; and a retirement plan. On occasion, clergy may earn extra money through teaching, writing or officiating at ceremonies, such as weddings.

EMPLOYMENT AND OUTLOOK

There were approximately 225,000 clergy serving congregations nationally in 2012. Employment is expected to grow about as fast as the average for all occupations through the year 2022, which means employment is projected to increase 6 percent to 12 percent. Most job openings will stem from the need to replace clergy who leave the ministry, retire or die.

Related Occupations
- Marriage & Family Therapist
- Religious Activities & Education Director
- School Counselor

Related Military Occupations
- Chaplain

Conversation With . . .

REV. Dr. ANDREA AYVAZIAN

Senior Pastor, Haydenville Congregational Church
Haydenville MA, 10 years
Clergy, 19 years

1. What was your individual career path in terms of education/training, entry-level job, or other significant opportunity?

I didn't go to divinity school until I was in my 40s—I'm 63—and before that I had several careers. I was a nurse in labor and delivery, and an anti-racism educator. I have a bachelor's degree from Oberlin College, another from the University of North Carolina, a master's in nursing from Duke University and a PhD in racial and ethnic studies from the Union Institute in Cincinnati. I hold a Master of Divinity from Yale University.

Before landing at divinity school, I experienced a call, a pull, like I was being beckoned. I was in my 30s. The call to ministry was hard to trust and, due to doubts, I couldn't justify it. I even applied to Harvard Divinity School and got funding, but it's a process that filled me with questioning. So I went to divinity school in my 40s, when I started to believe this was where I was meant to be.

While I was in divinity school, I was to intern in the Chaplain's office at Mount Holyoke Colleger. That summer, she left. So Mount Holyoke College hired me to be the Protestant Chaplain. Then Mount Holyoke created a position called Dean of Religious Life. Even though I didn't have my Master of Divinity yet, I applied for the job and was chosen. I stayed 10 years. I developed a program so all nine active faith groups on campus had a chaplain, and I was allowed to dismantle the traditional Christian style of the chapel's pews and pulpit to create an interfaith sanctuary.

When I came to th Hadenville Congregational Church, the historic 1851 building was a wreck and there were only 15 people in the congregation. It was broken down and sad. Because I believe in resurrection, I felt I was meant to save the group. Today the building is beautiful and we have 250 people in the congregation. I have been involved with major construction in two settings; they don't talk about that in divinity school.

2. What are the most important skills and/or qualities for someone in your profession?

You really need to have a deep and abiding faith to see you through the hard places of ministry. Every day, I wish I was more patient. And if you are going to run a church—you might work in a different setting—you need administrative skills because you are running a little village. You have to be empathetic and passionate. And you need both a thick and a thin skin: thin so you can cry and connect with people, and thick because they say difficult things and you will encounter conflict.

3. What do you wish you had known going into this profession?

I wish I had known it would entail this much administrative work. Divinity school doesn't tell you that developing the budget is going to take forever or that staff will quit suddenly or there might be a contentious meeting.

4. Are there many job opportunities in your profession? In what specific areas?

It's hard to get a church in New England—there are a lot of ordained people. But there are other opportunities, such as hospice work, pastoral counseling and hospital work.

5. How do you see your profession changing in the next five years, what role will technology play in those changes, and what skills will be required?

Technology is big in church now. If we want to reach out to younger people we need a stronger social media presence. Twitter, Facebook, Instagram—all of that is considered part of your job. We have an Associate Pastor who does most of that. Fewer and fewer people are going to church. Pastors are going to have to be in the community much more, not tucked away in churches. The emerging church movement is all about involving young people, and I think church in America is really changing.

6. What do you enjoy most about your job? What do you enjoy least about your job?

What I love most is connecting with people, baptizing babies, visting people, sitting at their kitchen tables, going to nursing homes or to the hospital — the hands-on ministry. What I like least is how much work it takes to keep a church community thriving. Today is the first day of Lent and I am going to church to do an Ash Wednesday service. In the meantime, I'm dealing with conflict in my church and with a church member who is divorcing. It's hard to find time to pull away and take the sustaining quiet time that makes you good at everything else.

I think that there's too much administrative work, such as staff evaluation, budget preparations, and fundraising.

7. Can you suggest a valuable "try this" for students considering a career in your profession?

If you're thinking about ministry, follow some ministers. Find someone at a small rural church and at an urban church, and see how they spend their days.

SELECTED SCHOOLS

Many colleges and universities have bachelor's degree programs in religious studies. The student may also attend a religious institute or theological school. Consult with your school guidance counselor or research area post-secondary programs to find the right fit for you.

MORE INFORMATION

Association for Clinical Pastoral Education
1549 Clairmont Road, Suite 103
Decatur, GA 30033
404.320.1472
www.acpe.edu

Catholic Campus Ministry Association
1118 Pendleton Street, Suite 300
Cincinnati, OH 45202-8805
888.714.6631
www.ccmanet.org

Chaplaincy Institute Interfaith Ordination Program
2138 Cedar Street
Berkeley, CA 94709
510.843.1422
www.chaplaincyinstitute.org

Corporate Chaplains of America
1300 Corporate Chaplain Drive
Wake Forest, NC 27587
919.570.0700
www.chaplain.org

Jewish Reconstructionist Federation
Beit Devora
101 Greenwood Avenue, Suite 430
Jenkintown, PA 19046
215.885.5601
www.jrf.org

Military Chaplains Association
P.O. Box 7056
Arlington, VA 22207
703.533.5890
www.mca-usa.org

Price Grisham/Editor

Employment Specialist

Snapshot

Career Cluster: Business Administration; Human Services

Interests: Human resources, career research, working with people, helping others

Earnings (Yearly Average): $56,630

Employment & Outlook: Average Growth Expected

OVERVIEW

Sphere of Work

Employment specialists, also referred to as staffing specialists or job placement professionals, provide job placement support services to individuals and staffing support services to employers. Employment specialists may recruit workers for employers, conduct initial job interviews, and refer clients for jobs. Employment specialists may work with recent college graduates, people interested in changing careers, unemployed adults, or adults living in situations that impact or limit employment options. Employment

specialists also support clients in their efforts to develop career goals and apply for job training and employment.

Work Environment

Employment specialists spend their workdays seeing clients in a wide variety of settings, including employment agencies, human resources offices, and college and university career counseling offices. Employment specialists may have a fixed office where they see clients, or they may travel to meet potential job candidates or attend job fairs. Given the diverse demands of employment specialist work, employment specialists may need to work days, evenings, and weekends to meet client needs.

Profile

Working Conditions: Work Inside
Physical Strength: Light Work
Education Needs: Bachelor's Degree
Licensure/Certification:
  Recommended
Physical Abilities Not Required: No
  Heavy Labor
Opportunities For Experience:
  Internship, Military Service, Part-Time
  Work
Holland Interest Score*: SEC

* See Appendix A

Occupation Interest

Individuals drawn to the employment specialist profession tend to be intelligent and have the ability to quickly assess situations and people, find resources, and solve problems. Those most successful in this profession display traits such as good time management, initiative, and tact. Employment specialists should enjoy matching people with jobs and have a background in human resources.

A Day in the Life—Duties and Responsibilities

The daily occupational duties and responsibilities of employment specialists will be determined by the individual's area of specialization and work environment. Specialties in employment counseling include recruiting, vocational assessment, staffing, and first-round interviewing.

An employment specialist's daily duties and responsibilities may include meeting with employers to discuss their staffing needs; developing a candidate pool of executive, professional, technical, managerial, and clerical workers; recruiting job candidates for specific employers; and conducting initial candidate interviews. They may also meet with job seekers to assess their vocational aptitude, work history, and job readiness, help them develop professional goals and objectives, and match them with available jobs. At temporary staffing agencies, employment specialists may continue mediating the relationship between employer and employee after a position is filled. Employment specialists are responsible for completing required documentation, such as job referral forms, on a daily basis, and they must stay informed about current labor laws, trends, and regulations.

Duties and Responsibilities

- Reviewing completed applications and evaluating applicants' work history, education, training, skills, desired salary and qualifications
- Recording skills, knowledge, abilities, interests and test results
- Searching files of employer job orders to match requirements to qualifications
- Informing applicant of job duties, pay, benefits, conditions and opportunities
- Referring applicants to interview with prospective employers
- Testing or arranging for tests of skills and abilities
- Keeping informed of labor market developments, educational and occupational requirements, labor laws, government training programs and various regulations
- Maintaining case files on job seekers and completing counseling activity reports

OCCUPATION SPECIALTIES

Recruiters

Recruiters identify and interview individuals in order to recruit them for organizations. They advise individuals on matters concerning career opportunities, incentives, rights and benefits, and advantages of a particular career or organization.

Placement Specialists

Placement Specialists match employers with qualified jobseekers. They search for candidates who have the skills, education, and work experience needed for jobs, and they try to place those candidates with employers. They also may help set up interviews.

WORK ENVIRONMENT

Physical Environment

AThe immediate physical environment of employment specialists varies based on their caseload and area of specialization. They spend their workdays seeing clients in a wide variety of settings, including employment agencies, human resources offices, job training and placement programs, and college and university career counseling offices.

Human Environment

Employment specialists work with a wide variety of people and should be comfortable meeting with employers, potential job candidates, colleagues, staff, supervisors, college and university students, and unemployed people.

Relevant Skills and Abilities

Communication Skills
- Expressing thoughts and ideas
- Speaking effectively
- Writing concisely

Interpersonal/Social Skills
- Cooperating with others
- Working as a member of a team

Organization & Management Skills
- Making decisions
- Performing duties that change frequently

Research & Planning Skills
- Developing evaluation strategies
- Using logical reasoning

Technological Environment

Employment specialists use computers, cell phones, cars, and Internet communication tools to perform their job. For instance, employment specialists must be comfortable using computers to access student and client records, as well as for posting job listings and navigating online forums.

EDUCATION, TRAINING, AND ADVANCEMENT

High School/Secondary

High school students interested in pursuing a career as an employment specialist should prepare themselves by developing good study habits. High school courses in foreign languages, psychology, and writing will provide a strong foundation for work as an employment specialist. High school students interested in this career path will benefit from seeking internships or part-time work that exposes the students to managerial roles and diverse professions.

Suggested High School Subjects
- Applied Communication
- College Preparatory
- Composition
- Computer Science

- English
- Foreign Languages
- Psychology

Famous First

The first employment office established by a city was the office established in Seattle in 1894. Initially set up in a simple wooden shanty consisting of a single small room, the office soon moved to larger quarters in City Hall.

College/Postsecondary

Postsecondary students interested in becoming employment specialists should work toward a bachelor's degree in human resource management or a related field. Coursework in psychology, business administration, and foreign languages may also prove useful in their future work. Postsecondary students can gain work experience and potential advantage in their future job searches by securing internships or part-time employment in career placement or job training programs.

Related College Majors
- Human Resources Management

Adult Job Seekers

Adults seeking work as employment specialists should have a bachelor's degree and preferably some experience in business or personnel administration. Adult job seekers should educate themselves about the educational and professional licensure requirements of their home states and the organizations where they seek employment. Professional employment associations, such as the American Staffing Association and the National Association of Professional Employer Organizations, generally offer job-finding workshops and maintain lists and forums posting available jobs.

Professional Certification and Licensure

Certification for employment specialists is voluntary but may be required as a condition of employment or promotion at professional employment agencies. The American Staffing Association and the National Association of Personnel Services offer the leading voluntary certification options for employment specialists. The American Staffing Association's Certified Staffing Professional designation and the Technical Services Certified designation are each earned by completing training requirements and passing a national examination. The Certified Staffing Professional credential demonstrates competency in general labor and employment law, while the Technical Services Certified credential demonstrates competency in labor and employment laws applicable to technical, IT, and scientific staffing. The National Association of Personnel Services' Certified Personnel Consultant designation, Certified Temporary-Staffing Specialists designation, Certified Employee Retention Specialist designation, and Physician Recruiting Consultant designation are also earned through completing training requirements and passing national examinations. State licensing is not generally required for employment specialists.

Additional Requirements

 Successful employment specialists engage in ongoing professional development to maintain their certifications. A high degree of personal integrity and professionalism are required of employment specialists because they have access to the personal information of employment candidates and influence over the hiring or job placement process. Membership in professional human resources associations is encouraged among all employment specialists as a means of building professional community and networking.

EARNINGS AND ADVANCEMENT

Earnings depend on the type, size and geographic location of the employer and the employee's education and experience. Employment specialists in personnel consulting firms are usually paid on a commission basis, while those in temporary help service companies receive a salary. Commissions are usually based on the type, as well as on the number, of placements. Those who place more highly skilled or hard-to-find employees usually earn more

Median annual earnings of employment specialists were $56,630 in 2013. The lowest ten percent earned less than $33,240, and the highest ten percent earned more than $96,470.

Employment specialists may receive paid vacations, holidays, and sick days; life and health insurance; and retirement benefits. These are usually paid by the employer.

Metropolitan Areas with the Highest
Employment Level in this Occupation

Metropolitan area	Employment[1]	Employment per thousand jobs	Hourly mean wage
New York-White Plains-Wayne, NY-NJ	9,830	1.88	$32.62
Washington-Arlington-Alexandria, DC-VA-MD-WV	7,040	2.97	$36.22
Atlanta-Sandy Springs-Marietta, GA	5,580	2.42	$30.34
Phoenix-Mesa-Glendale, AZ	5,510	3.10	$27.03
Los Angeles-Long Beach-Glendale, CA	5,460	1.37	$29.57
Dallas-Plano-Irving, TX	5,000	2.33	$30.64
Houston-Sugar Land-Baytown, TX	4,300	1.56	$30.71
Philadelphia, PA	4,190	2.28	$31.45
Chicago-Joliet-Naperville, IL	4,020	1.09	$29.48
Minneapolis-St. Paul-Bloomington, MN-WI	3,730	2.08	$28.93

[1]Does not include self-employed. Source: Bureau of Labor Statistics

EMPLOYMENT AND OUTLOOK

Employment specialists held about 200,000 jobs nationally in 2012. Most employment specialists worked in the private sector in the areas of administrative and support services; professional, scientific and technical services; manufacturing; health care and social assistance; and finance and insurance firms. Employment is expected to grow as fast as the average for all occupations through the year 2022, which means employment is projected to increase 9 percent to 15 percent. Increasing efforts throughout all industries to recruit and retain quality employees should create many jobs for employment specialists.

Employment Trend, Projected 2010–20

Business Operations Specialists: 15%

Employment Specialists: 13%

Total, All Occupations: 11%

Note: "All Occupations" includes all occupations in the U.S. Economy. Source: U.S. Bureau of Labor Statistics, Employment Projections Program

Related Occupations
- Human Resources Specialist/ Manager
- Rehabilitation Counselor
- School Counselor
- Social Worker
- Vocational Rehabilitation Counselor

Related Military Occupations
- Personnel Manager
- Personnel Specialist
- Recruiting Specialist

Conversation With . . .
STACY KYLE

Program Specialist
AHEDD, Camp Hill, Pennsylvania
Employment Specialist field, 21 years

1. What was your individual career path in terms of education/training, entry-level job, or other significant opportunity?

I majored in psychology with a concentration in deafness, and after I graduated, worked at a group home for delinquent girls. After two years, I moved to a job as a vocational counselor at a private rehab facility. I was an agent of the insurance company and helped people who had been on Workers' Compensation for more than a year find suitable jobs. I worked there for about two years, but didn't like that type of vocational counseling. Many clients had lawyers, which required me to send any communication to the lawyer, not the individual. This seriously hampered success because it caused delays and many opportunities were time-sensitive. In my current job with Association for Habilitation and Employment of Developmentally Disabled (AHEDD), I hire and train staff, manage projects, write grants, do data management and reporting, and do public speaking.

2. What are the most important skills and/or qualities for someone in your profession?

It's not just about finding jobs. The best employment specialists learn to ask the right questions. They are adept at talking to customers and understanding their concerns. They gain knowledge about external factors like Social Security benefits that can impact an individual's willingness to work or to work full time. You must have attention to detail and a willingness to learn. You have to understand how services are funded, so that you can work effectively with limited resources. You must constantly learn about different industries and employer expectations. You have to be able to effectively manage your own schedule, and be flexible enough to change your focus when unexpected needs arise.

The skills of those who perform well in this role are often under-appreciated. Sometimes staff are really good on the people end of things, but may not be good at assertively working the marketing/outreach side of things to find or create job opportunities.

3. What do you wish you had known going into this profession?

I knew the money was not big in this industry. I knew the supports available for clients don't always meet their needs, that program guidelines aren't always easy to understand, and that you can't always get the best results.

I think some employment specialists are surprised by the level of performance and outcomes expected. Here at AHEDD, of course we care about the satisfaction of the individuals with disabilities who are our clients, but we also have to meet the performance expectations of taxpayers, businesses, sponsors, etc. It's not good enough to just get people jobs. We want them to be working toward the maximum independence possible.

4. Are there many job opportunities in your profession? In what specific areas?

In current workforce development budgets, employment services for people with disabilities get a very small piece of the pie.

5. How do you see your profession changing in the next five years? What role will technolo-gy play in those changes, and what skills will be required?

Technology is huge. We have moved to a cloud environment, allowing staff easier access to data and other resources necessary to do their jobs in the community. We're working on an improved data system with participant-specific information outcomes. More and more, data will drive who gets money.

AHEDD is piloting an app that could help better quantify success in training individuals, by tracking their job performance and appropriate behaviors. This will help us make better decisions about whether to continue supporting someone in a specific position, and to justify requests for additional hours. The creator of this app is interested in trying out the use of remote job coaching, via webcam and other technology. That could reduce overall costs for employment services and, when appropriate, allow job coaches or employment specialists to be less obtrusive when an individual is trying to be integrated and accepted into his or her work environment.

6. What do you enjoy most about your job? What do you enjoy least about your job?

Hearing success stories is really my favorite part. When you learn that someone has been able to move out on their own, buy a car, or even take a friend out for lunch, it really drives home the purpose of AHEDD. Work gives people choices and power. The actual task I love most is doing presentations and selling employers on the value of working with us.

Documentation, while necessary, is my least favorite.

7. Can you suggest a valuable "try this" for students considering a career in your profession?

Customer service jobs can be a great opportunity, especially in an environment that requires you to deal with a variety of people who don't always understand things or are sometimes angry.

Selling or marketing jobs would also be helpful, because you have to learn about your potential customers and identify concerns or questions they might have with your product or program.

SELECTED SCHOOLS

Many colleges and universities have bachelor's degree programs in human resources management, counseling, and related subjects. The student may also gain an initial grounding at a technical or community college. Consult with your school guidance counselor or research area post-secondary programs to find the right fit for you.

MORE INFORMATION

American Staffing Association
277 South Washington St., Suite 200
Alexandria, VA 22314
703.253.2020
www.staffingtoday.net

Association of Executive Search Consultants
12 East 41st Street, 17th Floor
New York, NY 10017
212.398.9556
www.aesc.org

Human Resources Certification Institute
1800 Duke Street
Alexandria, VA 22314
866.898.4724
www.hrci.org

International Association of Workforce Professionals
1801 Louisville Road
Frankfort, KY 40601
888.898.9960
www.iawponline.org

National Association of Personnel Service
131 Prominence Lane, Suite 130
Dawsonville, GA 30534
706.531.0060
www.recruitinglife.com

Simone Isadora Flynn/Editor

Fitness Trainer & Instructor

Snapshot

Career Cluster: Sport & Athletics; Hospitality & Tourism; Personal Services

Interests: Exercise, being active, motivating others

Earnings (Yearly Average): $36,900

Employment & Outlook: Average Growth Expected

OVERVIEW

Sphere of Work

Fitness trainers and instructors design, organize, and lead exercise and sports programs that allow individuals to improve their health through cardiovascular activity, strength training, and stretching exercises. They usually offer private lessons as well as group instruction. They teach the fundamentals of fitness by presenting clients with various techniques, helping them set individually tailored fitness goals, and motivating them physically and mentally to reach those goals. Fitness trainers and instructors often focus on one or more areas of fitness, such as aerobics, weight lifting, yoga, or Pilates.

Work Environment

Fitness trainers and instructors work in a variety of settings, from health clubs and exercise studios to resorts and universities. Some travel to clients' homes to provide regular instruction, while others organize fitness programs for large businesses. The majority of fitness trainers and instructors work indoors in cool climates; however, some offer instruction in pleasant outdoor environments. Most fitness trainers and instructors work full time with irregular hours, as they must cater to the schedules of their clients. They often work early in the morning, at night, on weekends, and during holidays. Fitness trainers and instructors spend most of their time standing, walking, and participating in physical activities.

Profile

Working Conditions: Work both Indoors and Outdoors
Physical Strength: Medium Work
Education Needs: High School Diploma, Technical/Community College, Bachelor's Degree
Licensure/Certification: Recommended
Physical Abilities Not Required: No Heavy Labor
Opportunities For Experience: Internship, Volunteer Work
Holland Interest Score*: ESR

* See Appendix A

Occupation Interest

Those looking to become fitness trainers and instructors must be in excellent physical condition and have natural athletic ability. They should have a passion for instructing and motivating individuals. Sometimes clients are reluctant or unwilling to participate in specified activities, so fitness trainers and instructors should be firm, persuasive, and encouraging. Creativity and patience are also valuable traits. Fitness trainers and instructors must have strong customer service skills in order to find and maintain their clientele.

A Day in the Life—Duties and Responsibilities

Fitness trainers and instructors spend most of their day working with clients to achieve and build upon specified fitness goals. They begin by evaluating the physical strengths and weaknesses of each individual and providing corrective feedback for improvement. Fitness trainers and instructors design appropriate exercise programs based on the skill level, strength, and endurance of each client. They keep detailed records of clients' progress and advancement, noting accomplishments as well as areas that need improvement. Many fitness trainers and instructors have a background in nutrition and often advise clients on suitable diets, weight control techniques, and lifestyle modifications. They are responsible for informing clients of safety procedures and regulations related to sports and aerobic activities, as well as the proper use of exercise machines and other equipment.

When instructing large groups of people, fitness trainers and instructors plan lessons and routines, select music, and create innovative exercise programs. They must keep lessons and classes exciting, challenging, and safe for all participants. Because the skill levels of participants vary greatly, fitness trainers and instructors must offer alternative fitness regimens to accommodate all individuals within the group. They usually demonstrate a particular exercise method or sequence, observe participants in action, and correct any mistakes in order to prevent injury. Fitness trainers and instructors must also treat minor injuries, administer first aid, and refer clients to specialty physicians as needed.

Duties and Responsibilities

- Developing fitness programs for individuals or groups
- Conducting fitness training either one-on-one or before a group
- Making dietary and nutritional suggestions
- Recommending and purchasing equipment
- Monitoring exercise programs and making changes as necessary
- Hiring additional staff members

OCCUPATION SPECIALTIES

Group Fitness Instructors

Group Fitness Instructors organize and lead group exercise sessions, which can include aerobic exercise, stretching, muscle conditioning, or meditation. Some classes are set to music. In these classes, instructors may select the music and choreograph an exercise sequence.

Personal Fitness Instructors

Personal Fitness Instructors work with a single client or a small group. They may train in a gym or in the clients' homes. Personal fitness trainers assess the clients' level of physical fitness and help them set and reach their fitness goals.

Specialized Fitness Instructors

Specialized Fitness Instructors teach popular conditioning methods such as Pilates or yoga. In these classes, instructors show the different moves and positions of the particular method. They also watch students and correct those who are doing the exercises improperly.

Fitness Directors

Fitness Directors oversee the fitness-related aspects of a gym or other type of health club. They often handle administrative duties, such as scheduling personal training sessions for clients or creating workout incentive programs. They often select and order fitness equipment for their facility.

WORK ENVIRONMENT

Physical Environment

Most fitness trainers and instructors work indoors at fitness centers, health clubs, and exercise studios. Others work in hospitals, country clubs, resorts, and clients' homes. Gym environments are generally cool, clean, and well ventilated. Fitness trainers and instructors who lead outdoor fitness classes tend to work in warm weather conditions.

Human Environment

Fitness trainers and instructors mostly interact with their clients, regularly seeing individuals at least once a week and often more. Many are self-employed; however, those who work in fitness or health clubs typically report to fitness directors or gym managers.

Relevant Skills and Abilities

Communication Skills
- Speaking effectively

Interpersonal/Social Skills
- Being sensitive to others
- Cooperating with others
- Motivating others
- Providing support to others
- Working as a member of a team

Organization & Management Skills
- Coordinating tasks
- Managing people/groups
- Organizing information or materials

Technical Skills
- Working with your hands

Other Skills
- Being physically active

Technological Environment

Fitness trainers and instructors commonly use balance boards and discs, exercise balls, fitness weights, pedometers, and first aid kits in their daily activities. In order to track sessions and schedule clientele, they may use accounting, calendar, and project management software.

EDUCATION, TRAINING, AND ADVANCEMENT

High School/Secondary

High school students who are interested in becoming fitness trainers and instructors can prepare by taking courses not only in physical education but also in sciences such as biology, physiology, and chemistry. They should study business, English, nutrition, psychology, and basic math. Interested students can join school sports teams, participate in local sports leagues, or take individual lessons to learn the fundamentals of physical activity. Aspiring fitness trainers and instructors can gain experience by volunteering or working part time for a private gym, resort, or health club, or the gym of a local hospital, country club, or university.

Suggested High School Subjects

- Applied Math
- Biology
- Business
- Chemistry
- English
- First Aid Training
- Foods & Nutrition
- Health Science Technology
- Physics
- Physiology
- Psychology

Famous First

The first sport and fitness trainer to work full-time at an athletic facility was Bob Rogers of the New York Athletic Club, starting in 1883. Rogers had previously been a trainer with the London Athletic Club. Both organizations were exclusive "gentlemen's clubs" specializing in such activities as fencing, rowing, platform tennis, squash, and water polo. Eventually they diversified, in terms of both their sports programs and their clientele. New York Athletic Club members have won over 230 Olympic medals, more than 120 of which have been gold.

Postsecondary

After high school, prospective fitness trainers and instructors may pursue various modes of training for their area of desired specialization. They often enroll in classes that will qualify them for professional certification. Once certified, many fitness trainers and instructors work with or shadow an experienced trainer to better understand the practical applications of fitness instruction. After a period of time, new fitness trainers and instructors begin to establish their own clientele. Instructors looking to teach group classes must usually audition to teach at a particular gym or club. Those specializing in a certain method of exercise may need additional training or specialty certification.

An associate's or bachelor's degree in physical education, kinesiology, health, or exercise science is sometimes beneficial for new fitness trainers and instructors. In some cases, employers allow fitness trainers and instructors to substitute a postsecondary degree for professional licensure. Those looking to advance to management positions at health clubs or fitness centers should study exercise science, kinesiology, business administration, and accounting.

Related College Majors
- Exercise Science/Physiology/Movement Studies
- Health & Physical Education
- Parks, Recreation & Leisure Studies
- Physical Education Teaching & Coaching
- Sport & Fitness Administration/Management
- Sports Medicine & Athletic Training

Adult Job Seekers

Fitness trainers and instructors entering the job market should begin by contacting local health centers and other potential employers to determine their various needs. They are expected to be able to fulfill all of the job functions at the time of employment, without the need for on-the-job training. Many fitness trainers and instructors participate in part-time internships, apprenticeships, and job shadowing opportunities with experienced instructors at local health and fitness centers to gain necessary skills before beginning full-time work.

Professional Certification and Licensure

Certification in the fitness field is not always required; however, many employers prefer to hire fitness trainers and instructors who are certified. Candidates must have a high school diploma, maintain cardiopulmonary resuscitation (CPR) certification, and successfully complete an exam comprising both written and practical components related to physiology and exercise programs. Fitness trainers and instructors must be recertified every two years. Because there are many certifying organizations within the fitness field, candidates should first verify an organization's validity with the National Association for Certifying Agencies.

Additional Requirements

Employers in the fitness industry look for outgoing, dynamic, and confident staff. Communication is one of the most important aspects of the job, so fitness trainers and instructors should be comfortable addressing, leading, and motivating individuals and larger groups. They should also be sensitive to the needs and concerns of their clients while inspiring them to challenge themselves and improve their physical health.

EARNINGS AND ADVANCEMENT

Individuals can advance by locating jobs in more prestigious settings and by obtaining jobs with more responsibilities. Those who continually improve their skills by attending workshops, seminars, training sessions and classes will advance more quickly.

Mean annual earnings of fitness trainers and instructors were $36,900 in 2012. The lowest ten percent earned less than $18,094, and the highest ten percent earned more than $67,204. Persons in charge of large fitness programs and those who work in business environments earned the most.

Fitness trainers and instructors may receive paid vacations, holidays, and sick days; life and health insurance; and retirement benefits. These are usually paid by the employer.

Metropolitan Areas with the Highest
Employment Level in this Occupation

Metropolitan area	Employment	Employment per thousand jobs	Hourly mean wage
Chicago-Joliet-Naperville, IL	11,900	3.27	$15.21
New York-White Plains-Wayne, NY-NJ	9,510	1.84	$31.64
Los Angeles-Long Beach-Glendale, CA	5,790	1.49	$22.84
Boston-Cambridge-Quincy, MA	5,630	3.29	$21.92
Washington-Arlington-Alexandria, DC-VA-MD-WV	5,540	2.36	$19.85
Philadelphia, PA	4,490	2.46	$14.26
Seattle-Bellevue-Everett, WA	3,950	2.80	$21.03
Baltimore-Towson, MD	3,550	2.82	$15.77

Source: Bureau of Labor Statistics

EMPLOYMENT AND OUTLOOK

Fitness trainers and instructors held about 235,000 jobs nationally in 2012. About ten percent were self-employed, mostly as personal trainers. Employment is expected to grow faster than the average for all occupations through the year 2022, which means employment is projected to increase 12 percent to 22 percent. An increasing number of people spend more time and money on fitness to remain active, lose weight and have healthy lifestyles. This trend is seen in young people, baby boomers and the elderly alike. In addition, more businesses are recognizing the benefits of recreation and fitness programs and other services, such as wellness programs, for their employees.

Employment Trend, Projected 2012–22

Personal Care and Service Occupations: 21%

Fitness Trainers & Instructors: 13%

All Bus Drivers: 11%

Note: "All Occupations" includes all occupations in the U.S. Economy. Source: U.S. Bureau of Labor Statistics, Employment Projections Program

Related Occupations
- Health & Fitness Center Manager
- Recreation Program Director

Conversation With . . .
BRIAN JOHNSON

Fitness Trainer, 3 years

1. What was your individual career path in terms of education/training, entry-level job, or other significant opportunity?

I was in corporate America for almost 20 years. I became unemployable because I topped out on the rate scale. My last job was running a Safeway distribution center. I asked myself: what's the one thing I've always done? And that's go to the gym. So I got my certification and started training people. I had enough money saved up so I was living off my savings, but the motivating piece was, I didn't want to work for anybody else ever again. I did a 12-week online course to get my certification in 8 weeks. I joined networking groups, which is how I got my clients.

I have my own gym. I trained my first client outside at the park across the street. I used an eight foot chain TRX and a five dollar fitness map. I migrated from individual clients into boot camps, which just makes sense because you're leveraging your time and working with 20 people for $15 each, as opposed to one person at $80.

Through all my marketing and networking, I got hooked up with a couple of wedding vendors. The clients walk in there, see my business cards, and the next thing you know I'll have a bridal party boot camp that usually lasts about two months. I also am starting a two-hour ultimate boot camp challenge, that also has a 5K mudrun, live music, vendors…a fitness festival. We have one coming up in May in Annapolis, and I'm talking about doing one with a guy on Long Island, NY, and a guy in Raleigh, NC. My goal is to do one a month across the nation.

2. What are the most important skills and/or qualities for someone in your profession?

The ability to inspire, motivate and hold people accountable, that's the most important piece. Without that, whether you're working in a gym or doing your own gig, you're never going to retain people.

3. What do you wish you had known going into this profession?

How difficult it would be to get clients. I thought it would be easy. In the fitness industry, word of mouth is everything, networking and social media. You've got to get your name out there. I do Business Networking International and other local area mixers. You have to identify the best social media for your industry. For mine, it's Facebook. For a banker, it's LinkedIn. At the end of the day, I have a very extensive and elaborate website but the majority of my clients come from word of mouth.

Also, in hindsight, I would have trained at a gym for two or three months to gain that confidence level to train people. I only charged my first client $30 a session. Now, I charge $80 for a private session. You need to research what other people are charging. You don't want to devalue yourself, or overprice yourself out of business. You've got to find that balance and test the market.

4. Are there many job opportunities in your profession? In what specific areas?

Yes. I say that because I've seen constant turnover at the gyms. They're always looking for quality instructors.

5. How do you see your profession changing in the next five years? What role will technology play in those changes, and what skills will be required?

I think a lot of it's going to go online. I can already see that shift happening. My vision is, you have this ten-by-ten room, you have a nice camera in there, people log in every day, and I instruct them for an hour. For $1, I have 1,000 people logging in for an hour.

6. What do you enjoy most about your job? What do you enjoy least?

Getting people to their goals, whether somebody is morbidly obese or somebody is already fit and training for a tough event. At my gym, we have a whiteboard where everybody writes their goals. I have a 61-year-old lady flipping a 200-pound tractor tire. It helps to motivate everyone.

What I like least is that you're always on. It's hard to shut it off. Not that I ever would, but God forbid if I ever wanted to go to McDonalds and have a cheeseburger. Too many people in this town know me! But it's a blessing. If I was working for a gym training someone, I would leave there at the end of the day and be done.

7. Can you suggest a valuable "try this" for students considering a career in your profession?

Try it at a gym first. Don't try it on your own. Write out all the pros and cons and make sure it's right for you, because it's not right for everybody.

SELECTED SCHOOLS

Although training beyond high school is not necessarily expected of beginning fitness trainers and instructors, interested parties may obtain training in fitness and exercise science at selected technical/community colleges or at privately run programs designed to prepare students for certification. Selected four-year college programs, too, offer degrees in this field.

MORE INFORMATION

American Alliance for Health, Physical Education, Recreation & Dance
1900 Association Drive
Reston, VA 20192-1598
800.213.7193
www.aahperd.org

American Council on Exercise
4851 Paramount Drive
San Diego, CA 92123
888.825.3636
www.acefitness.org

American Fitness Professionals and Associates
1601 Long Beach Boulevard
P.O. Box 214
Ship Bottom, NJ 08008
800.494.7782
www.afpafitness.com

International Fitness Professionals Association
14509 University Point Place
Tampa, FL 33613
www.ifpa-fitness.com

International Health, Racquet, and Sportsclub Association
70 Fargo Street
Boston, MA 02210
617.951.0055
www.ihrsa.org

National Board of Fitness Examiners
1650 Margaret Street
Suite 302-342
Jacksonville, FL 32204
www.nbfe.org

National Gym Association
P.O. Box 970579
Coconut Creek, FL 33097
954.344.8410
www.nationalgym.com

National Strength and Conditioning Association
1885 Bob Johnson Drive
Colorado Springs, CO 80906
800.815.6826
www.nsca.com

**Society of State Directors
of Health, Physical Educ. &
Recreation**
1900 Association Drive, Suite 100
Reston, VA 20191-1599
703.390.4599
www.thesociety.org

Yoga Alliance
1701 Clarendon Boulevard
Suite 100
Arlington, VA 22209
571.482.3355
www.yogaalliance.org

1500 E. Broward Boulevard
Suite 250
Fort Lauderdale, FL 33301
888.484.8771
unitedstatespilatesassociation.com

Briana Nadeau/Editor

Healthcare Social Worker

Snapshot

Career Cluster: Health Care; Human Services

Interests: Social work, counseling, crisis intervention, mental health, case management, psychology

Earnings (Yearly Average): $50,820

Employment & Outlook: Faster Than Average Growth Expected

OVERVIEW

Sphere of Work

Healthcare social work is a specialty of the social work profession. While social workers are generalists committed to improving the social and behavioral lives of individuals, families, and communities, healthcare social workers, also called medical or public health social workers, are trained to assist patients and their families in medical settings. Healthcare social workers help patients and their families develop emotional and psychological coping strategies; resolve problems and conflicts with doctors, medical staff, and insurance providers; and

secure treatment opportunities. Healthcare social workers work with individual clients and their families to lessen the impact of illness and disease.

Work Environment

Healthcare social workers spend their workdays seeing clients in hospitals, out-patient medical clinics, public health agencies, nursing homes, psychiatric facilities, substance abuse clinics, and residential rehabilitation facilities. In addition to regular work hours, healthcare social workers often work in an on-call capacity. Healthcare social workers may have a fixed office where they see clients or may be on the road, traveling to meet with clients. Given the diverse demands of the healthcare social work profession, healthcare social workers may need to work days, evenings, and weekends to meet client or caseload needs.

Profile

Working Conditions: Work Indoors
Physical Strength: Light Work
Education Needs: Bachelor's Degree, Master's Degree
Licensure/Certification: Required
Physical Abilities Not Required: No Heavy Labor
Opportunities For Experience: Internship, Part-Time Work
Holland Interest Score*: ESA

* See Appendix A

Occupation Interest

Individuals drawn to the healthcare social work profession tend to be intelligent and socially conscious people who have the ability to quickly assess people and situations, find resources, demonstrate caring, and solve problems. Those who succeed in healthcare social work display traits such as leadership, knowledge of human behavior, comfort around illness, initiative, project management, and concern for individuals and society. Healthcare social workers should enjoy spending time with a wide range of people, particularly those suffering acute, chronic, or terminal illnesses and conditions.

A Day in the Life—Duties and Responsibilities

The healthcare social worker's area of specialization and work environment determine his or her daily occupational duties and responsibilities. There is a wide range of possible duties and responsibilities, so each day can be different depending on client needs. Healthcare social workers facilitate patient admissions and discharge processes; plan meetings and facilitate relationships between individuals facing the same medical challenges; discuss quality of life issues with patients and their families; and offer grief counseling to patients and their families. At times they provide substance abuse counseling; coordinate health-related transportation and housing needs for patients; conduct psycho-social assessment and evaluation of patients, including mental status exams; and collaborate with the patient's medical team, including specialists, general practitioners, and other case managers. Other responsibilities may include overseeing patients' long- and short-term medical care planning; assessing patients' home or residential facility health care options and future medical needs; providing financial and insurance benefit counseling to patients and their families; and educating clients and families on legal issues such as medical power of attorney or drawing up a living will. In addition, healthcare social workers may provide end of life psychological support to patients and their families; lead patient support groups for transplant, cancer, or substance abuse patients; offer crisis intervention services; participate in physical or sexual abuse investigations; and plan public health education campaigns for communities and special interest groups.

All healthcare social workers are responsible for completing patient charts and required documentation, such as patient discharge or insurance paperwork, on a daily basis. Because they help patients find services that enable them to return home sooner, healthcare social workers play a pivotal role in coordinating hospital discharges, which in turn affects hospital costs and patient quality of life.

Duties and Responsibilities

- **Working with patients and their families to restore and maintain patient health**
- **Advising patients about available resources and best practices**
- **Arranging for patient care at home or in a recovery facility**
- **Working on teams with other healthcare and medical professionals**
- **Filling out and maintaining case records on each patient**

WORK ENVIRONMENT

Physical Environment

A healthcare social worker's immediate physical environment varies based on caseload and specialization. Healthcare social workers spend their workdays seeing clients in a wide variety of settings including hospitals, out-patient medical clinics, public health agencies, nursing homes, psychiatric facilities, substance abuse clinics, and residential rehabilitation facilities

Relevant Skills and Abilities

Communication Skills
- Speaking effectively
- Writing concisely

Interpersonal/Social Skills
- Being sensitive to others
- Cooperating with others
- Having good judgment
- Providing support to others
- Working as a member of a team

Organization & Management Skills
- Coordinating tasks
- Handling challenging situations
- Making decisions
- Paying attention to and handling details

Human Environment

Healthcare social workers work with a wide variety of people and should be comfortable meeting with colleagues, medical staff, patients' families, and patients with acute, chronic and terminal illnesses. Healthcare social workers provide counseling, lead meetings, provide workshops, and collaborate on patient teams. Due to the wide range of human interactions required of healthcare social workers, they are often called on to use patience, empathy, leadership, tact, mediation, and negotiation.

Technological Environment

Healthcare social workers use computers, cell phones, and Internet communication tools to perform their work. For instance, healthcare social workers must be comfortable using computers to access client records and cell phones to ensure availability and accessibility during on-call hours.

EDUCATION, TRAINING, AND ADVANCEMENT

High School/Secondary

High school students interested in pursuing a career in healthcare social work should prepare themselves by developing good study habits. High school coursework in foreign languages, sociology, psychology, biology, and education will provide a strong foundation for college-level work in healthcare social work. Due to the diversity of healthcare social work specialties, high school students interested in this career will benefit from seeking internships or part-time work that expose the students to diverse groups of people, healthcare issues, and social needs.

Suggested High School Subjects
- Applied Communication
- Biology
- Chemistry
- English
- Foreign Languages
- Health Science Technology
- Mathematics
- Psychology
- Social Studies
- Sociology
- Statistics

Famous First

The first hospital to employ medical social workers was Massachusetts General Hospital in Boston, in the early 1900s. Dr. Richard Clarke Cabot, head of the outpatient department, believed that economic, social, family, and psychological conditions influenced patient health and recovery, especially in the case of illnesses such as tuberculosis, diabetes, and syphilis. The hospital, however, would not pay for the hiring of social workers, forcing Cabot, pictured with his team, to pay the wages of the two healthcare workers—a man and a woman—himself.

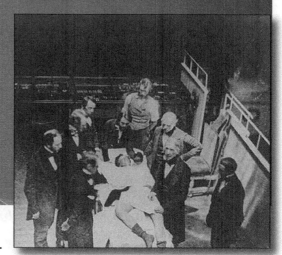

College/Postsecondary

Postsecondary students interested in becoming healthcare social workers should work towards the bachelor's of social work degree. Coursework in education, psychology, biology, and foreign languages may also prove useful in their healthcare social work practice. Postsecondary students can gain work experience and potential advantage in their future job searches by securing internships or part-time employment in medical settings or public health agencies.

Related College Majors
- Clinical & Healthcare Social Work
- Psychiatric/Mental Health Tech Services
- Psychology, General
- Social Work
- Sociology

Adult Job Seekers

Adults seeking employment as healthcare social workers should have earned, at a minimum, a bachelor's of social work degree or related field such as psychology or sociology. Healthcare social work jobs increasingly require a master of social work degree and second language proficiency. Adult job seekers should educate themselves about the educational and professional license requirements of their home states and the organizations where they seek employment.

Adult job seekers may benefit from joining professional associations to help with networking and job searching. Professional social work associations, such as the Action Network for Social Work Education and Research and the Center for Clinical Social Work, generally offer job-finding workshops and maintain lists and forums of available jobs.

Professional Certification and Licensure

Professional certification and licensure is required of all practicing healthcare social workers. The social work licensure process varies by state and specialty. Certifications include Licensed Social Work Associate (LSWA), Licensed Social Worker (LSW), Licensed Certified Social Worker (LCSW), and Licensed Independent Clinical Social Worker (LICSW). Each requires different amounts and types of education and supervised work experience. In general, healthcare social workers interested in clinical social work practice need the highest amount of supervised hours (approximately 3,000 hours) to earn their clinical license. Consult credible professional associations within the field and follow professional debate as to the relevancy and value of any certification program.

Additional Requirements

Individuals who find satisfaction, success, and job security as healthcare social workers are knowledgeable about the profession's requirements, responsibilities and opportunities. Successful healthcare social workers engage in ongoing professional development. Healthcare social workers must have high levels of integrity and ethics as they interact with vulnerable people and have access to personal records. Membership in professional social work associations is encouraged among junior and senior healthcare social workers as a means of building status in a professional community and networking.

EARNINGS AND ADVANCEMENT

Median annual earnings of healthcare social workers were $50,820 in 2013. The lowest ten percent earned less than $31,790, and the highest ten percent earned more than $75,140.

Healthcare social workers may receive paid vacations, holidays, and sick days; life and health insurance; and retirement benefits. These are usually paid by the employer.

Metropolitan Areas with the Highest Employment Level in this Occupation

Metropolitan area	Employment[1]	Employment per thousand jobs	Hourly mean wage
New York-White Plains-Wayne, NY-NJ	6,860	1.31	$29.67
Boston-Cambridge-Quincy, MA	4,390	2.51	$28.65
Los Angeles-Long Beach-Glendale, CA	3,740	0.94	$30.90
Philadelphia, PA	3,180	1.73	$24.45
Chicago-Joliet-Naperville, IL	2,760	0.75	$24.42
St. Louis, MO-IL	2,440	1.89	$21.91
Phoenix-Mesa-Glendale, AZ	1,910	1.07	$25.24
Baltimore-Towson, MD	1,880	1.47	$28.15
Atlanta-Sandy Springs-Marietta, GA	1,860	0.81	$23.62
Minneapolis-St. Paul-Bloomington, MN-WI	1,710	0.95	$25.44

[1] Does not include self-employed. Source: Bureau of Labor Statistics

EMPLOYMENT AND OUTLOOK

Healthcare social workers held about 146,000 jobs nationally in 2012. Employment is expected to grow much faster than the average for all occupations through the year 2022, which means employment is projected to increase 25 percent or more. This is primarily the result of the aging population creating greater demand for health services. As hospitals increasingly emphasize early discharge of patients in an effort to control costs, more healthcare social workers will be needed to ensure that the necessary medical and social services are in place when individuals leave the hospital. Employment is growing in home health care services as well, not only because hospitals are releasing patients earlier, but because a large number of people have impairments or disabilities that make it difficult to live at home without some form of assistance.

Employment Trend, Projected 2010–20

Healthcare Social Workers: 27%

Social Workers (All): 19%

Total, All Occupations: 11%

Note: "All Occupations" includes all occupations in the U.S. Economy. Source: U.S. Bureau of Labor Statistics, Employment Projections Program

Related Occupations
- Psychologist
- Rehabilitation Counselor
- School Counselor
- Social Worker

Conversation With . . .
PETER DRAGO

Mental Health Specialist
Crescent Care Health, New Orleans, LA
Health Care Social Worker, 25 years

1. What was your individual career path in terms of education/training, entry-level job, or other significant opportunity?

I decided to return to school for a Master's in Social Work after spending 10 unfulfilling years working for a major oil company with my bachelor's degree in computer science. I followed the clinical track in my new degree program. I knew my strength was being present with people in need and providing comfort in difficult situations. This was because I had spent four years volunteering at a residential facility with people with HIV/AIDS who, at that time, were dying quickly after diagnosis and in overwhelming numbers. I became fascinated with end-of-life situations and the perspectives of people going through them, as well as their loved ones witnessing these processes. I recognized my passion and knew that by enhancing it with a theoretical background, I could be even more effective.

My career focus has been primarily HIV. After graduating, I started at an HIV outpatient clinic doing case management and counseling. Shortly after, a professional partner and I opened our own residential facility for people with HIV bcause New Orleans had a shortage of that resource. I then spent three years in the Peace Corps with the initial assignment of counseling adolescents who did not qualify for formal high school and were in a vocational setting. Even there, I managed to steer myself into HIV work and helped create some care plans and policies to address the emerging HIV needs of the country where I was assigned. When I returned home, I went back to work for the HIV outpatient clinic in their palliative care program doing case management and counseling for that specific population. I had another short stint for an HIV case management agency. Then I went to work for a hospice agency doing end-of-life work as the bereavement counselor. Feeling a need for a break in my career track, I spent a little while being a counselor at an outpatient mental health clinic. That led to my current position as Mental Health Specialist at an agency serves people who are HIV-infected, with an emphasis on families, women and children.

2. What are the most important skills and/or qualities for someone in your profession?

Compassion, an open-mindedness, patience and a capacity for analyzing people and behaviors.

3. What do you wish you had known going into this profession?

When I entered the academic training for my (new) profession, all I knew was that I was compassionate and enjoyed people and helping them. I don't think there is anything I wish I had known that I did not get from formal training and hands-on experience.

4. Are there many job opportunities in your profession? In what specific areas?

I can only speak to my local area. Available jobs tend to be in school or health settings, and the mental health / addiction field.

5. How do you see your profession changing in the next five years, what role will technology play in those changes, and what skills will be required?

Again, I can only speak to my local area, but I see changes connected to the Affordable Care Act as well as a continuous loss of mental health services. I have worked mostly with an indigent population, limited in financial resources and education. They are also limited in understanding the core aspects of ACA; insurance has been a foreign concept to them because most received care at our "Charity Hospital" — lost after Hurricane Katrina — where services were delivered with little regard to people having insurance or the ability to pay for services. Getting my clients to accept and participate with ACA has been challenging because it's hard to educate them, and it also requires them to give up the long-standing tradition of free care in New Orleans.

The latest technology strategies use texting to remind clients of their medical and mental health appointments, as well as various programs for education and incentives to encourage clients to enter and stay in care.

6. What do you enjoy most about your job? What do you enjoy least about your job?

I most enjoy when the client I am working with gets to the point where they realize what the process is about and can acknowledge they have attained a goal or made some progress. I least like the barriers brought on by political agendas, funding shortages and loss of services. They make a difficult situation even more difficult.

7. Can you suggest a valuable "try this" for students considering a career in your profession?

Even 25 years after obtaining my MSW degree, I value the four years prior to that when I volunteered in HIV, the area I knew interested me. This experience had a significant impact on my decision to return to school. I would strongly encourage anyone considering a career in human services to test the waters by volunteering in an area that specifically interests you.

SELECTED SCHOOLS

Many colleges and universities have bachelor's degree programs in subjects related to health care and social work. The student may also gain an initial grounding at a technical or community college. Consult with your school guidance counselor or research area post-secondary programs to find the right fit for you. For a list of top schools in the field of social work, of which health care social work is a subcategory, see the entry "Social Worker" in the present volume.

MORE INFORMATION

American Board of Examiners in Clinical Social Work
241 Humphrey Street
Marblehead, MA 01945
www.abecsw.org

American Case Management Association
10310 West 36th Street
Little Rock, AR 72205-1579
501.907.2262
www.acmaweb.org

Center for Clinical Social Work
27 Congress Street, Suite 501
Salem, MA 01970
www.centercsw.org

Council on Social Work Education
1701 Duke Street, Suite 200
Alexandria, VA 22314-3457
703.683.8080
www.cswe.org

National Association of Social Workers
750 First Street NE, Suite 700
Washington, DC 20002-4241
202.408.8600
www.naswdc.org

Society for Social Work Leadership in Health Care
100 N. 20th Street, Suite 400
Philadelphia, PA 19103
866.237.9542
www.sswlhc.org

Simone Isadora Flynn/Editor

Health Information Technician

Snapshot

Career Cluster: Health Care; Human Services

Interests: Medical records and terminology, data entry, detailed work, problem solving

Earnings (Yearly Average): $34,970

Employment & Outlook: Faster Than Average Growth Expected

OVERVIEW

Sphere of Work

Health information technicians, sometimes referred to as medical records technicians, maintain medical information systems. They are responsible for the compilation and organization of medical records, including patient lab results, medical histories, and x-rays. Under the direction and supervision of medical records administrators, technicians process and maintain records that may be used and accessed by medical personnel and patients, as well as medical researchers, government inspectors or regulatory agencies, and insurance companies.

Work Environment

Health information technicians spend their workdays in the offices of hospitals, medical or dental practices, rehabilitation facilities, insurance companies, pharmaceutical companies, government health agencies, and medical laboratories. Technicians generally work forty-hour weeks but may be required to work evening or night shifts to meet the facility's constant need to access medical records.

Profile

Working Conditions: Work Indoors
Physical Strength: Light Work
Education Needs:
  Technical/Community College,
  Bachelor's Degree
Licensure/Certification:
  Recommended
Physical Abilities Not Required: No
Heavy Labor
Opportunities For Experience:
  Internship, Apprenticeship, Military
  Service, Part-Time Work
Holland Interest Score*: CSI

* See Appendix A

Occupation Interest

Individuals drawn to the profession of health information technician tend to be organized and detail oriented. They must be accurate and thorough, with the ability to identify and solve problems quickly. Health information technicians should be self-motivated and enjoy working in a medical environment.

A Day in the Life—Duties and Responsibilities

Health information technicians are responsible for the compilation, organization, and maintenance of medical records. These records may include lab results, medical histories, physical exam reports, x-rays, prescriptions, treatment plans and orders, and records of surgeries and hospitalizations. Technicians enter patient data into medical information systems, review the records for accuracy and completeness, and report any errors or omissions in medical records, at times requesting additional information from medical professionals and administrators. They then respond to requests for specific records by providing access or copies to medical personnel or patients. They may also respond to information requests from researchers studying various diseases or injuries, regulatory agencies inspecting the facility, or insurance companies verifying claims.

Some health information technicians choose to specialize in a particular area of recordkeeping. Those working in medical coding are responsible for assigning standardized classifications to procedures noted in medical records, which can then be easily interpreted by insurance companies for billing and reimbursement purposes. Other specialists may update national disease databases, such as the patient cancer registry, with patient information and pathology data.

Health information technicians may also work with their supervisors to create and implement practices and procedures for health information organization, classification, analysis, and retrieval. They may assist in the transition from paper medical records to electronic health records. Experienced technicians may also train office staff in electronic health record software.

As the work involves constant handling of private medical information, technicians must ensure the confidentiality and security of records within the medical information system. All health information technicians, regardless of specialty, are responsible for educating themselves about the administrative, physical, and technical patient privacy safeguards

Duties and Responsibilities

- Contacting medical personnel to obtain missing data on medical records
- Coding, indexing and filing records of diagnoses, diseases, operations and treatment
- Compiling medical care and census data for statistical reports
- Preparing reports on admissions, births, deaths, transfers and charges
- Transcribing medical records
- Releasing information to persons and agencies according to regulations
- Organizing, analyzing, and evaluating health records according to established standards
- Reviewing medical records for completeness, accuracy and compliance with requirements

WORK ENVIRONMENT

included in the federal Health Insurance Portability and Accountability Act.

Physical Environment

Health information technicians generally work in comfortable offices within hospitals, medical or dental practices, rehabilitation facilities, insurance companies, pharmaceutical companies, government health agencies, and medical laboratories. Although their interaction with patients is generally minimal, they may risk exposure to infectious diseases.

Human Environment

Health information technicians should be comfortable interacting with physicians, insurance representatives, laboratory staff, government inspectors, office staff, supervising medical records administrators, and patients. Due to the sensitive nature of medical diagnosis and treatment, health information technicians must be empathetic and tactful when interacting with patients and their families and must uphold patient confidentiality.

Relevant Skills and Abilities

Communication Skills
- Speaking effectively
- Writing concisely

Interpersonal/Social Skills
- Cooperating with others
- Working as a member of a team

Organization & Management Skills
- Following instructions
- Organizing information or materials
- Paying attention to and handling details

Research & Planning Skills
- Analyzing information
- Using logical reasoning

Technological Environment

In the course of their work, health information technicians use a wide variety of tools and equipment, including computers, electronic medical records software, medical coding charts, insurance rate charts and books, printers, calculators, photocopying machines, telephones, word processing software, facsimile machines, and scanners. Some technicians, particularly those specializing in coding, may need

EDUCATION, TRAINING, AND ADVANCEMENT

to have a basic understanding of medical equipment in order to categorize procedures properly.

High School/Secondary

High school students interested in pursuing a career as a health information technician should study typing and bookkeeping, which will provide a strong foundation for work in the field. Students interested in this career path may benefit from seeking volunteer positions, administrative internships, or part-time clerical work with local hospitals or other medical facilities.

Suggested High School Subjects
- Applied Communication
- Biology
- Business & Computer Technology
- Business Data Processing
- English
- Health Science Technology
- Keyboarding
- Mathematics

Famous First

The first centralized system of medical records for hospitals was developed by Dr. Henry Plummer and Mabel Root at the Mayo Clinic, Rochester, Minnesota, in 1907. The system provided a file for each patient that contained all records of hospital treatment, including lab test results, enabling medical staff to review the patient's entire history. (Previously, each department maintained its own files on patients.)

College/Postsecondary

Postsecondary students interested in becoming health information technicians should obtain an associate's degree in health information technology, medical secretarial science, or a related field from a program accredited by the Commission on Accreditation of Allied Health Education Programs (CAAHEP). Coursework in medical terminology, mathematics, and business may also prove useful. Students can gain work experience and potential advantage in their future job searches by securing administrative internships or part-time clerical employment with medical facilities.

Related College Majors
- Medical Office Management
- Medical Records Administration
- Medical Records Technology

Adult Job Seekers

Adults seeking employment as health information technicians should have, at a minimum, an associate's degree from a CAAHEP-accredited program. Some senior health information technician positions require extensive experience and bachelor's degrees, so job seekers should educate themselves about the educational and professional requirements of their prospective employers. Professional medical administration associations, such as the American Health Information Management Association (AHIMA) and the Association of Medical Secretaries, Practice Managers, Administrators and Receptionists (AMSPAR), may offer workshops, job postings, and networking opportunities.

Professional Certification and Licensure

Certification and licensure is not legally required for health information technicians, but it may be required as a condition of employment, salary increase, or promotion. Some technicians may choose to obtain the Registered Health Information Technician (RHIT) designation offered by AHIMA. This credential is available to individuals who have completed a training program accredited by the Commission on Accreditation for Health Informatics and Information Management Education (CAHIIM) and pass an examination. Health information technicians interested in pursuing certification should consult credible professional associations within the field and follow professional debate as to the relevancy and value of any voluntary certification program.

Additional Requirements

As professionals in this role have access to confidential medical records, health information technicians must possess a high level of integrity and professional ethics.

EARNINGS AND ADVANCEMENT

Earnings of health information technicians depend on the geographic location of the employer and the employee's experience and occupational specialty. Median annual earnings of health information technicians were $39,970 in 2013. The lowest ten percent earned less than $22,700, and the highest ten percent earned more than $57,320.

Health information technicians may receive paid vacations, holidays, and sick days; life and health insurance; and retirement benefits. These are usually paid by the employer.

Metropolitan Areas with the Highest
Employment Level in this Occupation

Metropolitan area	Employment[1]	Employment per thousand jobs	Hourly mean wage
Chicago-Joliet-Naperville, IL	4,870	1.31	$19.10
Los Angeles-Long Beach-Glendale, CA	4,580	1.15	$20.41
Houston-Sugar Land-Baytown, TX	4,540	1.65	$19.62
New York-White Plains-Wayne, NY-NJ	4,390	0.84	$22.17
Phoenix-Mesa-Glendale, AZ	3,490	1.96	$17.21
Boston-Cambridge-Quincy, MA	3,450	1.97	$21.03
Dallas-Plano-Irving, TX	2,860	1.33	$18.67
Philadelphia, PA	2,830	1.54	$17.54
Cleveland-Elyria-Mentor, OH	2,260	2.24	$19.34
St. Louis, MO-IL	2,250	1.74	$18.63

[1] Does not include self-employed. Source: Bureau of Labor Statistics

EMPLOYMENT AND OUTLOOK

There were approximately 185,000 health information technicians employed nationally in 2012. Over one-third of jobs were in hospitals. The rest were employed mostly in physicians' offices, nursing care facilities, outpatient care centers and home healthcare services. Employment of health information technicians is expected to grow faster than the average for all occupations through the year 2022, which means employment is projected to increase 20 percent to 28 percent. This is due to rapid growth in the number of medical tests, treatments, and procedures, and because medical records will be increasingly scrutinized by third party payers, courts and consumers.

Employment Trend, Projected 2010–20

Health Technologists and Technicians (All): 24%

Health Information Technicians: 22%

Total, All Occupations: 11%

Note: "All Occupations" includes all occupations in the U.S. Economy. Source: U.S. Bureau of Labor Statistics, Employment Projections Program

Related Occupations
- Clinical Laboratory Technologist
- Dental Assistant
- Library Technician
- Medical Assistant
- Medical Records Administrator

Related Military Occupations
- Health Services Administrator
- Medical Record Technician

Conversation With . . .
CORRINA HALLORAN
Health Information Director/Privacy Officer
20 years

1. What was your individual career path in terms of education, entry-level job, or other significant opportunity?

A community health center saved my son's life. My son didn't have health insurance and I was a cosmetologist. It was a catch-22. When we went to the community health center, on our first or second visit while I was waiting, I applied for a job as a managed care coordinator. I gave it a shot and they hired me. After that, I started taking classes at night and on weekends. Over time, I earned a certificate in Public Health Management and then, after working there for a decade, a grant opportunity from the Massachusetts League of Community Health Centers allowed me to use my years at the community health center as credits. I have an undergraduate degree in business administration and a master's degree in Public Administration (MPA).

2. Are there many job opportunities in your profession? In what specific areas?

Yes, absolutely. You need to learn new skills and know medical terminology and understand various applications. With the Electronic Records Act and the Health Insurance Portability and Accountability Act (HIPAA), jobs aren't going away but there are higher standards. Ten years ago, medical records was an entry level job. Now, it's not; you need to know insurance policies and government applications. In my department, instead of a medical records clerk we now have four roles: a medical records supervisor, two coordinators, and someone who can perform very technical audits.

3. How do you see your profession changing in the next five years?

The federal government mandates patient rights and privacy rights and they are very different. Patient rights are everywhere: you must treat everybody with dignity and respect. These rights are expanding every day and have policies and procedures attached to them that need to be managed as part of medical records work. There are federal and state laws that deal with the protection of patients' confidentiality. Privacy rights go more to HIPAA – for example, you have a right to restrict medical records. Health care providers will want or need a specialist in the area of the Health Insurance Accountability Act (HIPAA) to protect patients as well as employees from any liability that may arise.

4. What role will technology play in those changes, and what skills will be required?

HIPAA and the HITECH Act (the federal Health Information Technology Act) required some health care facilities to transfer paper records to electronic records. A whole lot of new regulations were attached to the transfer of paper to electronic records. Once the process has been implemented successfully, there are a lot of training and policy changes that come into play. Once you have electronic records, you will need an effective IT team to assist in glitches as this progresses.

For example, our system just added a fourth application, so now we have a scanning department to bring in records from the outside; practice management, which schedules appointments; EMR, which is the actual medical record, and QSI, for dental electronic records.

5. Do you have any general advice or additional insights to share with someone interested in your profession?

I have worked in the private sector and in public health. I find working in community health centers and serving the under-served to be far more rewarding than working in the private sector. There are days that are quite challenging but it is a great feeling when you can help someone who just got lost in the health care system, even if it is as easy as explaining a procedure or process to help them navigate their way to the high quality care we all deserve. I still love my job! It feels like I'm giving back to the community what the community gave me.

You do have to have a strong mind, empathy, compassion and attention to detail to really make a difference in this area. The medical records staffs work with a variety of people such as patients, providers and administrators so they do need "people skills." It is not likely you will be working alone!

6. Can you suggest a valuable "try this" for students considering a career in your profession?

Many medical records offices no longer take on volunteers due to the highly sensitive nature of the position.

MORE INFORMATION

**American Academy of
Professional Coders**
2480 South 3850 West, Suite B
Salt Lake City, UT 84120
800.626.2633
www.aapc.com

**American Health Information
Management Association**
233 North Michigan Avenue
Suite 2150
Chicago, IL 60601-5800
312.233.1100
www.ahima.org

**Commission on Accreditation
for Health Informatics and
Information Management
Education**
233 North Michigan Avenue
21st Floor
Chicago, IL 60601-5800
www.cahiim.org

Simone Isadora Flynn/Editor

Home Health Aide

Snapshot

Career Cluster: Health Care

Interests: Patient Care, Health Care

Earnings (Yearly Average): $21,794

Employment & Outlook: Faster Than Average Growth Expected

OVERVIEW

Sphere of Work

Home health aides provide patient care in patient homes and in residential facilities such as nursing homes and rehabilitation centers. The range of services provided by home health aides includes preventative care, personal hygiene, cooking and household chores, routine medical care, medical appointment transportation, and socio-emotional support. Home health aides are generally paid hourly and are employed by individuals, insurance companies, social service agencies, public health agencies, hospitals, and residential facilities.

Work Environment

Home health aides spend their workdays seeing patients in a wide variety of settings, including patient homes, nursing homes, rehabilitation centers, and adult daycare facilities. Home health aides may work with one patient at a time or travel each day to care for multiple patients in their homes or medical facilities. Given the diverse demands of the home health aide profession, home health aides may work days, evenings, nights, weekends, and on-call hours to meet patient or caseload needs.

Profile

Working Conditions: Work Indoors
Physical Strength: Light Work, Medium Work
Education Needs: High School Diploma Or G.E.D. Licensure/Certification Required
Licensure/Certification: Usually Not Required
Physical Abilities Not Required: No Strenuous Labor
Opportunities For Experience: Volunteer Work
Holland Interest Score*: SRI

* See Appendix A

Occupation Interest

Individuals drawn to the profession of home health aide tend to be physically strong, nurturing, competent, patient, and intelligent people who have the ability to quickly assess situations, demonstrate caring, and solve problems. Those who succeed as home health aides tend to exhibit traits such as empathy, patience, resourcefulness, responsibility, time management, and concern for individuals. Home health aides should find satisfaction in improving the quality of life for a wide range of people, including the disabled, the elderly, and the terminally ill.

A Day in the Life—Duties and Responsibilities

The daily occupational duties and responsibilities of home health aides will be determined by the individual's job specialization. Home health aides may specialize in pediatric care, elder care, management of chronic illness, psychiatric care, Alzheimer or dementia care, or hospice or end-of-life care. The range of possible duties and responsibilities is wide, but some experiences are common to all, such as care in the patient's home, assistance with basic tasks relative to personal care, nutrition, and daily medication.

Some home health-care aids may assist in housekeeping, transportation to the grocery store or medical visits, and physical therapy or exercise. They will be an integral member of the patient care team, which may include family members, social workers, medical professionals, and other home health aides.

For home-bound patients, home health-care workers may do the shopping and meal preparation, as well as track routine medical information such as blood pressure and pulse rate and coordinate in-home medical care. For those home health aides who work with social service agencies or long-term-care facilities, more regulatory tasks may be required, such as conducting background interviews with patients to record their health history, educating clients about public health services and resources, providing emotional support, teaching them practical life skills, and providing patient updates to agency supervisors and client families.

In addition to the range of responsibilities described above, home health aides may also be responsible for completing patient charts and required documentation on a daily basis.

Duties and Responsibilities

- Assisting clients with daily needs
- Bathing and shampooing clients
- Helping clients with dressing and grooming
- Helping clients to move around their homes
- Checking client blood pressure, respiration, and temperature
- Helping clients with exercises
- Assisting clients with medication and artificial limbs
- Helping clients transfer between chairs, wheelchairs, and beds
- Helping elderly or disabled clients with toileting as needed
- Doing cleaning and laundering in client homes or rooms
- Shopping for food and preparing meals for clients
- Attending to bed-bound clients as needed
- Providing moral support

OCCUPATION SPECIALTIES

Home Health Aides

Home Health Aides typically work for certified home health or hospice agencies that receive government funding and therefore must comply with regulations. They work under the direct supervision of a medical professional, usually a nurse. These aides keep records of services performed and of the client's condition and progress. They report changes in the client's condition to the supervisor or case manager. Aides also work with therapists and other medical staff.

Personal Care Attendants

Personal Care Attendants, also called homemakers, caregivers, and companions—provide clients with companionship and help with daily tasks in a client's home. They are often hired in addition to other medical health workers, such as hospice workers, who may visit a client's home. Personal care aides do not provide any type of medical service.

WORK ENVIRONMENT

Physical Environment

The immediate physical environment of home health aides varies based on their caseload and employer. Home health aides spend their workdays seeing patients in patient homes, social service agencies, public health agencies, hospitals, and residential facilities such as assisted living residences, nursing homes, and rehabilitation centers.

Human Environment

Home health aides work with a wide variety of people and should be comfortable caring for children, the elderly, the chronically ill, the terminally ill, the disabled, and mentally ill people, as well as communicating with patient families, colleagues, and physicians.

Relevant Skills and Abilities

Communication Skills
- Speaking effectively
- Listening attentively

Interpersonal/Social Skills
- Being able to remain calm in stressful situations
- Being persistent
- Being sensitive to others
- Cooperating with others
- Providing support to others
- Working as a member of a team

Organization & Management Skills
- Adhering to a schedule
- Planning daily actions

Other Skills
- Preparing food
- Being comfortable with people who are ill or disabled

Technological Environment

Home health aides use activity logs (often in paper form) and other record-keeping forms to keep track of client status for supervising nurses or other medical personnel. They may sometimes use computers and telecommunication tools to perform their jobs. In addition, home health aides use medical equipment, such as glucose monitors, wheelchair lifters, and blood pressure cuffs, to care for patients.

EDUCATION, TRAINING, AND ADVANCEMENT

High School/Secondary

High school students interested in pursuing a career as a home health aide should prepare themselves by developing good study habits. High school-level study of psychology and biology will provide a strong foundation for work as a home health aide or college-level work in the field. Due to the diversity of home health aide duties, high school students interested in this career path will benefit from seeking internships or part-time work that expose the students to the nursing community and people facing physical and mental challenges. High school students may be able to secure employment as a home health aide directly out of high school.

Suggested High School Subjects
- Applied Biology/Chemistry
- Applied Communication
- Child Care
- English
- First Aid Training
- Foods & Nutrition
- Health Science Technology
- Medical Assisting
- Nurse Assisting
- Psychology
- Sociology
- Speech

Famous First

The first visiting nurse service was established by Lillian Wald (pictured), pioneering nurse and humanitarian, in New York City's Lower East Side tenement district in 1893. Wald and another nurse rented a room in the district to be closer to their patients. The service soon drew the attention of donors and public officials and eventually grew large enough to operate in all five boroughs plus Nassau and Westchester counties.

Library of Congress
photograph by Harris & Ewing

Postsecondary

Generally, postsecondary education is not necessary for a career in home health care. Those students interested in pursuing an associate's degree may consider focusing their course of study in the areas of nursing or a related field such as psychology or gerontology. Coursework in nutrition, anatomy, physiology, and psychology may also prove useful in their future work. Postsecondary students can gain work experience and potential advantage in their future job searches by securing internships or part-time employment as home health aides or nursing assistants.

Related College Majors
- Home Health Aide Training
- Human Anatomy & Physiology
- Pre-Nursing Training

Adult Job Seekers

Adults seeking employment as home health aides should have, at a minimum, a high school degree. Adult job seekers in the home health or nursing field will benefit from joining professional associations to help with networking and job searching. Professional home health associations, such as the National Association for Home Care and Hospice, generally offer career workshops and maintain lists and forums of available jobs.

Professional Certification and Licensure

The federal government has guidelines for home health aides whose employers receive reimbursement from Medicare. Federal law requires home health aides to pass a competency test covering basic subjects related to patient care. Home health aides may receive training before taking the competency test. Federal law suggests at least 75 hours of classroom and practical training, supervised by a registered nurse. Training and testing programs may be offered by the employing agency, but must meet the standards of the Center for Medicare and Medicaid Services. Training programs vary with state regulations.

Professional certification and licensure of home health aides is voluntary in some states. Home health aides may choose to pursue certification as certified nurse assistants (CNAs). The CNA certification, which is earned through a state-based competency exam and completed state-approved training program, will provide increased work opportunities in residential facilities, a higher salary, and greater opportunities for advancement. Other home health aide certification options include programs administered by local chapters of the American Red Cross and the Visiting Nurse's Association of America.

Additional Requirements

Individuals who find satisfaction, success, and job security as home health aides will be knowledgeable about the profession's requirements, responsibilities, and opportunities. Integrity, empathy, patience, and personal and professional ethics are required of home health aides as they interact with vulnerable people and have access to patient's personal information and their homes. Home health aides should generally have a driver's license and be sufficiently strong to lift and move patients as needed.

EARNINGS AND ADVANCEMENT

Home health aides and personal care attendants receive slight pay increases with experience and added responsibility. Usually, they are paid only for the time worked in the home; normally, they are not paid for travel time between jobs. Median annual earnings of aides and attendants were $21,794 in 2012. The lowest ten percent earned less than $17,278, and the highest ten percent earned more than $31,153. Depending on full-time or part-time status, home health aides and personal care attendants may receive paid vacations, holidays, and sick days; life and health insurance; and retirement benefits.

Metropolitan Areas with the Highest
Concentration of Jobs in this Occupation
(Home Health Aide)

Metropolitan area	Employment (1)	Employment per thousand jobs	Hourly mean wage
New York-White Plains-Wayne, NY-NJ	96,340	18.68	$9.74
Chicago-Joliet-Naperville, IL	30,940	8.50	$11.10
Philadelphia, PA	20,580	11.29	$10.68
Minneapolis-St. Paul-Bloomington, MN-WI	16,690	9.54	$11.65
Cleveland-Elyria-Mentor, OH	15,830	15.92	$9.87

(1) Does not include Nursing Aides or self-employed. Source: Bureau of Labor Statistics, 2012

Metropolitan Areas with the Highest
Concentration of Jobs in this Occupation
(Personal Care Attendant)

Metropolitan area	Employment (1)	Employment per thousand jobs	Hourly mean wage
New York-White Plains-Wayne, NY-NJ	79,770	15.47	$10.80
Minneapolis-St. Paul-Bloomington, MN-WI	33,540	19.17	$11.46
McAllen-Edinburg-Mission, TX	20,730	91.05	$8.15
Dallas-Plano-Irving, TX	18,520	8.83	$8.37
San Antonio-New Braunfels, TX	17,900	20.76	$8.20

(1) Does not include Nursing Aides or self-employed. Source: Bureau of Labor Statistics, 2012

EMPLOYMENT AND OUTLOOK

Home health aides held about 840,000 jobs nationally in 2012. Another 985,000 jobs were held by personal care attendants. Most aides and attendants are employed by home health services agencies, homemaker assistance agencies, visiting nurse associations, residential care facilities with home health departments, hospitals, public health and welfare departments, community volunteer agencies, and temporary help firms. Self-employed home health aides work with no agency affiliation and accept clients, set fees, and arrange work schedules on their own.

Employment of home health aides and personal care attendants is expected to grow much faster than the average for all occupations through the year 2020, which means employment is projected to increase as much as 70 percent. This is a result of both growing demand for home health-care services from an aging population and efforts to contain health-care costs by moving patients out of hospitals and nursing care facilities as quickly as possible. In addition, a preference by most people for care in the home and improvements in medical technologies for in-home treatment will contribute to job growth.

Employment Trend, Projected 2010–20

Personal Care Aides: 70%

Home Health Aides: 69%

Other Personal Care and Service Workers: 35%

Health-Care Support Occupations: 34%

Total, All Occupations: 14%

Note: "All Occupations" includes all occupations in the U.S. Economy. Source: U.S. Bureau of Labor Statistics, Employment Projections Program

Related Occupations
- Childcare Worker
- Licensed Practical Nurse (LPN)
- Medical Assistant
- Nursing Aide

Conversation With . . .
BAILEY McDONALD,
Home Health Aide, 18 months

1. What was your individual career path in terms of education, entry-level job, or other significant opportunity?

I began nursing school at Quincy College. During my first semester there, I started getting clinical experience where I was able to put my skills to use.

During that time, I completed the Certified Nursing Assistant/Home Health Aide course offered by the Red Cross, and passed the written and practical CNA exam to be licensed by the Commonwealth of Massachusetts. A few months after that, I started my job with Right at Home.

2. Are there many job opportunities in your profession? In what specific areas?

There are quite an extensive amount of jobs for Certified Nursing Assistants (CNAs) in the industry because they are certified in the skills required to work in a hospital setting, nursing home, acute care rehab or home care. Home Health Aides are certified to work in long-term care facilities or provide home care, but not to work in hospitals. Having the CNA license gives you many more opportunities for jobs A lot of home health care clients only want a licensed person to care for them. A third type of job is Personal Care Assistant (PCA). Most home health agencies also offer homemaker/companion services to clients as well, and those services are provided by an unlicensed person.

3. What do you wish you had known going into this profession?

One thing someone should know about going into someone's home to care for them is that you need to be a patient, compassionate, professional person. You will need a lot of patience every day because you never know how a client will be feeling when you're with them and many times they cannot fully communicate. They may be in pain, but unable to communicate that to you. They may be upset about something, but unable to tell you why. You need to be professional in the sense that your own personal problems and issues need to be left at the door because the elderly can sense your mood quickly and it can easily influence their own mood negatively.

4. How do you see your profession changing in the next five years?

With the aging of the baby boomers, I anticipate that in the next five years the demand for Home Heath Aides and Certified Nursing Assistants will grow.

5. What role will technology play in those changes, and what skills will be required?

One interesting way my company is implementing technology in accordance with Massachusetts state law is paying Home Health Aides and Certified Nursing Assistants for travel time by tracking the mileage with new mapping software. In the past, they would give CNAs a flat stipend for travel time. I also foresee home health clients specifically requesting aides in their home who have at least basic computer skills. This way they can turn to their home health aides for help keeping in touch with their families, their grandchildren, and their friends. My best advice is to at least have a basic knowledge of computers because it can only help you with any career goal.

6. Do you have any general advice or additional professional insights to share with someone interested in your profession?

Being a Home Health Aide is a great job for a student in nursing school. It allows you to put into practice some of the things you learn in class, and applying the knowledge helps you remember what you learned in ways that you can't always achieve from reading a text book. You can also work a very flexible schedule as a Certified Nursing Assistant, and that's a plus for a student..

7. Can you suggest a valuable "try this" for students considering a career in your profession?

If someone is considering a career with home health care or wants to complete the HHA/CNA course, I would suggest volunteering at a local hospital or nursing home. They always need extra hands and being around the geriatric population is good exposure for what you can expect working in the industry. Another suggestion would be to contact either the Red Cross or another facility that offers training and request to observe a class before actually paying and signing up for the course.

SELECTED SCHOOLS

Many technical and community colleges offer programs in professional health care or pre-nursing. Interested students are advised to consult with a school guidance counselor or research area postsecondary schools. Also advisable is contacting your state health department and/or local American Red Cross along with hospitals, nursing homes, and residential care facilities to learn first-hand about training opportunities—and CNA certification—in your area.

MORE INFORMATION

American Health Care Association
1201 L Street NW
Washington, DC 20005
202.842.4444
www.ahcancal.org

National Association for Home Care and Hospice
228 7th Street SE
Washington, DC 20003
202.547.7424
pubs@nach.org
www.nahc.org

National Association of Health Care Assistants
501 E. 15th Street
Joplin, MO 64080
417.623.6049
www.nahcacares.org

National Network of Career Nursing Assistants
3577 Easton Road
Norton, OH 44203
330.825.0342
cna-network.org

Briana Nadeau/Editor

Marriage & Family Therapist

Snapshot

Career Cluster: Human Services

Interests: Counseling, family counseling, human relationships, conflict resolution, psychology, health

Earnings (Yearly Average): $48,160

Employment & Outlook: Faster Than Average Growth Expected

OVERVIEW

Sphere of Work

Marriage and Family Therapists (MFTs), are specialists who use a variety of psychotherapeutic models to treat dysfunctional marriages, provide premarital counseling, and offer divorce and post-divorce counseling. Some MFTs may choose to specialize in diagnosing and treating couples, families, or specific age groups. Some of the most common problems they see are related to communication, trust, and intimacy. When a problem is beyond their professional scope, they may refer clients to psychiatrists, medical personnel, clergy, lawyers, or other professionals. While it is common for clergy

members and others to give advice to couples, only MFTs are licensed counseling professionals.

Work Environment

Most marriage and family therapists work independently in private practices. Daytime office hours are typical, although MFTs are often required to be on call for emergencies during nights, weekends, and holidays. They may choose to meet clients at those times as well. Their offices are usually arranged with comfortable furnishings conducive to communicating with their clients.

Profile

Working Conditions: Work Indoors
Physical Strength: Light Work
Education Needs: Master's Degree, Doctoral Degree
Licensure/Certification: Required
Physical Abilities Not Required: No Heavy Labor
Opportunities For Experience: Internship
Holland Interest Score*: SEC

* See Appendix A

Occupation Interest

The marriage counseling profession attracts people who want to help others and who value the role of marriage both in society and in achieving personal satisfaction. They must have excellent listening and reasoning skills, oral and written communication, and the ability to handle sensitive issues confidentially and professionally. Therapists must be willing to treat couples without discrimination. Objectivity and critical thinking are imperative to the work. As the job can entail a high level of stress, marriage and family therapists must also be strong emotionally and physically.

A Day in the Life—Duties and Responsibilities

Marriage and family therapists treat clients who have taken the initiative to receive counseling and those who have been referred to them by doctors, judges, or clergy members. Most often, a couple, or one partner, contacts a marriage therapist when the relationship is at a critical stage, although premarital counseling and post-divorce counseling are also becoming common. The average counseling session lasts one hour each week. A marriage therapist may hold weekly sessions with clients over the course of several weeks or months. Short-term therapy, lasting twelve weeks or less, is typical. A busy therapist must be able to respond to the needs of multiple couples each day.

The goal of premarital counseling is to ensure that a couple is compatible; to uncover any emotional problems that might later get in the way of a successful, fulfilling marriage; and to teach a couple useful skills for dealing with conflict resolution and communication. Some therapists offer group sessions for many couples at once.

The goal of marriage counseling is to get a couple to work out the issues that are threatening their marriage. The therapist's first task is to diagnose the heart of the problem. He or she may give the couple a test or survey and then use those results as a springboard for discussions. The therapist listens, questions, observes, and takes notes. He or she may assign homework, such as reading a chapter in a book or asking the couple to practice certain communication techniques. As the treatment plan unfolds, the therapist assesses its progress. At some point, the therapist may decide to switch to another therapy model or to meet with the individuals separately in addition to the regular session.

Preparatory work for each session may involve reviewing notes, reading select professional materials, or consulting with other professionals. Post-session work may involve billing or submitting a claim to an insurance company.

Duties and Responsibilities

- Collecting data about clients by using testing, interview, discussion and observational techniques
- Evaluating data to determine the nature and sources of clients' concerns
- Determining the advisability of counseling clients or referring them to other specialists in such
- fields as medicine, psychiatry or legal aid Counseling clients on concerns such as unsatisfactory relationships between marriage partners,
- divorce and separation, child rearing, home management and financial difficulties
- Assisting clients in understanding and gaining insight into the causes of their problems, defining goals and planning action to eliminate or correct problems

WORK ENVIRONMENT

Physical Environment

Marriage and family therapists usually work in comfortable office settings that pose few environmental risks. Most work independently in private practices. Some therapists form partnerships or group practices. Others work in mental health centers.

Relevant Skills and Abilities

Communication Skills
- Expressing thoughts and ideas
- Speaking effectively
- Writing concisely

Interpersonal/Social Skills
- Being sensitive to others
- Cooperating with others
- Counseling others
- Providing support to others

Organization & Management Skills
- Coordinating tasks
- Making decisions
- Managing people/groups
- Performing duties that change frequently

Research & Planning Skills
- Developing evaluation strategies
- Using logical reasoning

Human Environment

Marriage and family therapists interact most often with their clients. Depending on the size of the practice, interaction with others may be minimal or may involve communicating with a full staff of office personnel, such as a receptionist, billing clerk, therapists, and other mental health professionals. Some may report to an administrator or director, while experienced therapists may oversee interns.

Technological Environment

Marriage and family therapists depend heavily on computers for scheduling, billing, record keeping, research, and other procedures. Cell phones, answering machines, and other standard office equipment are also commonly used.

EDUCATION, TRAINING, AND ADVANCEMENT

High School/Secondary

As certification and licensing for marriage and family therapists requires postsecondary work, interested high school students should prepare themselves by pursuing a strong college preparatory course with an emphasis on English and the social sciences, including psychology, sociology, and religion.

Suggested High School Subjects
- Child Growth & Development
- College Preparatory
- English
- Psychology
- Sociology

Famous First

The first annulment of a marriage by court decree was that of James Luxford of Boston in 1639. The court noted that Luxford, "being presented for haveing two wives," was to be divorced from his second wife and, moreover, was "not to come to the sight of her whom hee last tooke, and hee to be sent away to England by first opportunity; all that he hath is appointed to her whom hee last married for her and her children; he is also fined 100 t. and to bee set in the stocks an houre upon a market day..."

College/Postsecondary

Most states require at least the completion of a master's degree in
marriage and family therapy, counseling, psychology, or similar field,
and at least two years of postgraduate experience for the MFT license.
An internship is a requirement of the master's degree. A doctorate
degree is usually needed for administrative positions, professorships,
or consulting. Undergraduate students should research and apply to
masters and doctoral programs that are accredited by the Commission
on Accreditation for Marriage and Family Therapy Education
(COAMFTE).

Related College Majors
- Individual & Family Development Studies
- Psychology, General

Adult Job Seekers

Marriage and family therapy can be a good fit for those with a
background in psychology, social work, or education. The lengthy and
expensive educational requirements may be a major drawback for
those with family responsibilities of their own; some scholarships and
distance education courses can help.

Advancement is highly dependent on experience and education. A
therapist employed in a large practice or institution may be able to
advance to an administrative or managerial position, or establish his
or her own practice, where the earnings tend to be the highest. Other
opportunities for advancement include teaching, consulting, and
research.

Professional Certification and Licensure

All states and the District of Columbia require a license to practice
marriage counseling. Licensure candidates must meet certain
educational requirements and acquire mandatory clinical experience.
In addition, a passing score on a state or nationally administered
exam, such as the MFT Exam offered by the Association of Marital
and Family Therapy Regulatory Boards, is required. Some states also
mandate more experience or the completion of continuing education
credits.

Additional certification may be required or desired for some jobs, obtained from a professional association such as the National Board for Certified Therapists or the American Association for Marriage and Family Therapy. Requirements for certification are similar to licensure requirements. Consult credible professional associations within the field and follow professional debate as to the relevancy and value of any certification program.

Additional Requirements

Marriage and family therapists must have a high level of integrity and ethics as they work with their clients' personal information; members of professional associations must conform to their associations' Code of Ethics. Those who intend to establish private practices also need business skills and knowledge about health plan policies and procedures.

EARNINGS AND ADVANCEMENT

Earnings of marriage and family therapists depend on whether or not they are in private practice, their level and area of education and their experience. Those in private practice tend to earn the highest salaries. Some marriage and family therapists work for social service agencies and have a private practice or do consulting and research work to supplement their incomes.

Median annual earnings of marriage and family therapists were $48,160 in 2013. The lowest ten percent earned less than $29,180 and the highest ten percent earned more than $78,580.

Marriage and family therapists may receive paid vacations, holidays, and sick days; life and health insurance; and retirement benefits. These benefits are usually paid by the employer. Self-employed marriage and family therapists pay for any benefits themselves.

Metropolitan Areas with the Highest Employment Level in this Occupation

Metropolitan area	Employment[1]	Employment per thousand jobs	Hourly mean wage
Los Angeles-Long Beach-Glendale, CA	2,140	0.54	$23.11
New York-White Plains-Wayne, NY-NJ	1,090	0.21	$30.34
Newark-Union, NJ-PA	1,070	1.12	$34.45
Edison-New Brunswick, NJ	930	0.95	$34.10
Baltimore-Towson, MD	840	0.66	$23.78
Camden, NJ	680	1.36	$34.43
Washington-Arlington-Alexandria, DC-VA-MD-WV	610	0.26	$27.81
Santa Ana-Anaheim-Irvine, CA	570	0.39	$27.34
Miami-Miami Beach-Kendall, FL	520	0.51	$22.84
Minneapolis-St. Paul-Bloomington, MN-WI	520	0.29	$23.50

[1] Does not include self-employed. Source: Bureau of Labor Statistics

EMPLOYMENT AND OUTLOOK

There were about 38,000 marriage and family therapists employed nationally in 2012. Employment is expected to grow much faster than the average for all occupations through the year 2022, which means employment is projected to increase 29 percent or more. This is due to increasing social pressures on marriages and families and a growing tendency to seek outside help to solve marital problems. Rapid growth is projected in private practice and community and social service agencies alike.

Employment Trend, Projected 2010–20

Marriage and Family Therapists: 31%

Mental Health Counselors (All): 29%

Total, All Occupations: 11%

Note: "All Occupations" includes all occupations in the U.S. Economy. Source: U.S. Bureau of Labor Statistics, Employment Projections Program

Related Occupations
- Case Worker/Social Services Assistant
- Clergy
- Educational Therapist
- Forensic Scientist
- Psychologist
- Rehabilitation Worker
- Religious Worker
- Social Worker
- Substance Abuse Therapist
- Vocational Rehabilitation Therapist

Conversation With . . .
ELI KARAM, Ph.D., LMFT

Private Practice Clinician, Louisville, KY
Associate Professor, University of Louisville
Raymond A. Kent School of Social Work
Marriage and Family Therapist, 14 years

1. What was your individual career path in terms of education/training, entry-level job, or other significant opportunity?

I studied undergraduate psychology at Northwestern University in Chicago. The program was very research-based, so we were in labs studying theories based on a patient's psychopathology and deficit. I became disenchanted by the time I was 21 or 22 because I wanted the direct application of a systemic approach, which taps into a person's strength and health. I lost my father at 18; it was a significant event that was quite unexpected, so my family had worked with a Marriage and Family Therapist. They work in a systemic way, looking for a client's strength and health. That attracted me.

After graduating, I took a year off and became a coordinator at a recreation center in Hilton Head, SC working with kids and teenagers. One of the best things you can do is have relevant experience in a field.

When I came back, I went to the Family Institute at Northwestern University. I got to work with very affluent families on the North Shore of Chicago, and in the Cabrini-Green projects in Chicago. The more I worked with these different populations, the more I got curious about how people change. I went back later and got a Ph.D. from Purdue University's Dept. of Child Development and Family Studies. Now, I'm a tenured professor at the University of Louisville, as well as a clinician in my own practice.

2. What are the most important skills and/or qualities for someone in your profession?

You have to be somebody who thinks systemically, meaning you wonder how people are impacted by a combination of bio-psycho-social factors. This includes the biology of the family of origin and the social environment a person is part of. You have to be open to feedback from your supervisor and your peers because that is part of your licensure as a MFT, and it also is helpful afterwards in your own practice. Also, you need to be a person who will find a good work-life balance, and be able to make a commitment to take care of yourself.

3. What do you wish you had known going into this profession?

Change doesn't happen as quickly as you think. You need to have patience, and you need to meet patients (or clients, as they're also called) where they are.

4. Are there many job opportunities in your profession? In what specific areas?

Marriage and Family Therapy was named by U.S. News & World Report as one of the fastest growing professions, and it's growing because people see useful extensions of our approach in other areas. For example, in medical settings doctors who sometimes don't have the greatest bedside manner are being trained in our systemic approach, in how to be more empathetic towards patients and families. It's also being used in military and VA (Veteran's Administration medical facility) settings.

5. How do you see your profession changing in the next five years, what role will technology play in those changes, and what skills will be required?

A significant number of Marriage and Family Therapists are getting older and aging out. We have a huge mission to reach out to Millennials. We need to offer them choice and make them feel included, and that means considering how to use technology to do that. We will see more distance supervision via applications like Skype, more online courses and MFP programs, and we'll also see more clients wanting e-therapy. That being said, this will always be a face-to-face profession; technology will supplement.

6. What do you enjoy most about your job? What do you enjoy least about your job?

I'm a passionate and hopeful person, and when something really works, it's really powerful. It's a great feeling to be part of that. When something does not end well, or you're working with people who, through no fault of their own — say, somebody has died — are not amenable to change, it can be difficult. You need to accept what you can't change, and help clients move to acceptance and tolerance.

7. Can you suggest a valuable "try this" for students considering a career in your profession?

Be comfortable with your own family narrative: what do you like, what don't you like, and what's influenced you? Do your own self-exploration.

Also, find someone who is early in their career — in that period between graduation and licensure — who is in the trenches who can be a mentor.

SELECTED SCHOOLS

Many colleges and universities have bachelor's degree programs in counseling and related subjects. The student may also gain an initial grounding in the field at a technical or community college. Consult with your school guidance counselor or research area post-secondary programs to find the right fit for you. The web site of the American Association for Marriage and Family Counseling (see below) contains a directory of accredited programs.

MORE INFORMATION

American Association for Marriage and Family Therapy
112 S. Alfred Street
Alexandria, VA 22314-3061
703.838.9808
www.aamft.org

American Counseling Association
5999 Stevenson Avenue
Alexandria, VA 22304
800.347.6647
www.counseling.org

American Mental Health Counseling Association
801 N. Fairfax Street, Suite 304
Alexandria, VA 22314
703.548.6002
www.amhca.org

National Board for Certified Therapists
3 Terrace Way, Suite D
Greensboro, NC 27403-3660
336.547.0607
www.nbcc.org

Sally Driscoll/Editor

Music Therapist

Snapshot

Career Cluster: Health Care; Human Services

Interests: Music, playing instruments, singing, patient rehabilitation, planning and organizing musical activities, therapeutic programs and services

Earnings (Yearly Average): $43,180

Employment & Outlook: Average Growth Expected

OVERVIEW

Sphere of Work

Music therapists are trained professionals who work within the health industry to help people manage pain, overcome an emotional issue, build self-esteem, facilitate communication and social interaction, and improve well-being. Music therapy treatments may include singing, playing instruments, or listening to music. Practitioners of musical therapy are considered recreational therapists, along with art, dance, and writing therapists.

Work Environment

Music therapists work in private practice and in hospitals, schools, nursing homes, mental health clinics, prisons, and other environments. They tend to specialize in clients with physical disabilities or illnesses, cognitive problems, or emotional issues. Some music therapists treat all conditions. Full-time therapists work about a forty-hour week, usually with some evenings, nights, and weekends. They might travel from site to site or work at one institution. They interact mostly with their clients and other professionals.

Profile

Working Conditions: Work Indoors
Physical Strength: Light Work
Education Needs: Bachelor's Degree
Licensure/Certification: Required
Physical Abilities Not Required: No Heavy Labor
Opportunities For Experience: Internship, Volunteer Work
Holland Interest Score*: ESI

* See Appendix A

Occupation Interest

People attracted to the music therapy profession are usually musicians who are passionate about music and enjoy putting their talents and skills to use to help others. The ability to sing and play instruments and a familiarity with music theory, notation, and various genres (including classical, jazz, and popular music) are crucial. In addition to musical ability, therapists are excellent communicators, empathetic, patient, creative, and mentally and emotionally strong.

A Day in the Life—Duties and Responsibilities

Music therapists spend most of their work time engaged in activities with clients. The first meeting with a client usually involves assessing his or her needs and setting goals.

If a client has been referred by a doctor or psychiatrist, as is often the case, the therapist begins by devising a treatment plan intended to meet the prescribed goals. For example, a child with autism may need to work on some cognitive issues, such as basic math skills or how to tie shoes, but is difficult to reach through normal methods of communication and traditional instructional techniques. The music therapist might select or compose songs to sing with the child that are both engaging and instructional.

Some music therapists work in hospices, where patients are often depressed and frightened of death. The therapist might play soothing tunes on an instrument, such as a guitar or harp, or sing songs that bring back positive memories.

Other common treatment plans include drumming sessions, songwriting, and dancing to music, which might be done in conjunction with a dance therapist. Music therapists also sometimes teach clients how to sing or play an instrument. Occasionally, they may organize concerts involving groups of patients.

As part of the treatment plan, the therapist takes notes that will help him or her to evaluate its success and prepares assessment documents. Most therapists are also responsible for maintaining instruments and audio equipment. Therapists who own their own practices have additional business responsibilities.

Duties and Responsibilities

- Planning musical activities for patients or groups
- Playing music for patients to soothe them or get them physically active
- Working with disabled patients
- Assessing the needs of patients, choosing the appropriate treatment and evaluating patients' progress
- Using rhythmic exercises with patients

WORK ENVIRONMENT

Physical Environment

Music therapists usually work inside, in recreation rooms, classrooms, studios, offices, or private homes, but they may choose to conduct sessions outside in good weather. Some locations may be soundproofed for noise and privacy reasons.

Human Environment

Music therapists spend most of their time interacting with their clients and collaborate regularly with other therapists, teachers, or health professionals. Unless self-employed, they report to a supervisor. They may oversee part-time employees or interns. Those who own their own practices may be responsible for scheduling or bookkeeping staff.

Relevant Skills and Abilities

Creative/Artistic Skills
- Being skilled in art, music or dance

Interpersonal/Social Skills
- Being patient
- Being sensitive to others
- Cooperating with others
- Providing support to others
- Working as a member of a team

Research & Planning Skills
- Creating ideas

Technological Environment

Music therapists work with a variety of audio equipment, including portable stereo systems and mp3 players. They may also use recording equipment, such as a computer outfitted with a microphone and interfaced with an electronic keyboard or electric guitar. They must also know how to play a variety of instruments.

EDUCATION, TRAINING, AND ADVANCEMENT

High School/Secondary

A college preparatory program strong in the sciences, health, English, social sciences, and music courses will provide the necessary foundation for further studies. Interested high school students should supplement their coursework with extracurricular music activities, such as orchestra or choral group. A student must be proficient on at least one instrument—ideally piano, guitar, or voice—for admission into a music therapy program. Volunteer experience in a school, hospital, or recreational center is also recommended.

Suggested High School Subjects
- Biology
- English
- Health Science Technology
- Instrumental & Vocal Music
- Psychology
- Sociology

Famous First

The first large-scale study of the effects of music therapy on children was done at the University of Pennsylvania in 1962. The project was begun under music professor Paul Nordoff, who eventually collaborated with Dr. Clive Robbins, a special education expert. The focus of their study was piano and vocal improvisation as applied to children on the autistic spectrum, but a variety of other musical forms and young subjects were examined as well. The Nordoff-Robbins approach soon became the standard in the field.

College/Postsecondary

A bachelor's degree in music therapy from an American Music Therapy Association (AMTA) approved program is the minimum requirement for board certification. The curriculum typically includes coursework in the social and behavioral sciences, biology, anatomy, music therapy, and music (theory, performance, piano, guitar, voice). These programs also require 1,200 hours of clinical training, including an internship.

A master's or doctorate degree is required for advancement to supervisory positions and also for teaching, research, or administrative work. Most music therapists who establish their own practices have an advanced degree and many years of experience.

Related College Majors
- Dance Therapy
- Music Therapy
- Psychology, General
- Sociology

Adult Job Seekers

Adults with a bachelor's degree or higher in another discipline may choose to complete the music therapy degree equivalency program. Program participants take only those courses that are necessary and fulfill internship and other clinical training requirements. Musicians and music teachers may find that music therapy fits well with their other interests and responsibilities.

Professional Certification and Licensure

State licensing requirements vary for music therapists. In some states, applicants are licensed as creative arts therapists or recreational therapists and may need a master's degree.

The Certification Board for Music Therapists (CBMT) offers national board certification for music therapists. To become a Music Therapist-Board Certified (MT-BC), an individual must hold a bachelor's degree in music therapy or degree equivalent, complete clinical training, and earn a passing grade on the examination. Certification renewal usually involves continuing education.

Additional Requirements

Some music therapists may need a driver's license. Those seeking employment in public schools need a teaching certificate. Music therapists must also abide by the CBMT Code of Professional Practice.

Fun Fact

Music therapy may sound a bit new age-y, but not only did Aristotle and Plato recognize the healing properties of music, but after both World Wars, amateur and professional musicians visited veterans' hospitals around the country. Doctors and nurses noticed that music truly was a salve for the soul, and insisted that staff musicians be hired.

Source: http://www.musictherapy.org/about/history/

EARNINGS AND ADVANCEMENT

Advancement opportunities to supervisory or administrative positions limit the contact music therapists have with patients. Advancement is available in research, teaching, private practice, and consulting. Earnings are generally highest in the New England and Western states and lowest in the South Central states. Those employed in hospices or who specialize in gerontology tend to earn the least.

Median annual earnings of music therapists were $43,180 in 2013. The lowest ten percent earned less than $27,120, and the highest ten percent earned more than $68.950.

Music therapists may receive paid vacations, holidays, and sick days; life and health insurance; and retirement benefits. These are usually paid by the employer.

Metropolitan Areas with the Highest Employment Level in this Occupation

Metropolitan area	Employment[1]	Employment per thousand jobs	Hourly mean wage
New York-White Plains-Wayne, NY-NJ	980	0.19	$25.67
Philadelphia, PA	580	0.32	$21.61
Chicago-Joliet-Naperville, IL	560	0.15	$21.94
Boston-Cambridge-Quincy, MA	510	0.29	$18.60
Nassau-Suffolk, NY	380	0.31	$23.94
Los Angeles-Long Beach-Glendale, CA	340	0.09	$30.24
Atlanta-Sandy Springs-Marietta, GA	320	0.14	$19.87
Washington-Arlington-Alexandria, DC-VA-MD-WV	300	0.13	$23.55
Warren-Troy-Farmington Hills, MI	260	0.23	$24.54
St. Louis, MO-IL	230	0.18	$20.05

[1]Does not include self-employed. Source: Bureau of Labor Statistics

EMPLOYMENT AND OUTLOOK

Recreational therapists, of whom music therapists are a part, held about 20,000 jobs nationally in 2012. Employment is expected to grow about as fast as the average for all occupations through the year 2022, which means employment is projected to increase 10 percent to 16 percent. Overall, the outlook for music therapists is growing as the older population increases. There are demands in nursing homes, rehabilitation centers, and extended care facilities. It is gaining acceptance and popularity as the medical profession and the public recognize the benefits of this alternative form of therapy in patient healing and recovery.

Employment Trend, Projected 2010–20

Health Diagnosing and Treating Practitioners: 20%

Recreational and Music Therapists: 13%

Total, All Occupations: 11%

Note: "All Occupations" includes all occupations in the U.S. Economy. Source: U.S. Bureau of Labor Statistics, Employment Projections Program

Related Occupations
- Art Therapist
- Occupational Therapist
- Recreational Therapist

Conversation With . . .
ANDREA YUN-SPRINGER

Music Therapist
Toneworks Music Therapy, Minneapolis, MN
Music therapist, 2 years

1. What was your individual career path in terms of education/training, entry-level job, or other significant opportunity?

When I first went to college, I was a psychology major and I got a job doing research. I realized that doing data collection and sitting behind a desk was not what I wanted to do. I had been a musician since I was 3 years old. My primary instruments are violin, piano and guitar, and I just kind of picked up the ukulele. A family friend had gotten her PhD in music therapy from the University of Minnesota Twin Cities (UMTC) and I decided to see what the program was about. I didn't really know what music therapy was about. When I realized it combined my two interests — music and helping people reach their potential — I decided to go back to school. At UMTC, if your first degree was not in music, you can't go into the master's program, so I got another bachelor's degree. After I graduated, I created Toneworks with my business partner, Lyndie Walker, who's also a music therapist. We go anywhere from assisted living facilities to early childhood centers.

2. What are the most important skills and/or qualities for someone in your profession?

First, you do have to be a competent musician, because if no one wants to hear you sing or play your instrument, you're not going to get anyone to connect. You have to have a strong learning base in how music therapy works and be interested in always knowing more about how it works. You don't have to be an extrovert necessarily, but you do develop long-term relationships with people. It's important to have a deep respect for people of all abilities and in all walks of life as you provide music therapy.

3. What do you wish you had known going into this profession?

I just wish I had known about it earlier, so that I could have gotten my bachelor's in music therapy the first time around! I wish I had known that anyone can be an advocate for anyone else. Sometimes you have to advocate for clients who are non-verbal or for caregivers who feel they can't ask for the resources they need.

Also, you shouldn't be intimidated by the idea of starting your own business. In a sense, even when you're going for a job interview, you're always pitching yourself.

4. Are there many job opportunities in your profession? In what specific areas?

Yes, there are jobs. Music therapy is a growing field. There are more opportunities in states that have less music therapists and are just gaining awareness, but have an increasing demand for services.

5. How do you see your profession changing in the next five years? What role will technology play in those changes, and what skills will be required?

I see the field growing in hospice settings. I see more opportunities for early intervention with little children who are, say, just diagnosed with autism. There's been a lot of press about music therapy lately and it's seen as less of an "out there" kind of thing. People can see how it actually works. As licensure requirements are enacted, I see the field growing. Technology has already played a role. Social media has helped spread the word; there were pictures of Gabby Giffords doing music therapy. There's an ethical issue with providing Skype sessions, but if it's in a rural area, that may be someone's only access. Already we record digitally with clients and make recordings with clients and show them how to share those recordings.

6. What do you enjoy most about your job? What do you enjoy least about your job?

I love seeing how music affects clients. Some of them can tell me how it affects them, and maybe write a song about how happy music makes them. Some of them smile; some sign me; some point to the happy face on their iPad. With a hospice patient, it might be slow, steady breathing instead of a look of pain on their face. What I enjoy least is going from place to place and driving around Minnesota.

7. Can you suggest a valuable "try this" for students considering a career in your profession?

Try searching for music therapists by state using Google or cbmt.org. Once you find one in your area, call and ask if you can volunteer in one of the groups. They may just have you help hand out instruments and sit in the circle, but you'll have an idea of what it's like.

SELECTED SCHOOLS

Many colleges and universities have bachelor's degree programs in recreational therapy or related subjects; a number of them have programs specifically in music therapy. The student may also gain an initial grounding at a technical or community college. Consult with your school guidance counselor or research post-secondary programs in your area. The online Therapeutic Recreation Directory (see below) contains a listing of accredited recreational therapy schools and programs; and the web site of the American Music Therapy Association has additional resources.

MORE INFORMATION

American Music Therapy Association
8455 Colesville Road, Suite 1000
Silver Spring, MD 20910
301.589.3300
www.musictherapy.org

Certification Board for Music Therapists
506 E. Lancaster Avenue, Suite 102
Downingtown, PA 19335
800.765.2268
www.cbmt.org

National Association of Schools of Music
11250 Roger Bacon Drive, Suite 21
Reston, VA 20190-5248
703.437.0700
info@arts-accredit.org
nasm.arts-accredit.org/index.jsp

National Council for Therapeutic Recreation Certification
7 Elmwood Drive
New City, NY 10956
845.639.1439
nctrc@nctrc.org
www.nctrc.org

National Federation of Music Clubs
1646 Smith Valley Road
Greenwood, IN 46142
317.882.4003
www.nfmc-music.org

Sally Driscoll/Editor

Occupational Therapist

Snapshot

Career Cluster: Health Care; Human Services

Interests: Health, biology, psychology, anatomy, record keeping, physical therapy

Earnings (Yearly Average): $76,940

Employment & Outlook: Faster Than Average Growth Expected

OVERVIEW

Sphere of Work

Occupational therapists provide therapeutic services aimed at helping variously disabled people perform everyday tasks in their life and work. Occupational therapists treat people with temporary and chronic motor function impairments caused by mental, physical, developmental, or emotional issues. An occupational therapist may help patients with skills such as self-care (dressing, eating), household care (cleaning, cooking), using communication devices such as telephones and computers, and such

basic activities as writing, problem-solving, memory, and coordination. Occupational therapists develop patient treatment plans that attempt to maintain, develop, or recover a patient's daily functioning, productivity, and quality of life.

Work Environment

Occupational therapists work in settings such as rehabilitation facilities, hospitals, nursing homes, occupational therapy clinics, and schools. In medical environments, occupational therapists generally partner with medical and social service professionals, such as doctors and social workers, to increase patients' physical and mental abilities and overall independence. In school settings, occupational therapists partner with educational professionals such as teachers and special education coordinators to address the physical or mental issues of students with special needs. Occupational therapy is a common component of a special needs child's individualized education plan (IEP). Occupational therapists generally work a standard 40-hour week, and scheduled appointments are the norm.

Profile

Working Conditions: Work Indoors
Physical Strength: Medium Work
Education Needs: Master's Degree
Licensure/Certification: Required
Physical Abilities Not Required: No Heavy Labor
Opportunities For Experience: Internship, Military Service, Part-Time Work
Holland Interest Score*: SRE

* See Appendix A

Occupation Interest

Individuals attracted to the field of occupational therapy tend to be physically capable people who enjoy hands-on work and close interaction with others. Individuals who excel as occupational therapists exhibit traits such as intellectual curiosity, problem solving, a desire to help, patience, and caring. Occupational therapists must be good at science and able to work as part of a team to meet patient needs.

A Day in the Life—Duties and Responsibilities

An occupational therapist's daily occupational duties and responsibilities include full days of hands-on patient interaction and treatment as well as administrative duties. Patients seen by occupational therapists include those experiencing physical limitations caused by accident or injury, stroke, or congenital conditions such as cerebral palsy or muscular dystrophy; other patients may require services due to developmental delays, learning disabilities, or mental retardation.

As a medical or therapeutic professional, occupational therapists interact with patients or clients on a daily basis. Daily work responsibilities may include conducting patient assessments; developing patient treatment plans; providing patients with special instruction in life skills; advising patients on the use of adaptive equipment such as wheelchairs or orthopedic aids; providing early intervention services to young children with physical and social delays and limitations; building adaptive equipment for patients with special needs not met by existing options; providing instruction in self-care such as dressing and eating; counseling patients on technical or physical adaptations that will allow the patient to continue to work at his or her chosen occupation; and meeting with patient treatment team or patient families.

An occupational therapist's daily administrative responsibilities include the record keeping involved with patient evaluation and treatment. Occupational therapists must draft treatment plans, record notes following patient treatment sessions, provide written updates to patient treatment teams, and provide insurance companies with patient records and progress notes as required. Independent occupational therapists working outside of a school or medical clinic may also be responsible for patient appointment scheduling and billing.

Duties and Responsibilities

- **Testing and evaluating patients' physical and mental abilities**
- **Designing special equipment to aid disabled patients**
- **Instructing and informing patients how to adjust to home, work and social environments**
- **Evaluating patients' progress, attitudes and behavior**

OCCUPATION SPECIALTIES

Directors of Occupational Therapy

Directors of Occupational Therapy plan, direct and coordinate occupational therapy programs in hospitals, institutions and community settings to facilitate the rehabilitation of those who are physically, mentally or emotionally disabled.

Industrial Therapists

Industrial Therapists arrange salaried, productive employment in an actual work environment for disabled patients, to enable them to perform medically prescribed work activities and to prepare them to resume employment outside of the hospital environment.

WORK ENVIRONMENT

Physical Environment

Occupational therapists work in rehabilitation facilities, hospitals, nursing homes, therapy clinics, and schools. Therapeutic office settings used by occupational therapists may be shared with other therapeutic professionals such as physical, recreational, or speech and language therapists.

Human Environment

Examples of patients needing occupational therapy to increase their independence and quality of life include people suffering balance and strength issues caused by cerebral palsy, spinal cord injuries, or muscular dystrophy; stroke victims experiencing memory loss or coordination problems; people experiencing mental health problems; and children or adults with developmental disabilities. Occupational therapists usually work as part of a patient treatment team that includes patient families, social workers, teachers, doctors, and other therapists. As a member of a treatment team, occupational therapists participate in frequent team meetings and are responsible for communicating patient progress to fellow team members.

Relevant Skills and Abilities

Interpersonal/Social Skills

- Being able to remain calm
- Cooperating with others
- Teaching others
- Working as a member of a team

Organization & Management Skills

- Coordinating tasks
- Demonstrating leadership
- Making decisions
- Managing people/groups
- Meeting goals and deadlines
- Paying attention to and handling details
- Performing duties that change frequently

Research & Planning Skills

- Creating ideas

Technological Environment

Occupational therapists use a wide variety of technology in their work. Computers and Internet communication tools are a ubiquitous part of occupational therapy work. Occupational therapists often introduce specialized computer programs to patients that need help with their reasoning, problem solving, memory, and sequencing. In addition, occupational therapists generally learn how to use and teach adaptive devices such as wheelchairs, orthopedic aids, eating aids, and dressing aids.

EDUCATION, TRAINING, AND ADVANCEMENT

High School/Secondary

High school students interested in pursuing the profession of occupational therapy in the future should pursue coursework in biology, psychology, anatomy, sociology, and mathematics to prepare for college-level studies. Students interested in the occupational therapy field will benefit from seeking internships or part time work with occupational therapists or people with physical, developmental, or social problems that have an impact on their daily lives.

Suggested High School Subjects
- Algebra
- Applied Biology/Chemistry
- Applied Communication
- Arts
- Biology
- Chemistry
- College Preparatory
- Composition
- Crafts
- English
- Health Science Technology
- Physical Education
- Physical Science
- Physiology
- Psychology
- Science
- Sociology

Famous First

The first occupational therapy program began at Johns Hopkins University, pictured, in the early 20th century. At that time it was called "habit training," and its goal was to provide persons with mental disabilities the basic skills they needed to handle everyday tasks and live a productive life. Patients were given goal-directed activities such as weaving, broom-making, or bookbinding to focus their efforts and allow them to develop industrious habits.

College/Postsecondary

Occupational therapists are typically required to have a master's degree or higher in their field. Interested college students should complete coursework in occupational therapy, if offered by their school, as well as courses in physical therapy, special education, biology, psychology, anatomy, sociology, and mathematics. Students interested in attending graduate school in occupational therapy will benefit from seeking internships or work with occupational therapists, people with impaired functioning, or as occupational therapy assistants or special education aides. A student membership in the American Occupational Therapy Association may provide networking opportunities and connections.

Related College Majors

- Anatomy
- Exercise Science/Physiology/Movement Studies
- Human & Animal Physiology
- Occupational Therapy

Adult Job Seekers

Adult job seekers in the occupational therapy field should generally have completed master's or doctoral training in occupational therapy from an accredited university (as determined by the Accreditation Council for Occupational Therapy Education (ACOTE)), as well as earned the necessary professional licensure. Occupational therapists seeking employment will benefit from the networking opportunities, job workshops and job lists offered by professional occupational therapy associations such as the American Occupational Therapy Association.

Professional Certification and Licensure

Occupational therapists are required to have a professional occupational therapy license prior to beginning their professional practice. Upon completion of an accredited master's or doctoral program in occupational therapy, candidates take a national occupational therapy licensing exam and, if successful, earn the Occupational Therapist Registered (OTR) title. In addition to national licensing, occupational therapists are required to register with their state health board and engage in continuing education as a condition of their license. State licensing boards generally have additional requirements for occupational therapists choosing to specialize in early education, mental health, or gerontological occupational therapy.

Additional Requirements

Occupational therapists fundamentally enjoy helping other people achieve greater freedom and independence in their daily lives. They find satisfaction working in health care or educational environments with special needs populations. High levels of integrity and ethics are required of occupational therapists, as they work with confidential and personal patient information. Membership in professional occupational therapy associations is encouraged among junior and senior occupational therapists as a means of building status within a professional community and networking. Successful occupational therapists engage in ongoing professional development.

Fun Fact

The young profession of occupational therapy became more widely known after World War I, when "restorative activities were found to be beneficial for rehabilitating war veterans with severe injury."

Source: http://www.therapy-directory.org.uk/articles/occupational-therapy.html

EARNINGS AND ADVANCEMENT

Earnings of occupational therapists depend on the individual's education and experience and the type and geographic location of the employer. Those in private practice generally earned more than salaried workers. Occupational therapists in public elementary or secondary schools were sometimes classified as teachers and received pay accordingly, which averaged less than their hospital counterparts.

Median annual earnings of occupational therapists were $76,940 in 2013. The lowest ten percent earned less than $51,310, and the highest ten percent earned more than $109,380.

Occupational therapists may receive paid vacations, holidays, and sick days; life and health insurance; and retirement benefits. These are usually paid by the employer.

Metropolitan Areas with the Highest Employment Level in this Occupation

Metropolitan area	Employment[1]	Employment per thousand jobs	Hourly mean wage
New York-White Plains-Wayne, NY-NJ	4,900	0.93	$39.02
Chicago-Joliet-Naperville, IL	3,200	0.87	$35.45
Boston-Cambridge-Quincy, MA	2,310	1.32	$37.04
Los Angeles-Long Beach-Glendale, CA	2,210	0.56	$44.43
Philadelphia, PA	1,950	1.06	$36.51
Dallas-Plano-Irving, TX	1,770	0.82	$43.77
Atlanta-Sandy Springs-Marietta, GA	1,730	0.75	$35.63
Denver-Aurora-Broomfield, CO	1,570	1.23	$37.45
Houston-Sugar Land-Baytown, TX	1,540	0.56	$37.05
Minneapolis-St. Paul-Bloomington, MN-WI	1,540	0.86	$32.11

[1] Does not include self-employed. Source: Bureau of Labor Statistics

EMPLOYMENT AND OUTLOOK

There were approximately 113,000 occupational therapists employed nationally in 2012. The largest numbers of jobs were in ambulatory healthcare services, which employed about one-third of occupational therapists. Other major employers included hospitals, offices of health care practitioners, school systems and nursing care facilities. Employment is expected to grow much faster than the average for all occupations through the year 2022, which means employment is projected to increase 29 percent or more. Job growth will occur as a result of an aging population that requires increased occupational therapy services and from advances in medicine that allow people to survive serious illness and injury and need rehabilitative therapy.

Employment Trend, Projected 2010–20

Occupational Therapists: 29%

Health Diagnosing and Treating Practitioners: 20%

Total, All Occupations: 11%

Note: "All Occupations" includes all occupations in the U.S. Economy. Source: U.S. Bureau of Labor Statistics, Employment Projections Program

Related Occupations
- Activities Therapist
- Art Therapist
- Music Therapist
- Occupational Therapy Assistant
- Physical Therapist
- Recreational Therapist
- Rehabilitation Counselor
- Respiratory Therapist

Related Military Occupations
- Physical & Occupational Therapist

Conversation With . . .
AMY LAMB

Vice President, American Occupational Therapy Association
Assistant Professor, Eastern Michigan University
Occupational Therapy Program, Ypsilanti, MI
Occupational Therapist, 17 years

1. What was your individual career path in terms of education/training, entry-level job, or other significant opportunity?

When I went to college, I initially studied psychology. I loved it, but felt something was missing. I wanted to do more to help people overcome their challenges, which led me to look at the therapy world. The roots of occupational therapy are in mental health because the mind and body are interconnected and occupational therapy addresses both. I changed my major and got my bachelor's degree in occupational therapy. Today you have to have a master's degree to enter the profession.

After graduating, I worked in a hospital until I was laid off due to significant changes in the healthcare system. I went back to school, got my doctoral degree and started my own practice, which allowed me to use my occupational therapy knowledge in new ways. I practice in a variety of settings, such as in schools, where students might be having challenges focusing. I evaluate what's happening with the students and maybe adapt the environment. Perhaps you get them a standing desk with a little foot shelf so they can swing one of their feet, which provides them with the sensory stimulation they need to focus. You can't jump to the conclusion that a student's issue is behavioral; maybe it's sensory. We also help people in the community "age in place" by doing things such as making sure older drivers know how to use all the bells and whistles on their cars. Occupational therapy is a health and wellness profession; it's much broader than rehabilitation. One of the things that attracted me is that I can move between practice areas without an additional degree. I still have my own practice, but my full-time job now is as a program director and professor, teaching the next generation of occupational therapists.

2. What are the most important skills and/or qualities for someone in your profession?

You have to be adaptable. You may say, 'I'm going to work with this patient with this plan today," but they might not want that. You need plans B, C, and D. This is not a rote profession. You need to be creative and be able to problem solve. You need to be compassionate and to truly want other people to be successful.

3. What do you wish you had known going into this profession?

Nothing prepares you for the fact that you are going to help an individual shower or get dressed, and you're going to see things you didn't anticipate. That's hard for people. You want to protect modesty and dignity, and you're helping a person with their modesty and dignity by helping them learn to do this on their own. You're helping them gain independence, and that's a huge gift.

4. Are there many job opportunities in your profession? In what specific areas?

Occupational therapists are in high demand due to several things. To meet the needs of aging baby boomers, we have to help them stay in their homes and be safe. Then there are changes under the Affordable Care Act, which is projected to add about 31 million people to the healthcare system with no added infrastructure to care for them. And there are jobs working with children and youth, including in schools, helping students be mentally healthy and handle the challenges that everyday life brings.

5. How do you see your profession changing in the next five years, what role will technology play in those changes, and what skills will be required?

Occupational therapy is going to become less of a mystery: we are learning to better define it in ways that are accessible to the general public. You're going to find it used in places such as community-based organizations — not just in rehabilitation centers — to help people develop healthy lifestyles and maintain independence. The forefront of technology is, how we can help people grow old in their homes, rather than enter a nursing home? For instance, a smart mirror installed in your bathroom literally tells you – via voice or screen message – to take your medicine. We can use these sorts of devices to help people who might have mild cognitive challenges stay home longer and be safe.

6. What do you enjoy most about your job? What do you enjoy least about your job?

I most enjoy helping people get to where they need to be, and where they want to be. It's pretty awesome to have that kind of impact on people. My least favorite thing is probably the paperwork. It takes a lot of time to do it right and it's a necessary part of the equation, yet on the surface it doesn't seem like it's where you want to be spending your time. I would much rather be with my clients.

7. Can you suggest a valuable "try this" for students considering a career in your profession?

Volunteer in a community organization where you can begin to understand people's different needs. In a place like a nursing home, for example, you see a bigger picture that what you know from your own life at home and school.

SELECTED SCHOOLS

Many colleges and universities have bachelor's degree programs in counseling and rehabilitation therapy, often with a specialization in occupational therapy. The student may also gain an initial grounding in the field at a technical or community college. Consult with your school guidance counselor or research area post-secondary programs to find the right fit for you. Below are listed some of the more prominent schools in this field.

Boston University
233 Bay State Road
Boston, MA 02215
617.353.2300
www.bu.edu

Colorado State University
Fort Collins, CO 80523
970.491.6444
www.colostate.edu

Indiana University, Bloomington
107 S. Indiana Avenue
Bloomington, IN 47405
812.855.4848
www.iub.edu

Tufts University
419 Boston Avenue
Medford, MA 02155
617.628.5000
www.tufts.edu

University of Florida
Gainesville, FL 32611
352.392.3261
www.ufl.edu

University of Illinois at Chicago
1200 W. Harrison Street
Chicago, IL 60607
312.996.7000
www.uic.edu

University of Kansas
1450 Jayhawk Boulevard
Lawrence, KS 66045
785.864.2700
www.ku.edu

University of Pittsburgh
4200 Fifth Avenue
Pittsburgh, PA 15260
412.624.4141
www.pitt.edu

University of Southern California
University Park Campus
Los Angeles, CA 90089
213.740.1111
www.usc.edu

Washington University in Saint Louis
1 Brookings Drive
Saint Louis, MO 63130
314.935.5000
wustl.edu

MORE INFORMATION

American Occupational Therapy Association
4720 Montgomery Lane
P.O. Box 31220
Bethesda, MD 20824-1220
301.652.2682
www.aota.org

Simone Isadora Flynn/Editor

Physical Therapist

Snapshot

Career Cluster: Health Care, Health and Wellness

Interests: Anatomy and Physiology, Sports Medicine, Physical Education

Earnings (Yearly Average): $80,889

Employment & Outlook: Faster Than Average Growth Expected

OVERVIEW

Sphere of Work

Physical therapists (PTs) provide therapeutic services to patients who have temporary or chronic physical conditions or illnesses that limit physical movement and mobility, thereby negatively affecting

patients' life and work. When working with patients, a physical therapist may use techniques such as therapeutic exercise, manual therapy techniques, assistive devices, adaptive devices, hydrotherapy, and electrotherapy. Physical therapists develop patient treatment plans designed to help maintain or recover a patient's physical mobility, lessen pain, increase productivity and independence, and improve quality of life.

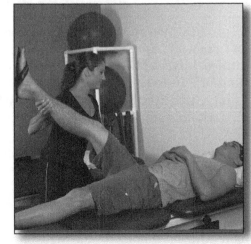

Work Environment

Physical therapists work in rehabilitation facilities, hospitals, nursing homes, physical therapy clinics, and schools. In medical environments, physical therapists work with a team of medical and social service professionals to increase a patient's physical abilities and overall independence. In school settings, physical therapists partner with educational professionals, such as teachers and special education coordinators, to address a student's physical issues. Physical therapists generally work a standard forty-hour workweek, and scheduled appointments are the norm.

Profile

Working Conditions: Work Indoors
Physical Strength: Light Work
Education Needs: Doctoral Degree
Licensure/Certification: Required
Physical Abilities Not Required: No Heavy Labor
Opportunities For Experience: Military Service
Holland Interest Score*: IES

* See Appendix A

Occupation Interest

Individuals attracted to the field of physical therapy tend to be physically strong people who enjoy hands-on work and close interaction with people from diverse backgrounds. Those who excel as physical therapists exhibit traits such as physical stamina, problem solving, empathy, patience, and caring. Physical therapists should enjoy learning, stay knowledgeable about changes in therapeutic techniques, and expect to work as part of a team to effectively address patient needs.

A Day in the Life—Duties and Responsibilities

A physical therapist's daily duties and responsibilities include full days of hands-on patient interaction and treatment, as well as administrative duties. Physical therapists' patients include those experiencing physical limitations and effects from neck and spinal cord injuries, traumatic brain injury, arthritis, burns, cerebral palsy, muscular dystrophy, strokes, limb or digit amputation, or work- or sports-related injuries.

As medical or therapeutic professionals, physical therapists interact with patients or clients on a daily basis and strive to understand the particular challenges faced by each individual. Treatment typically includes a blend of physical techniques and emotional encouragement, since the patient may be in the process of adjusting to a major life change. Some of a physical therapist's daily responsibilities include conducting patient assessments, developing patient treatment plans, and providing physical treatment to patients with severe physical limitations. Physical therapists frequently advise patients on the use of adaptive equipment, such as wheelchairs and orthopedic aids. Some provide early intervention services to young children experiencing physical delays and limitations. Others may offer consultation on or participate in building customized adaptive equipment for patients with special needs not met by existing options. Physical therapists also instruct individuals and groups on physical exercises to prevent injury, lead fitness and health classes and workshops, and counsel patients on physical adaptations that can help the patient to continue to work at his or her chosen occupation. They may also supervise the activities of physical therapy assistants and aides.

During the course of treatment, a physical therapist will consult with a team of physicians, educators, social workers, mental health professionals, occupational therapists, speech therapists, and other medical professionals to help ensure that each patient receives comprehensive care.

A physical therapist's administrative responsibilities include documenting treatment sessions and ongoing patient evaluation. Physical therapists must draft treatment plans, record notes following patient treatment sessions, provide written updates to the other members of a patient's treatment team, and provide insurance companies with patient records and progress notes as required. Independent physical therapists who do not work as part of a school or medical clinic may also be responsible for scheduling appointments and for submitting bills to insurance companies or patients.

Duties and Responsibilities

- Evaluating the physician's referral and the patient's medical records to determine the treatment required
- Performing tests, measurements, and evaluations such as range-of-motion and manual-muscle tests, gait and functional analyses, and body-parts measurements
- Administering manual therapeutic exercises to improve or maintain muscle function
- Administering treatments involving the application of such agents as light, heat, water, and ice massage techniques
- Recording patients' treatments, responses, and progress

OCCUPATION SPECIALTIES

Physical Therapist Assistants

Physical Therapist Assistants help physical therapists provide care to
patients. Under the direction and supervision of physical therapists,
they give therapy through exercise; therapeutic methods, such as
electrical stimulation, mechanical traction, and ultrasound; massage;
and gait and balance training. Physical therapist assistants record
patients' responses to treatment and report the results of each
treatment to the physical therapist.

Physical Therapist Aides

Physical Therapist Aides help make therapy sessions productive,
under the direct supervision of a physical therapist or physical
therapist assistant. They usually are responsible for keeping the
treatment area clean and organized and for preparing for each
patient's therapy. They also help patients who need assistance moving
to or from a treatment area.

Directors of Physical Therapy

Directors of Physical Therapy plan, direct, and coordinate physical
therapy programs and make sure the program complies with state
requirements.

WORK ENVIRONMENT

Physical Environment

Physical therapists work in rehabilitation facilities, hospitals, nursing
homes, therapy clinics, and schools. Therapeutic office settings
used by physical therapists may be shared with other therapeutic
professionals, such as occupational, recreational, or speech and
language therapists.

Human Environment

Physical therapists work with patients who use physical therapy to improve their strength and mobility, as well as their independence and quality of life. This may include people experiencing balance and strength issues caused by cerebral palsy, spinal cord injuries, or muscular dystrophy; stroke victims experiencing coordination problems or paralysis; and children or adults suffering the physical effects of injuries, abuse, or accidents. Physical therapists usually work as part of a patient treatment team that includes patient families, social workers, teachers, doctors, and additional therapists.

Relevant Skills and Abilities

Communication Skills
- Expressing thoughts and ideas
- Speaking and writing effectively

Interpersonal/Social Skills
- Being patient
- Being sensitive to others
- Cooperating with others
- Working as a member of a team

Organization & Management Skills
- Coordinating tasks
- Managing people/groups
- Paying attention to and handling details
- Performing duties that may change frequently

Planning & Research Skills
- Developing evaluation strategies

Technical Skills
- Performing technical work
- Working with your hands

Technological Environment

Physical therapists use a wide variety of technology in their work. Computers and Internet communication tools are widely used in physical therapy work and practice. Specialized therapies, such as electrotherapy, hydrotherapy, and ultrasound therapy, require technical equipment and training. In addition, physical therapists must learn how to use and teach the use of adaptive devices, such as wheelchairs and orthopedic aids.

EDUCATION, TRAINING, AND ADVANCEMENT

High School/Secondary

High school students interested in pursuing the profession of physical therapy in the future should develop good study habits. High school courses in biology, psychology, anatomy, sociology, and mathematics will prepare students for college- and graduate-level studies. Students interested in the physical therapy field will benefit from seeking internships or part-time work with physical therapists or with people who have physical issues that affect their range of movement or daily life.

Suggested High School Subjects
- Algebra
- Applied Communication
- Applied Math
- Applied Physics
- Biology
- Chemistry
- College Preparatory
- English
- Geometry
- Health Science Technology
- Humanities
- Physical Education
- Physics
- Physiology
- Psychology
- Science
- Trigonometry

Famous First

The first physical therapy school was formed at Walter Reed Army Hospital in Washington, D.C., following the United States' entry into World War I. In 1921 the first research journal in physical therapy, *The PT Review*, was published, and in that same year the first professional organization for physical therapists, the American Physical Therapy Association, was established.

Library of Congress

College/Postsecondary

Postsecondary students interested in becoming physical therapists should complete coursework in physical therapy, if possible, as well as courses on occupational therapy, special education, biology, psychology, anatomy and physiology, sociology, and mathematics. Prior to graduation, college students interested in joining the physical therapy profession should apply to graduate-level physical therapy programs or secure physical therapy-related employment. Those who choose to pursue a master's degree tend to have better prospects for employment and advancement in the field. Membership in the American Physical Therapy Association may help provide postsecondary students with networking opportunities and connections.

Related College Majors
- Adapted Physical Education/Therapeutic Recreation
- Anatomy and Physiology
- Exercise Science/Physiology/Movement Studies
- Health & Physical Education, General
- Physical Therapy
- Sports Medicine & Athletic Training

Adult Job Seekers

Adult job seekers in the physical therapy field should have a master's degree in physical therapy from a college or university accredited by the Commission on Accreditation in Physical Therapy Education. They must also earn the necessary professional licensure. Physical therapists seeking employment may benefit from the networking opportunities, job workshops, and job lists offered by professional physical therapy associations, such as the American Physical Therapy Association and American Board of Physical Therapy Specialties. Advancement in the physical therapy field often depends on the individual's education and specialty certification.

Professional Certification and Licensure

Physical therapists are required to have earned a professional physical therapy (PT) license prior to beginning their professional practice. Upon completion of an accredited master's or doctoral program in physical therapy, candidates take the National Physical Therapy Examination (NPTE) administered by the Federation of State Boards of Physical Therapy. In addition to passing the NPTE, physical therapists are required to register with their state health board, pass a state exam, and engage in continuing education as a condition of their PT license.

Physical therapists may choose to pursue additional, specialized physical therapy certification from the American Board of Physical Therapy Specialties. Certification is available for the following specialties: cardiovascular and pulmonary, clinical electrophysiology, geriatrics, neurology, pediatrics, sports, and women's health.

Additional Requirements

Individuals who find satisfaction, success, and job security as physical therapists will be knowledgeable about the profession's requirements, responsibilities, and opportunities. Successful physical therapists engage in ongoing professional development related to changes in therapeutic techniques, ethical standards, and new technology. Because physical therapists work with vulnerable people and share confidential patient information with other medical professionals, adherence to strict professional and ethical standards is required.

Both entry-level and senior-level physical therapists may find it beneficial to join professional associations as a means of building professional community and networking.

Fun Fact

Brief bouts of dizziness with changes in position or movement of the head – positional vertigo – the most common cause of dizziness, is caused by dysfunction of the inner ear, and can successfully be treated in as little as one session with a physical therapist.

Source: http://www.athletico.com/2011/09/27/the-top-10-things-you-did-not-know-about-physical-therapy

EARNINGS AND ADVANCEMENT

Earnings of physical therapists depend on the type and size of the employer and the physical therapist's length of employment and level of responsibility. Physical therapists in private practice tend to earn more than salaried workers. Salaries are usually higher in rural areas as employers try to attract physical therapists to where there are severe shortages.

Median annual earnings of physical therapists were $80,889 in 2012. The lowest ten percent earned less than $56,837, and the highest ten percent earned more than $114,395.

Physical therapists may receive paid vacations, holidays, and sick days; life and health insurance; and retirement benefits. These are usually paid by the employer. Some employers also provide for paid educational leave.

Metropolitan Areas with the Highest
Employment Level in this Occupation

Metropolitan area	Employment (1)	Employment per thousand jobs	Hourly mean wage
New York-White Plains-Wayne, NY-NJ	7,610	1.48	$40.46
Chicago-Joliet-Naperville, IL	6,740	1.85	$37.33
Los Angeles-Long Beach-Glendale, CA	4,880	1.26	$42.51
Boston-Cambridge-Quincy, MA	3,430	2.00	$37.08
Philadelphia, PA	3,000	1.64	$36.78
Phoenix-Mesa-Glendale, AZ	2,960	1.71	$39.40
Dallas-Plano-Irving, TX	2,830	1.35	$45.41
Nassau-Suffolk, NY	2,570	2.10	$41.68

(1) Does not include self-employed. Source: Bureau of Labor Statistics, 2012

EMPLOYMENT AND OUTLOOK

There were approximately 192,000 physical therapists employed nationally in 2012. Another 120,000 worked as physical therapist assistants or aides. Employment of physical therapists is expected to grow much faster than the average for all occupations through the year 2020, which means employment is projected to increase 35 percent or more. As new medical technologies allow more people to survive accidents and illnesses, but who then require physical therapy, employment opportunities will increase. The rapidly growing elderly population will also contribute to this demand. A growing number of employers are using physical therapists to evaluate work sites, develop exercise programs and teach safe work habits to employees in the hope of reducing injuries.

Employment Trend, Projected 2010–20

Physical Therapists: 39%

Health Diagnosing and Treating Practitioners: 26%

Total, All Occupations: 14%

Note: "All Occupations" includes all occupations in the U.S. Economy. Source: U.S. Bureau of Labor Statistics, Employment Projections Program

Related Occupations
- Activities Therapist
- Athletic Trainer
- Chiropractor
- Occupational Therapist
- Recreational Therapist
- Respiratory Therapist

Related Military Occupations
- Physical & Occupational Therapist

Conversation With . . .
ASHLEY BURNS

Physical Therapist/Certified Orthopedic
Manual Therapist, 5 years

1. What was your individual career path in terms of education, entry-level job, or other significant opportunity?

I completed an entry-level 5½-year Master's in Science physical therapy program at Springfield College. The first two years were spent completing prerequisites; the last three years were the graduate school portion of the program. After graduating with a Master's in Physical Therapy (PT) in 2008, I passed my boards, and began working at Brigham & Women's Hospital. After working for two years, I entered the transitional Doctorate in Physical Therapy program at Massachusetts General's Institute of Health Professions, while still working full-time. Before and after my Doctor in Physical Therapy (DPT), I completed continuing education classes through Maitland Australian Physiotherapy Seminars (MAPS) and passed a two-day exam with three parts: practical, short-answer, and multiple-choice. With this completion, I earned the degree of Certified Orthopedic Manual Therapist. While working at the Brigham, I have had many educational opportunities, including teaching courses, lecturing at outside athletic programs, attending rounds/clinical education series, and publishing articles.

2. Are there many job opportunities in your profession? In what specific areas?

There are many job opportunities in the physical therapy profession, which can be broken down into four different areas: outpatient, inpatient, rehabilitation, and home-care. Within these areas, there are different categories, such as orthopedics, geriatric, neurological, oncology, and cardiopulmonary. There are job openings in all of these areas, but the biggest area in terms of available jobs currently is home care. This is due to the growing geriatric population, which is a result of people living longer, people living healthier lifestyles, and the effects of ever-changing and improving health care.

3. What do you wish you had known going into this profession?

I can honestly say that my education prepared me well for the job, and there weren't a lot of big surprises.

4. How do you see your profession changing in the next five years?

I think in the next five years, patients will be able to come directly to physical therapy without being required to have a referral from their primary care physician to satisfy health insurance requirements. Physical therapists will be more respected for having a doctorate in their field, and will have the ability to screen patients for red flags and determine whether they are appropriate for PT or require further diagnostic screening by a different specialist. (By 2015, all degree programs for physical therapists will be doctorate programs.) In addition, I think physical therapists will eventually be allowed to directly order imaging and to refer patients to other specialists as appropriate.

5. What role will technology play in those changes, and what skills will be required?

Technology is already changing the manner in which health care professionals interact with their patients, charge for billing, and record visits. We have to walk a fine line when seeing patients–typing in all the required information while also listening to a patient, making eye contact, and thinking critically: what is this patient's diagnosis? Physical therapists will need to be computer savvy to ensure all information is recorded accurately.

6. Do you have any general advice or additional professional insights to share with someone interested in your profession?

Physical therapy school is not easy. It is very hard work. You will go to class for eight hours some days, like a job. But it is worth all your time and effort. You will change people's lives by teaching them how to walk again, how to work without pain, return to their sport, or live more comfortably. The rewards of this profession are difficult to put into words. You will have patients who change your own perspective on life, who give you a greater insight into life and give your life meaning. You may think that you are changing their lives, but they effect change in yours. Each day is different from the next, full of variety and challenges. I am constantly learning. As more research is being produced, my evidence-based practice changes. You are keeping your mind active at all times. I honestly wouldn't want to be in any other profession.

7. Can you suggest a valuable "try this" for students considering a career in your profession?

I would suggest observing a physical therapist in a clinic for a few weeks. This will give you a better idea of what physical therapy is all about.

SELECTED SCHOOLS

Many colleges, universities, and professional schools offer programs in physical therapy. Below are listed some of the more prominent institutions in this field.

Emory University
Division of Physical Therapy
1462 Clifton Road NE, Suite 312
Atlanta, GA 30322
404.727.4002
www.rehabmed.emory.edu/pt

MGH Institute of Health Professions
Graduate Program in Physical Therapy
36 First Avenue
Boston, MA 02129
617.726.8009
www.mghihp.edu/academics/physical-therapy

Northwestern University
Department of Physical Therapy and Human Movement Science
645 N. Michigan Avenue, Suite 1100
Chicago, IL 60611
312.908.8160
www.medschool.northwestern.edu/nupthms

University of Delaware
Department of Physical Therapy
301 McKinly Laboratory
Newark, DE 19716
302.831.8910
www.udel.edu/PT

University of Iowa
Graduate Program in Physical Therapy
1-252 Medical Education Building
Iowa City, IA 52242
319.335.9791
www.medicine.uiowa.edu/physicaltherapy

University of Miami
Department of Physical Therapy
5915 Ponce de Leon Boulevard
Coral Gables, FL 33146
305.284.4535
pt.med.miami.edu

University of Pittsburgh
School of Health and Rehabilitation Sciences
4020 Forbes Tower
Pittsburgh, PA 15260
412.383.6558
www.shrs.pitt.edu

University of Southern California
Biokinesiology and Physical Therapy
1540 Alcatraz Street, CHP 155
Los Angeles, CA 90089
323.442.2900
pt/usc.edu

U.S. Army-Baylor University
Physical Therapy Department
3151 Scott Road
Fort Sam Houston, TX 78234
210.221.8410
www.baylor.edu/graduate/pt

Washington University in St. Louis
Program in Physical Therapy
4444 Forest Park Boulevard
St. Louis, MO 63108
314.286.1400
physicaltherapy.wustl.edu

MORE INFORMATION

American Physical Therapy Association
1111 N. Fairfax Street
Alexandria, VA 22314-1488
800.999.2782
www.apta.org

Commission on Accreditation of Allied Health Education Programs
1361 Park Street
Clearwater, FL 33756
727.210.2350
www.caahep.org

Federation of State Boards of Physical Therapy
124 West Street S, 3rd Floor
Alexandria, VA 22314
703.299.3100
www.fsbpt.org

Simone Isadora Flynn/Editor

Psychologist

Snapshot

Career Cluster: Education & Training; Health Care; Human Services

Interests: Mental health, human behavior, emotional issues, psychological counseling, behavior modification

Earnings (Yearly Average): $67,750

Employment & Outlook: Average Growth Expected

OVERVIEW

Sphere of Work

Psychologists study the human mind, and try to understand human behavior. Many people think of psychologists as people who provide counseling services to help people cope with issues in their lives, but that is only one area of specialization in this broad field. Psychologists may work directly with clients in an office, a hospital, or in a school; they may work for companies or organizations, figuring out how best to accomplish tasks or convey messages; or they may work at a university or research institution, conducting psychological research or

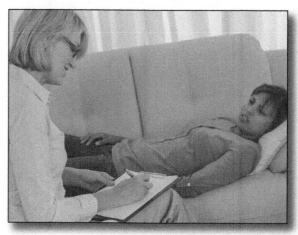

teaching psychology to others. These various areas of specialization are denoted by terms such as clinical psychology, school psychology, industrial/organizational psychology, developmental psychology, social psychology, research psychology, and others.

Work Environment

Psychologists are often self-employed, working as private practitioners or independent consultants. They may work from home or in private offices, where they set their own hours, sometimes working evenings and weekends to accommodate working clients. Others work in institutional team environments, such as in schools or with corporations, and provide their services during regular business hours. Research psychologists may work in labs carrying out various kinds of experiments and evaluating research results. Psychologists also work at hospitals, nonprofit organizations, and government agencies.

Profile

Working Conditions: Work Indoors
Physical Strength: Light Work
Education Needs: Master's Degree, Doctoral Degree
Licensure/Certification: Required
Physical Abilities Not Required: No Heavy Labor
Opportunities For Experience: Military Service, Volunteer Work
Holland Interest Score*: SIA

* See Appendix A

Occupation Interest

Psychology is an appropriate career pursuit for people who are interested in how the human mind works, and in how this knowledge can be used to improve people's lives. To varying degrees, depending on their area of specialization, psychologists should have good people skills (for one-on-one work with patients or other members of a team) as well as strong analytical skills (for conducting research or evaluating patients' needs). Psychologists usually have graduate degrees, and most commonly, a doctorate.

A Day in the Life—Duties and Responsibilities

Again, the typical day for a psychologist depends on his or her specialty. Clinical or counseling psychologists may spend their days helping clients cope with mental illness or simply managing the issues in their life—family or marital distress, bereavement, substance abuse, or problems at work or school. They may also work with medical patients trying to cope with illness or injury.

In the process of helping clients, psychologists conduct diagnostic testing and interviews that can help them pinpoint central issues and behavioral triggers. They provide various kinds of psychotherapy, or psychological counseling, sometimes over just a few sessions and sometimes on a longer-term basis. They may help clients develop behavior modification programs or other strategies to help achieve wellness. In most cases, psychologists are not qualified to prescribe medication, and may recommend other medical providers to patients who could benefit from medication.

Research psychologists and industrial/organizational psychologists do not typically provide services directly to individuals. Rather, they work for organizations or institutions, perhaps expanding knowledge and understanding through large research experiments, or helping develop work processes and approaches that help fulfill business-related needs, such as greater employee productivity or more effective product marketing. Research psychologists may conduct experiments on people or animals; they may administer surveys or conduct ongoing interviews with human volunteers; or they may study how animals react to various stimuli in order to learn more about very basic mental processes. Industrial/organizational psychologists may help companies develop more effective communication strategies between managers and employees, or assess other aspects of work life and generate recommendations for improvement.

Duties and Responsibilities

- Diagnosing and treating psychological conditions
- Collecting data using interviews, case histories, observational techniques and other methods
- Administering and interpreting psychological tests
- Counseling people individually and in groups
- Conferring with parents, counselors, administrators and others

OCCUPATION SPECIALTIES

Clinical Psychologists

Clinical Psychologists constitute the largest specialty; they help mentally and emotionally disturbed people adjust to life.

Counseling Psychologists

Counseling Psychologists use such techniques as interviewing and testing to advise people on how to deal with problems of everyday living — personal, educational, vocational and social.

School Psychologists

School Psychologists evaluate children within an educational system and plan and implement corrective programs. They work with teachers, parents and administrators to resolve students' learning and behavioral problems.

Psychometrists

Psychometrists administer, score and interpret intelligence, aptitude, achievement and other psychological tests.

Experimental Psychologists

Experimental Psychologists conduct experiments with human beings and animals, such as rats, monkeys and pigeons, in the prominent areas of experimental research that includes motivation, thinking, learning and retention, sensory and perceptual processes and genetic and neurological factors in behavior.

Industrial-Organizational Psychologists

Industrial-Organizational Psychologists develop and apply psychological techniques to administration, management and marketing problems. They are involved in policy planning, applicant screening, training and development, psychological test research, counseling and organizational development.

Forensic Psychologists

Forensic Psychologists use psychological principles in the legal and criminal justice system to help judges, attorneys, and other legal specialists understand the psychological aspects of a particular case. They often testify in court as expert witnesses. They typically specialize in family court, civil court, or criminal court.

Social Psychologists

Social Psychologists investigate the psychological aspects of human interrelationships to gain understanding of individual and group thought, feeling and behavior, using observation, experimentation and survey techniques.

WORK ENVIRONMENT

Relevant Skills and Abilities

Analytical Skills
- Analyzing data

Communication Skills
- Expressing thoughts and ideas
- Speaking effectively
- Writing concisely

Interpersonal/Social Skills
- Cooperating with others
- Working as a member of a team

Organization & Management Skills
- Managing time
- Meeting goals and deadlines
- Performing duties that may change frequently

Physical Environment

Psychologists usually see clients in comfortable and quiet office or home settings where there are few distractions. Research and organizational psychologists can be found in labs and office buildings, and other psychologists can be found in their respective places of specialization, such as schools, hospitals, and places of business.

Human Environment

Clinical and counseling psychologists work with clients who may be in various states of distress, and they also frequently collaborate with other psychologists, social workers,

Research & Planning Skills
- Developing evaluation strategies
- Using logical reasoning

Technical Skills
- Performing scientific, mathematical and technical work

psychiatrists, and other kinds of social service and health care providers. Research psychologists work with colleagues and other professionals, and teaching psychologists work with undergraduate and graduate students.

Technological Environment

Unless working in a research laboratory with humans, animals, and scientific equipment, psychologists mostly listen, ask questions, take notes, and often they use computers to keep records of their clients' status and progress.

EDUCATION, TRAINING, AND ADVANCEMENT

High School/Secondary

High school students can best prepare for a career in psychology by focusing on science, English, and math. Some high schools may offer advanced placement psychology as an elective. Otherwise, students should generally cultivate their skills in writing, speech, critical thinking, and scientific research. Biology is the science that is most relevant to psychology, and it is also useful to take classes in the social sciences.

High school guidance counselors can help students learn more about career and university offerings.

Suggested High School Subjects
- Algebra
- Child Growth & Development
- College Preparatory
- Composition
- English

- Psychology
- Social Studies
- Sociology
- Statistics

Famous First

The first use of psychodrama, in which the person under treatment (often along with others) is assigned a role to play in a dramatized scenario, was in Beacon, New York, in 1937. The treatment, developed by Dr. Jacob L. Moreno, was designed to enable the therapist to achieve a clear understanding of the patient's mental and emotional processes. Dr. Moreno was also a pioneer of group psychotherapy.

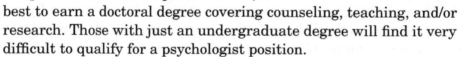

College/Postsecondary

In order to practice psychology, students need a master's or doctoral degree in the field. Since competition in this occupation is stiff, it is best to earn a doctoral degree covering counseling, teaching, and/or research. Those with just an undergraduate degree will find it very difficult to qualify for a psychologist position.

Universities all over the United States encourage psychology students to understand and conduct varying levels of analysis of written documents and the interpretation of scientific cases. Coursework includes topics such as critical thinking, psychopathology, the biological bases of behavior, psychological assessment, interpersonal behavior, psychophysiology, psychosocial adjustment, and research design and methodology.

The largest professional organization of U.S. psychologists, the American Psychological Association, normally requires a doctoral degree for full membership, and a master's degree for associate membership. Doctoral degrees available in psychology include: a regular doctorate, or PhD, the most wide-ranging option; a doctorate of psychology (PsyD), which is geared more toward clinical practice than research; and a doctorate of education (EdD) focused on psychology, usually counseling, developmental, or educational psychology.

Related College Majors
- Clinical Psychology
- Criminology
- Gerontology
- Psychology, General

Adult Job Seekers

For those adults with the appropriate education and training, who seek to update their professional credentials, it is important to have an up-to-date resume, and determine which courses may need to be taken or retaken. Other ways to enhance credentials include taking continuing education courses, applying for scholarships or grants, or getting involved in work with professional associations to make contacts for future employment opportunities.

Professional Certification and Licensure

Those psychologists who have their own practice need a license from the state in which they work. Getting a license requires education, work experience, and passing a qualifying test.

Additional Requirements

Psychologists are often empathetic and compassionate people, interested in the complexities of the mind and the individual's ability to navigate an increasingly complex world. Successful psychologists are discrete and patient, understanding that patient treatment is a complex process with both successes and failures. An ability to motivate others to continue to work towards long-term mental health is critical.

Fun Fact

Some say that the road to psychotherapy was paved by Austrian physician Dr. Franz Mesmer, who, back in 1774, theorized that physical and mental illness involved internal magnetic forces, which he called "animal magnetism." His cure, originally known as mesmerism, is now known as hypnosis.

Sources: http://allpsych.com/timeline/#.VQBz8UI-CqA

http://psychcentral.com/blog/archives/2011/05/09/psychologys-history-of-being-mesmerized/

EARNINGS AND ADVANCEMENT

Earnings depend on the employer and the individual's education and experience. Those having a doctoral degree earned more than those with a master's degree. Median annual earnings of clinical, counseling and school psychologists were $67,760 in 2013. Median annual earnings of industrial-organizational psychologists were $91,140 in 2013.

Psychologists usually receive paid vacations, holidays, and sick days; life and health insurance; and retirement benefits. These are usually paid by the employer.

Metropolitan Areas with the Highest
Employment Level in this Occupation

Metropolitan area	Employment[1]	Employment per thousand jobs	Hourly mean wage
Los Angeles-Long Beach-Glendale, CA	6,220	1.56	$34.97
New York-White Plains-Wayne, NY-NJ	6,090	1.16	$41.49
Chicago-Joliet-Naperville, IL	3,040	0.82	$31.61
Boston-Cambridge-Quincy, MA	2,180	1.25	$41.63
Philadelphia, PA	1,970	1.07	$38.53
Atlanta-Sandy Springs-Marietta, GA	1,760	0.76	$31.44
Houston-Sugar Land-Baytown, TX	1,580	0.57	$28.04
Washington-Arlington-Alexandria, DC-VA-MD-WV	1,580	0.67	$38.05
Baltimore-Towson, MD	1,550	1.21	$33.08
Minneapolis-St. Paul-Bloomington, MN-WI	1,520	0.85	$35.41

[1] Does not include self-employed. Source: Bureau of Labor Statistics

EMPLOYMENT AND OUTLOOK

Nationally, there were 160,000 psychologists employed in 2012. Approximately 145,000 of these were clinical, counseling, and school psychologists. After several years of experience, some psychologists, usually those with doctoral degrees, enter private practice or set up private research or consulting firms. About one-third were self-employed. Employment is expected to grow as fast as the average for all occupations through the year 2022, which means employment is projected to increase 12 percent. This is primarily due to the increased demand for psychological services in schools, hospitals, social service agencies, mental health centers, substance abuse treatment clinics, consulting firms and private companies. Demand should be particularly strong for persons holding an advanced degree in industrial-organizational psychology, as companies and organizations look for ways to maximize productivity. Psychologists with extensive training in quantitative research methods and computer science may have a competitive edge over applicants without this background.

Employment Trend, Projected 2010–20

Industrial-Organizational Psychologists: 53%

Psychologists (All): 12%

Clinical, Counseling, and School Psychologists: 11%

Psychologists, All Other: 11%

Total, All Occupations: 11%

Note: "All Occupations" includes all occupations in the U.S. Economy. Source: U.S. Bureau of Labor Statistics, Employment Projections Program

Related Occupations

- Human Resources Specialist/ Manager
- Marriage Counselor
- Medical Social Worker
- Neuropsychologist
- Psychiatrist
- Rehabilitation Counselor
- School Counselor
- Social Worker
- Substance Abuse Counselor
-

Related Military Occupations

- Psychologist

Conversation With . . .
SHARON SALINE, Psy.D.

Psychologist, 25 years
Northampton, MA

1. What was your individual career path in terms of education/training, entry-level job, or other significant opportunity?

I studied history and semiotics in college, and we read a lot of Freud and other post-modern theory. I was interested in theater and filmmaking and video production, and I began teaching drama in after school programs, was assistant director in some children's theater productions, and was also director of intergenerational videos for another children's theater company. I became more and more interested in people's stories than all the logistical stuff around these productions. I was in my mid 20s, and decided to get my master's degree in psychology. Then I worked two years as a staff therapist at an agency south of San Francisco which was great experience because I worked with kids and families at the agency, ran groups for kids in schools, and co-led trainings for teachers on cross cultural issues. I am very glad I went on and got my doctorate at the California School of Professional Psychology. The process of researching and writing a dissertation was interesting and compelling; I learned how to do assessments and understand statistics. Today, I don't do research but I can read it, refer to it, and understand it. I had my first child after the first year of my doctorate, finished school and then had my second child. A year later we moved back east to Amherst. I worked at an agency in Springfield, Mass and saw families, did school consultations, and later started a private practice. I specialize in ADHD and see 20-25 clients per week. At least half are children and families, and I do a lot of collateral work including calling teachers, pediatricians, and others who are involved in a child's life. In more recent years, I also do training, parent talks, and write. Because I have a strong theater background, I'm comfortable with public speaking. I do monthly talks with a pediatrician from a local practice for parents about ADHD, anxiety, preschool behaviors, sibling relationships, and similar issues.

2. What are the most important skills and/or qualities for someone in your profession?

Compassion, empathy, boundaries, a sense of humor, intellectual curiosity, and a real interest in people and their lives and a willingness to connect with them and share. Also, it's important to set up a network for yourself because this work is draining.

You need good self-care skills. I have been in therapy myself at times over the years, I see a clinical consultant once a month to talk about my challenging cases and other professional issues, and I started a consultation group of five clinicians to discuss clinical topics and questions, including anything related to running our own businesses.

3. **What do you wish you had known going into this profession?**

    The toll on the emotional and physical body. Some cases are hard; some people have intense issues in their lives and I'm carrying that with me. The other thing I didn't expect is how difficult it is to deal with insurance companies — reimbursements and that type of thing — and the major influence insurance companies have on the practice of psychology in terms of reimbursement, authorizations and length of treatment.

4. **Are there many job opportunities in your profession? In what specific areas?**

    Yes, there are plenty of opportunities. Areas include agency work, and in therapeutic schools, hospitals, and research.

5. **How do you see your profession changing in the next five years, what role will technology play in those changes, and what skills will be required?**

    Major trends are cultural competencies — what's happening with various racial and ethnic groups — plus gender identity, mindfulness, neuropsychology and neuroscience and partnering with primary care physicians. As for technology, some people use Skype or have a phone session but to me the benefit of therapy is face-to-face. I also feel things may be changing because the younger generation is too attached to their technology. Addressing changes in behavior and emotions from the increase in technology is another area of growth right now.

6. **What do you enjoy most about your job? What do you enjoy least about your job?**

    I really enjoy working with people, hearing their stories and helping them help themselves to make changes in their lives and grow and move on. It's extremely rewarding. Because I work with kids and families, I see people over many years. It's incredible to share their lives.

    What I don't like is feeling burdened sometimes. And I also don't like seeing parents or kids make choices which are clearly ineffective for them and create problems for them. We'll talk about it but they'll do it anyway; that is really hard. I also don't like dealing with health insurance companies.

7. **Can you suggest a valuable "try this" for students considering a career in your profession?**

Volunteer for an organization like a hotline — rape crisis, domestic violence — to get crisis training and actually talk to people who are having difficulty. Or volunteer in a classroom, an afterschool program, or at a nursing home so that you start to build some skills in building relationships and working with people in different settings.

MORE INFORMATION

American Psychological Association
Education Directorate
750 First Street, NE
Washington, DC 20002-4242
800.374.2721
www.apa.org

Association for Psychological Science
1133 15th Street NW, Suite 1000
Washington, DC 20005
202.293.9300
www.psychologicalscience.org

Mental Health America
2000 N. Beauregard Street, 6th Floor
Alexandria, VA 22311
800.969.6642
www.nmha.org

National Alliance on Mental Illness
3803 N. Fairfax Drive, Suite 100
Arlington, VA 22203
800.950.6264
www.nami.org

National Association of School Psychologists
4340 East West Highway, Suite 402
Bethesda, MD 20814
301.657.0270
www.nasponline.org

National Institute of Mental Health
6001 Executive Boulevard
Room 8184, MSC 9663
Bethesda, MD 20892-9663
866.615.6464
www.nimh.nih.gov

Susan Williams/Editor

Recreational Therapist

Snapshot

Career Cluster: Human Services

Interests: Recreational therapy, physical therapy, human development, psychology, assistive technology, physiology

Earnings (Yearly Average): $43,180

Employment & Outlook: Average Growth Expected

OVERVIEW

Sphere of Work

Recreational therapists provide therapeutic recreational services aimed at helping their patients improve emotional and mental well-being, build interpersonal relations, strengthen social skills, and increase confidence.

Recreational therapists develop and implement medically approved recreational therapies and programs to meet patient needs, abilities, and interests. The range of recreational therapies is vast and includes community integration, stress reduction, fitness, group sports, field trips, and arts and crafts. Recreational

therapists encourage their patients to socialize and use recreational and community resources.

Work Environment

Recreational therapists work in medical settings, such as hospitals, physical rehabilitation centers, substance abuse facilities, and psychiatric facilities, as well as community and institutional settings, including schools, parks and recreation departments, prisons, retirement facilities, and adult day care facilities. In medical environments, recreational therapists generally partner with medical and social service professionals to increase patients' social skills and confidence. In community and institutional settings, recreational therapists partner with educational and therapeutic professionals to address students' or patients' social or recreational needs.

Profile

Working Conditions: Work Indoors
Physical Strength: Light Work
Education Needs: Bachelor's Degree
Licensure/Certification:
 Recommended
Physical Abilities Not Required: No
 Heavy Labor
Opportunities For Experience:
 Internship, Volunteer Work, Part-Time
 Work
Holland Interest Score*: SEC

* See Appendix A

Occupation Interest

Individuals attracted to the field of recreational therapy tend to be physically strong and energetic people who have the ability to teach and lead a variety of activities. Individuals who excel as recreational therapists exhibit tact, creativity, problem solving, desire to help, patience, humor, and caring. Recreational therapists must be able to work as part of a team to meet patient needs.

A Day in the Life—Duties and Responsibilities

The daily duties and responsibilities of recreational therapists vary by the individual's area of job specialization and work environment. Recreational therapists attend to the therapeutic needs of their patients. Patients in recreational therapy may be part of inpatient medical facilities or may be seen on an outpatient basis, often by referral. The recreational therapist first conducts patient assessments. Once the patient's needs and abilities have been recorded, the recreational therapist develops patient treatment plans. He or she then provides therapy sessions and workshops that focus on the mental and physical well-being of patients.

Community integration, stress reduction, fitness, group sports, field trips, and arts and crafts are common types of recreational therapies. A recreational therapist might lead individuals and small groups in such community integration exercises as riding public transportation, placing orders in a restaurant, and asking for or giving directions. Recreational therapists might teach patients such stress reduction techniques as massage, meditation, and deep breathing. In various group settings, recreational therapists lead group activities on nature, performing arts, field trips, arts and crafts, stretching, aerobic exercise, strength training, or group sports such as volleyball and baseball. They are responsible for ensuring that all recreation program activities and events meet national requirements for safety and the Americans with Disabilities Act. This may mean overseeing the safety, upkeep, and maintenance of recreational equipment and facilities.

In all cases, recreational therapists must communicate regularly and effectively with patients, patient families, colleagues, and insurers. They interact with patients throughout the day in a friendly and supportive manner and advise patients on the use of recreational equipment. Some provide early intervention services to young children with mental and social delays and limitations. Recreational therapists evaluate, document, and communicate patient progress in therapeutic activities. They then meet with patient treatment teams or patient families and provide insurance companies with patient records and progress notes as required. Recreational therapists may also supervise recreation staff and volunteers.

Independent recreational therapists, who work outside of a medical or educational facility, may also be responsible for scheduling appointments and billing patients.

Duties and Responsibilities

- Observing the physical, mental and social progress of patients
- Contributing information and progress reports for use in meeting treatment goals
- Assisting patients in readjusting recreational needs to activities offered by the community in which they live
- Training groups of volunteers and students in techniques of recreation therapy
- Organizing athletic events, craft workshops, field trips, dances and concerts for patients
- Instructing patients in relaxation techniques
- Instructing patients in calisthenics and individual and group sports
- Developing a treatment plan, leading activities and monitoring patients' progress

WORK ENVIRONMENT

Physical Environment

Recreational therapists work in rehabilitation facilities, hospitals, nursing homes, therapy clinics, and schools. Therapeutic office settings used by recreational therapists may be shared with other therapeutic professionals such as physical, occupational, or speech and language therapists.

Human Environment

Recreational therapists interact with a wide variety of people and should be comfortable meeting with people with physical, mental, and emotional illnesses and special needs, the elderly, and children, as well as colleagues and supervisors. Recreational therapists usually work as part of a patient treatment team that includes families, social workers, teachers, doctors, and other therapists. As a member of a treatment team, recreational therapists participate in frequent team meetings and are responsible for communicating patient progress to fellow team members.

Relevant Skills and Abilities

Communication Skills
- Speaking effectively
- Writing concisely

Interpersonal/Social Skills
- Being sensitive to others
- Counseling others
- Providing support to others

Organization & Management Skills
- Coordinating tasks
- Managing people/groups
- Performing duties that change frequently

Technological Environment

Recreational therapists use a wide variety of technologies and equipment in their work. Recreational therapists use Internet communication tools, word-processing software, and spreadsheets. During therapy sessions, the equipment they use may include musical instruments, sports equipment, and adaptive technology such as wheelchairs.

EDUCATION, TRAINING, AND ADVANCEMENT

High School/Secondary

High school students interested in pursuing the profession of recreational therapy in the future should develop good study habits. High school coursework in physical education, psychology, and sociology can prepare students for undergraduate and master's level studies. Students interested in the recreational therapy field may benefit from seeking internships or part-time or volunteer work in recreational programs or with people with physical, developmental, or social problems that have an impact on their daily life.

Suggested High School Subjects
- Arts
- Biology

- Crafts
- English
- Health Science Technology
- Instrumental & Vocal Music
- Physical Education
- Physiology
- Psychology
- Social Studies

Famous First

The first major statement about the need for recreational therapy was made by Dr. Frank Wynn of Indianapolis in 1909. Wynn, pictured, wrote, "Recreation therapy—a type of psychotherapy—plays an important role in the management of functional neuroses. It is not enough to tell a patient to take a daily walk or to go to the theater. Ascertain what he enjoys. Fortunate is the [patient] who enjoys hunting or fishing; or, still better, the ocean or the mountains. The ceaseless lashing of the sea has a wonderfully calming effect upon the emotions; the inspiring grandeur of the mountains is also quieting and lifts one to higher mental levels."

College/Postsecondary

Postsecondary students interested in recreational therapy should complete coursework in recreational therapy, if offered by their school, and courses in related fields. Such coursework may include physical education, physical therapy, special education, abnormal psychology, human development, ethics, anatomy, physiology, and assistive technology. An internship is typically required for completion of an undergraduate program in recreational therapy. Those interested in attending graduate school in recreational therapy may benefit from seeking internships or work in recreational therapy programs or with people with physical or mental special needs. Membership in the American Therapeutic Recreation Association (ATRA) may provide networking opportunities. Prior to graduating, interested college students should apply to graduate school in recreational therapy or secure related employment as a therapy assistant or special education assistant.

Related College Majors
- Recreational Therapy

Adult Job Seekers

Adult job seekers in the recreational therapy field have generally completed bachelor's or master's degrees in recreational therapy from an accredited university as well as earned necessary professional certification. Recreational therapists seeking employment may benefit from the networking opportunities, job workshops, and job lists offered by professional therapy associations such as the ATRA.

Professional Certification and Licensure

Recreational therapy certification is a voluntary practice and not usually required for general recreational therapy practice. Recreational therapists seeking employment in clinical settings, such as hospital and rehabilitation facilities, will need to be certified by the National Council for Therapeutic Recreation Certification. The Certified Therapeutic Recreation Specialist (CTRS) credential requires completion of a bachelor's degree in recreational therapy, a supervised clinical internship, and a national examination. In addition, recreational therapists who choose a therapeutic specialty, such as art, music or aquatic therapy, need specialized certification as a condition of employment.

Requirements for professional licensure for recreational therapists vary by state. Interested individuals should check the requirements of their home state and the organizations where they seek employment.

Additional Requirements

Individuals who find satisfaction, success, and job security as recreational therapists will be knowledgeable about the profession's requirements, responsibilities, and opportunities. Successful recreational therapists engage in ongoing professional development. Recreational therapists must have a high level of integrity and ethics as they work with vulnerable people and have access to personal patient information. Membership in professional recreational therapy associations is encouraged among all recreational therapists as a means of building professional community and networking.

Fun Facts

Recreational therapy emerged from two schools of thought in the 1940s and 1950s. One held that recreation was a therapeutic tool for treatment. The second viewed recreation as a means to meet a specific human need for people who were institutionalized. The term "therapuetic recreation" was coined in the early 1950s.
Source: Glen E. Van Andel, Re.D

The Egyptians described "diversion and recreation as a means of treating the sick" as early as 2000-1500 BC. In the American colonies, Benjamin Franklin helped found the Pennsylvania Hospital in 1753, where "light manual labor such as spinning and carding wool" were among the therapeutic activities.
Source:http://www.recreationtherapy.com/history/rthistory1.htm

EARNINGS AND ADVANCEMENT

Earnings of recreational therapists depend on the type and geographic location of the employer, and the individual's education and experience. Advancement is mainly to supervisory or administrative positions. Median annual earnings of recreational therapists were $43,180 in 2013. The lowest ten percent earned less than $27,120, and the highest ten percent earned more than $68,950.

Recreational therapists may receive paid vacations, holidays, and sick days; life and health insurance; and retirement benefits. These are usually paid by the employer.

Metropolitan Areas with the Highest
Employment Level in this Occupation

Metropolitan area	Employment[1]	Employment per thousand jobs	Hourly mean wage
New York-White Plains-Wayne, NY-NJ	980	0.19	$25.67
Philadelphia, PA	580	0.32	$21.61
Chicago-Joliet-Naperville, IL	560	0.15	$21.94
Boston-Cambridge-Quincy, MA	510	0.29	$18.60
Nassau-Suffolk, NY	380	0.31	$23.94
Los Angeles-Long Beach-Glendale, CA	340	0.09	$30.24
Atlanta-Sandy Springs-Marietta, GA	320	0.14	$19.87
Washington-Arlington-Alexandria, DC-VA-MD-WV	300	0.13	$23.55
Warren-Troy-Farmington Hills, MI	260	0.23	$24.54
St. Louis, MO-IL	230	0.18	$20.05

[1] Does not include self-employed. Source: Bureau of Labor Statistics

EMPLOYMENT AND OUTLOOK

Recreational therapists held about 20,000 jobs nationally in 2012. About one-third worked in nursing care facilities. Others worked in hospitals, residential care facilities, community mental health centers, adult day care programs, correctional facilities, community programs for people with disabilities, substance abuse centers, and state and local government agencies. Employment of recreational therapists is expected to grow about as fast as the average for all occupations through the year 2022, which means employment is projected to increase 9 percent to 16 percent. Job demand will be created by the growing percentage of older adults who will require the services of recreational therapists to manage injuries, illnesses and decreased physical and sometimes mental ability.

Employment Trend, Projected 2010–20

Health Diagnosing and Treating Practitioners: 20%

Recreational Therapists: 13%

Total, All Occupations: 11%

Note: "All Occupations" includes all occupations in the U.S. Economy. Source: U.S. Bureau of Labor Statistics, Employment Projections Program

Related Occupations
- Activities Therapist
- Fitness Trainer & Aerobics Instructor
- Music Therapist
- Occupational Therapist
- Occupational Therapy Assistant
- Physical Therapist
- Sports Instructor/Coach

Conversation With . . .
CATHY O'KEEFE, M.ED., CTRS

Recreational Therapist
Retired Instructor, University of South Alabama
Therapeutic Recreation, 42 years

1. What was your individual career path in terms of education/training, entry-level job, or other significant opportunity?

I got an art degree in college, and in my senior year I volunteered in the unit for the criminally insane at our state psychiatric hospital. I took art projects to do with the patients and realized that it helped these people to express themselves through art.

That experience got me my first job at an inpatient psychiatric unit. At the interview, I was told, "If you can do this on the criminally insane unit, you can do it here." I worked as an activities therapist treating emotionally disturbed patients, drug addicts, and older adults with dementia.

Over the years, my jobs taught me different aspects of therapeutic recreation's value. Early in my career, I worked with disadvantaged youth at a local detention center and learned that using TR to develop skills in children and youth can diminish the negative effects of poverty, create potential for sound and healthy behavior, and bridge the socio-economic gaps that often keep people from recognizing their similarities.

I went on to establish a long-term care consultation practice in nursing homes, work with people with developmental disabilities to help them live actively within the community, and work with hospice.

I've always told my students that the best jobs I had came by way of volunteering. As with my first job, I got into teaching via another volunteer opportunity. A teacher at the university asked me to come do a guest lecture. At the time, she was trying to start a therapeutic recreation program and I was working in a hospital. I ended up being the first graduate in her program, and I taught at the university for 37 years, 30 of them full-time. I also was coordinator for the university's Leisure Studies Program, which includes general recreation and sports management as well as therapeutic recreation. I still do guest lectures, talks around the country, and I've kept my certification in therapeutic recreation.

2. What are the most important skills and/or qualities for someone in your profession?

It's important to be outgoing and to enjoy interacting with people. I had a creative nature, too, which made it easy to come up with new ideas and solutions. I was interested in activities ranging from music and art to civic leadership programs. You also need to be able to relate well to others, especially people with special needs. A sense of social justice is important.

3. What do you wish you had known going into this profession?

I wish I had grasped how powerful and important leisure and recreation are to a healthy, enjoyable, and meaningful life, and I wish I'd known doctors, nurses, and therapists who embraced this knowledge, too. Medical professionals today seem to understand that prevention and the promotion of healthy lifestyles and a good life/work balance are critically important.

At the time I went into the field, it had not occurred to people that the lifestyle you lead has an enormous amount to do with your wellbeing as a person. One of the ways to stay healthy is to regularly engage in things you really enjoy.

4. Are there many job opportunities in your profession? In what specific areas?

This field spans a range of human needs and age groups. Rehabilitation and psychiatric hospitals, nursing homes and assisted living facilities, community recreation and senior centers, schools, and outdoor programs/camps are among the most common employers, and some RTs have their own businesses, too.

5. How do you see your profession changing in the next five years, what role will technology play in those changes, and what skills will be required?

I'm seeing technology that allows people with disabilities to access more things. For example, if I can't play guitar anymore because I've had a stroke, I can get a guitar app on my iPad and play with one hand. If I love the outdoors, I can bring it inside via virtual reality apps and programs. A recreational therapist is going to have to stay up on adaptation apps that keep people in the game even if they have a limitation or impairment.

For children and adults with life-long disabilities, recreation starts as a teaching tool and eventually evolves into a full-time management framework for a good quality of life. For our veterans addressing post-deployment issues, recreation has become a valuable tool in adjustment and recovery and will continue to be expanded. Technology advancements, coupled with a need for personalized services, will prompt more entrepreneurial opportunities.

6. **What do you enjoy most about your job? What do you enjoy least about your job?**

I've loved the flexibility to change my work venue so it suited my personal life, as well as the chance to bring my personal interests and skills to the workplace. For instance, I designed a playroom and Child Life program at our children's hospital after I had children, so I used my personal knowledge of art, music, games, and play activities in my job.

What I've enjoyed least was working around medical professionals who were fixated on their own ego and status and failed to understand that their real purpose is serving their patients.

7. **Can you suggest a valuable "try this" for students considering a career in your profession?**

Volunteer! There are lots of opportunities, from summer camps for people with disabilities to nursing homes. Developing empathy is probably the best thing you could possibly do.

SELECTED SCHOOLS

Many colleges and universities have bachelor's degree programs in recreational therapy or related subjects. The student may also gain an initial grounding at a technical or community college. Consult with your school guidance counselor or research post-secondary programs in your area. The online Therapeutic Recreation Directory (see below) contains a listing of accredited schools and programs.

MORE INFORMATION

American Art Therapy Association
225 North Fairfax Street
Alexandria, VA 22314-1574
888.290.0878
www.arttherapy.org

American Dance Therapy Association
10632 Little Patuxent Parkway
Suite 108
Columbia, MD 21044
410.997.4040
www.adta.org

American Music Therapy Association
8455 Colesville Road, Suite 1000
Silver Spring, MD 20910
301.589.3300
www.musictherapy.org

American Therapeutic Recreation Association
629 North Main Street
Hattiesburg, MS 39401
601.450.2872
www.atra-online.com

National Center on Physical Activity and Disability
1640 W. Roosevelt Road
Chicago, IL 60608-6904
800.900.8086
www.ncpad.org

National Council for Therapeutic Recreation Certification
7 Elmwood Drive
New City, NY 10956
845.639.1439
www.nctrc.org

Simone Isadora Flynn/Editor

Rehabilitation Counselor

Snapshot

Career Cluster: Human Services

Interests: Counseling, mental health, physical rehabilitation, disability management, sociology, psychology

Earnings (Yearly Average): $34,230

Employment & Outlook: Faster Than Average Growth Expected

OVERVIEW

Sphere of Work

Rehabilitation counselors (also called case managers, rehabilitation specialists, and human services counselors) provide vocational, medical, housing, employment, and personal support services to individuals and groups with disabilities. In general, they work to help their clients become more independent, employable, and productive. Rehabilitation counselors support clients living with disabilities present since birth or impairments resulting from illness, disease, addiction, accident, or injury. For instance, individuals experiencing employment,

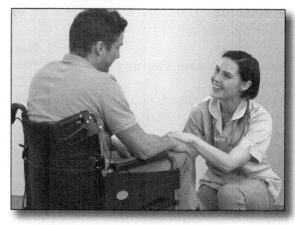

housing, or social complications and challenges related to HIV/ AIDS, schizophrenia, or intellectual disability are generally eligible for rehabilitation counseling under the Rehabilitation Act and the Americans with Disabilities Act. The range of counseling services provided by rehabilitation counselors includes coordinating counseling activities at residential facilities, overseeing job training and vocational counseling programs, and creating rehabilitation plans for clients.

Work Environment

Rehabilitation counselors spend their workdays seeing clients in a wide variety of settings, including public or private rehabilitation facilities, mental health facilities, schools and universities, insurance companies, job training and placement programs, prisons and hospitals, and private counseling practices. Rehabilitation counselors may have an office or may travel to see clients. Given the diverse demands of rehabilitative counseling, rehabilitation counselors may need to work days, evenings, weekends, and on-call hours to meet client or caseload needs.

Profile

Working Conditions: Work Indoors
Physical Strength: Light Work
Education Needs: Bachelor's Degree, Master's Degree
Licensure/Certification: Required
Physical Abilities Not Required: No Heavy Labor
Opportunities For Experience: Military Service, Volunteer Work, Part-Time Work
Holland Interest Score*: SEC

* See Appendix A

Occupation Interest

Individuals drawn to the rehabilitation counseling profession tend to be intelligent and socially conscious and able to quickly assess situations, find resources, demonstrate caring, and solve problems. Successful rehabilitation counselors display traits such as time management, knowledge of human behavior, initiative, and concern for individuals and society. Rehabilitation counselors should find satisfaction in spending time with a wide range of people, including those considered at-risk and those from diverse cultural, social, and educational backgrounds.

A Day in the Life—Duties and Responsibilities

A rehabilitation counselor's daily duties and responsibilities are determined by the individual's area of job specialization and work environment. Rehabilitation counseling specialties include physical rehabilitation, mental health counseling, substance abuse counseling, disability management, corrections, vocational assessment, forensic rehabilitation, pediatric rehabilitation, and geriatric rehabilitation.

Rehabilitation counselors work closely with clients to assess their situations and provide assistance. The rehabilitation counselor's first task is assessment. The rehabilitation counselor may complete client intake interviews for residential rehabilitation or medical facilities. He or she may also undertake client evaluations to assess physical, mental, academic, and vocational aptitude and readiness. The rehabilitation counselor then works with clients to develop counseling goals and objectives, oversees client job search efforts, and assists clients with employment, welfare, childcare, and food stamp applications. Depending on client needs, a rehabilitation counselor may also help clients obtain assistive devices, such as wheelchairs, that enable independence and employment, organize on-site job training for clients, help clients arrange transportation and housing, or lead workshops for clients in residential facilities.

Rehabilitation counselors act as liaisons for their clients. They participate in client team meetings and provide client updates to supervisors and client families. Rehabilitation counselors also develop connections and familiarity with community social service agencies, and refer clients to community services or agencies as needed.

All rehabilitation counselors ensure that rehabilitation programs meet the requirements of the Rehabilitation Act of 1973 and the Americans with Disabilities Act (ADA). In addition, all rehabilitation counselors are responsible for completing client records and required documentation, such as referral forms and insurance forms, on a daily basis.

Duties and Responsibilities

- Arranging tests and evaluations for rehabilitation purposes
- Conducting interviews with clients and their families
- Evaluating school and medical reports
- Working with physicians, psychologists, occupational therapists, and employers

WORK ENVIRONMENT

Physical Environment

The immediate physical environment of rehabilitation counselors vary based on their caseload and specialization. Rehabilitation counselors spend their workdays seeing clients in a wide variety of settings, including public or private rehabilitation facilities, mental health facilities, schools and universities, insurance companies, job training and placement programs, prisons and hospitals, and private counseling practices.

Relevant Skills and Abilities

Interpersonal/Social Skills
- Being able to work independently
- Being patient
- Having good judgment
- Motivating others
- Providing support to others

Organization & Management Skills
- Demonstrating leadership
- Making decisions
- Managing time
- Meeting goals and deadlines

Research & Planning Skills
- Predicting

Human Environment

Rehabilitation counselors interact with many people. They should be comfortable meeting with colleagues, staff, client families, incarcerated people, and people living with mental, physical, and emotional disabilities.

Technological Environment

Rehabilitation counselors use computers and a range of telecommunication tools to perform their job. They must be comfortable using computers to access client records. Rehabilitation counselors should also be comfortable traveling for work, as they may be required to frequently visit client homes and facilities.

EDUCATION, TRAINING, AND ADVANCEMENT

High School/Secondary

High school students interested in pursuing a career as a rehabilitation counselor should prepare themselves by developing good study habits. Coursework in foreign languages, public safety, sociology, psychology, and education can provide a strong foundation for college-level work in the rehabilitation counseling field. Due to the diversity of rehabilitation counseling specialties, high school students interested in this career path may benefit from seeking internships or part-time work that expose the students to diverse groups of people and social needs.

Suggested High School Subjects
- Applied Communication
- College Preparatory
- English
- Humanities
- Literature
- Psychology
- Social Studies
- Sociology

Famous First

The first rehabilitation counselors in the 1940s (and earlier) came from a variety of disciplines, including nursing, social work, and educational counseling. The field began to grow in the wake of World War II, as disabled veterans returned home. By the mid-1950s rehabilitation counseling was an established profession.

College/Postsecondary

Postsecondary students interested in becoming rehabilitation counselors should work towards an undergraduate degree in counseling or a related field, such as psychology or social work. Coursework in education, public safety, and foreign languages may also prove useful in their future work. Postsecondary students can gain work experience and potential advantage in their future job searches by securing internships or part-time employment in social service agencies or with individuals or groups living with physical, mental, or emotional disabilities.

Interested college students should also research and apply to master's degree programs for rehabilitation counseling. Master's degree programs in rehabilitative counseling typically include such courses as counseling theory, assessment, human development, ethics, evaluation, and case management; a practicum or internship is mandatory for degree completion.

Related College Majors
- Counselor Education/Student Counseling & Guidance Services
- Psychology, General
- Sociology

Adult Job Seekers

Adults seeking employment as rehabilitation counselors should have obtained a master's degree in rehabilitation counseling or a similar field, such as social work, psychology, or sociology, and earned national certification. Adult job seekers should educate themselves about the educational and professional license requirements of their home states and the organizations where they seek employment.

Adult job seekers may benefit from joining professional associations to help with networking and job searching. Professional rehabilitation counseling associations, such as the Commission on Rehabilitation Counselor Certification (CRCC), generally offer career workshops and maintain lists and forums of available jobs.

Professional Certification and Licensure

Professional certification and licensure is required of all practicing rehabilitation counselors. Specific licensure requirements—including additional coursework, continuing professional education, and supervision—vary by state.

The Certified Rehabilitation Counselor (CRC) designation is often an employment requirement. The CRC designation is awarded through the CRCC. Candidates must have a master's of rehabilitation counseling or related field, demonstrate work experience, and complete a written national examination. Certified rehabilitation counselors are eligible to apply for state mental health counselor licenses. Continuing education is required for certification renewal.

Additional Requirements

Individuals who find satisfaction, success, and job security as rehabilitation counselors will be knowledgeable about the profession's requirements, responsibilities, and opportunities. Successful rehabilitation counselors engage in ongoing professional development. Rehabilitation counselors must have high levels of integrity and ethics as they interact with at-risk people and groups and have access to personal information. Membership in professional counseling associations is encouraged among all rehabilitation counselors as a means of building status in a professional community and networking.

EARNINGS AND ADVANCEMENT

Rehabilitation counselors may advance with additional education. Those persons with a master's degree will have higher earnings. Median annual earnings of rehabilitation counselors were $34,230 in 2013. The lowest ten percent earned less than $21,170, and the highest ten percent earned more than $60,020.

Rehabilitation counselors may receive paid vacations, holidays, and sick days; life and health insurance; and retirement benefits. These are usually paid by the employer.

Metropolitan Areas with the Highest
Employment Level in this Occupation

Metropolitan area	Employment[1]	Employment per thousand jobs	Hourly mean wage
New York-White Plains-Wayne, NY-NJ	4,940	0.94	$19.25
Los Angeles-Long Beach-Glendale, CA	3,140	0.79	$16.43
Seattle-Bellevue-Everett, WA	2,620	1.81	$22.15
Philadelphia, PA	2,440	1.33	$19.24
Boston-Cambridge-Quincy, MA	2,190	1.25	$20.35
Minneapolis-St. Paul-Bloomington, MN-WI	1,810	1.01	$20.16
Chicago-Joliet-Naperville, IL	1,760	0.48	$18.49
Riverside-San Bernardino-Ontario, CA	1,600	1.33	$15.41
Washington-Arlington-Alexandria, DC-VA-MD-WV	1,590	0.67	$20.62
Tacoma, WA	1,370	5.24	$16.93

[1] Does not include self-employed. Source: Bureau of Labor Statistics

EMPLOYMENT AND OUTLOOK

Rehabilitation counselors held about 118,000 jobs nationally in 2012. Employment is expected to grow faster than the average for all occupations through the year 2022, which means employment is projected to increase 20 percent or more. The number of people who need rehabilitation services will rise as advances in medical technology allow more people to survive injury or illness and live independently again.

Employment Trend, Projected 2010–20

Rehabilitation Counselors: 20%

Community and Social Service Occupations: 17%

Total, All Occupations: 11%

Note: "All Occupations" includes all occupations in the U.S. Economy. Source: U.S. Bureau of Labor Statistics, Employment Projections Program

Related Occupations
- Employment Specialist
- Marriage Counselor
- Medical Social Worker
- Occupational Therapist
- Psychologist
- School Counselor
- Social Worker
- Vocational Rehabilitation Counselor

Conversation With . . .
JAMES HILL

Owner
Vocational Evaluation & Counseling Services
Oregon, Wisconsin
Rehabilitation Counselor, 43 years

1. What was your individual career path?

When I graduated from the University of Wisconsin/Madison in 1971 with a degree in education, there was a glut of teachers looking for work. I de-cided to try working at a small rehabilitation facility. I started "teaching" individuals with developmental disabilities, training them how to work. We worked on a production line that made, among other things, rat poison and Christmas decorations! The job was not what I expected, but it was fun, I loved the population I was working with, and so I went on to get a master's degree in rehabilitation psychology. I'm a Certified Rehabilitation Counselor (CRC). About 15 years ago, after working for the State of Wisconsin and a few private rehab companies, I got laid off and decided to go ahead and start my own rehabilitation consultant business.

2. What are the most important skills and qualities for someone in this profession?

A good rehabilitation counselor will have good listening abilities, patience, perseverance and a sense of humor. The ability to find positive features in everyone you meet is helpful. Good basic computer skills and the ability to write reports and observations are important.

3. What do you wish you had known going into this profession?

I wish I had known what it was! The career exploration activities we had in high school were very superficial, and myself and some of my classmates ended up drifting into things we liked without really knowing where we were going.

4. Are there many job opportunities in your profession? In what specific areas?

Individuals who are flexible about relocating and trying different types of job settings will have the best employment prospects. It's a field where you can go in a lot of different directions. Many of us in rehabilitation counseling have worked for a variety of employers before finding our niche. I have worked at a couple of rehabilitation facilities, worked for a state agency, helped a professor research and write a book, and worked at a couple of private rehabilitation companies that did work for attorneys and insurance companies, which is known as "forensic work."

Forensic work tends to be primarily litigious, writing depositions or testifying in court as an expert witness. You're doing "loss assessment." For instance, there might be a construction worker who can't do that type of work anymore due to a work injury or personal injury like a car accident. Often there is some type of legal settlement involved. When you have a medical difference of opinion, then you also have a vocational difference of opinion: What kind of transferrable skills does someone have? What is their work potential and earnings potential? This type of work is not for everyone. Typically, rehab counselors do something else first and evolve toward forensics. Most people coming out of school work in the public sector and do "direct service" work. It's good to move around. In the private sector, they emphasize quality. You have a smaller caseload and you have to get results.

My favorite area has been doing vocational evaluations, testing and career planning with individuals. I have friends who appreciate the team approach and the stability that goes with working for a state or federal agency or in a large hospital setting. You can expand your employability, and adventure, by trying a number of things. But there will always be strong demand for people who enjoy and can do job placement.

5. How do you see your profession changing in the next five years? What role will technology play?

Advances in medical treatment and in prosthetics/orthotics, as well as high tech developments for individuals with specific disabilities, will change the future for individuals with disabilities. We have gone well past the white cane for blind people, with, for example, GPS locators and devices that can read books aloud better than most of us can. Professionals in rehabilitation have to keep up with these developments and be tech savvy about maximizing them.

6. What do you enjoy most and least about your job?

I enjoy meeting new and interesting people all the time. It's great to realize that some of your efforts can actually make a difference in someone's life. I'm not crazy about writing reports and case notes, but you get quicker at it as time goes along, and I've discovered how to dictate work instead of typing it all myself.

7. What is a valuable "try this" for students?

Interview or shadow a rehabilitation counselor. You may want to visit a rehabilitation agency such as Goodwill, go to a center that does vocational evaluation testing, or visit specialty programs such as a substance abuse center. State agencies or the Veterans Administration might be a little more agreeable to helping you.

SELECTED SCHOOLS

Many colleges and universities have bachelor's degree programs in counseling and therapy, often with a specialization in rehabilitation counseling. The student may also gain an initial grounding in the field at a technical or community college. Consult with your school guidance counselor or research post-secondary programs in your area. Below are listed some of the more prominent schools in this field.

George Washington University
2121 I Street NW
Washington, DC 20052
202.994.1000
www.gwu.edu

Illinois Institute of Technology
3300 South Federal Street
Chicago, IL 60616
312.567.3000
web.iit.edu

Michigan State University
220 Trowbridge Roads
East Lansing, MI 48824
517.355.1855
www.msu.edu

Penn State University
University Park
State College, PA 16801
814.865.4700
www.psu.edu

San Diego State University
5500 Campanile Drive
San Diego, CA 92182
619.594.5200
www.sdsu.edu

Southern Illinois University
1263 Lincoln Drive
Carbondale, IL 62901
618.453.2121
siu.edu

University of Arizona
Tucson, AZ 85721
520.621.2211
www.arizona.edu

University of Iowa
Iowa City, IA 52242
319.335.3500
www.uiowa.edu

University of Wisconsin
Madison, WI 53706
608.263.2400
www.wisc.edu

Virginia Commonwealth
University
821 West Franklin Street
Richmond, VA 23284
804.828.0100
www.vcu.edu

MORE INFORMATION

American Counseling Association
5999 Stevenson Avenue
Alexandria, VA 22304
800.347.6647
www.counseling.org

**American Rehabilitation
Counseling Association**
www.arcaweb.org

**Association for Education and
Rehabilitation of the Blind and
Visually Impaired**
1703 N. Beauregard St., Suite 440
Alexandria, VA 22311
703.671.4500
www.aerbvi.org

**Commission on Rehabilitation
Counselor Certification**
1699 E. Woodfield Road, Suite 300
Schaumburg, IL 60173
847.944.1325
www.crccertification.com

**National Organization for Human
Services**
1600 Sarno Road, Suite 16
Melbourne, FL 32935
www.nationalhumanservices.org

**National Rehabilitation
Association**
PO Box 150235
Alexandria, VA 22315
703.836.0850
www.nationalrehab.org

Simone Isadora Flynn/Editor

Religious Activities & Education Director

Snapshot

Career Cluster: Human Services
Interests: Religious studies, social services, social work, psychology, education
Earnings (Yearly Average): $38,160
Employment & Outlook: Average Growth Expected

OVERVIEW

Sphere of Work

Religious activities and education directors work within spiritual communities. These communities are made up of people with a shared religion or spiritual belief system. They are often centered on a single church, mosque, temple, or other place of worship. Directors organize group functions such as community meals and fundraisers.

They also coordinate enrollment, staffing, and curriculums for faith-based education initiatives. While some religious activities and education directors are spiritual leaders or clergy members, it is not a requirement of the job. However, most directors share the faith or religious doctrine of the community they serve.

Work Environment

The work environment of a religious activities and education director varies. Directors can work at churches, temples, mosques, or other places of worship. Many work out of an office in or near a religious facility. Directors hold events in various locations, including cafeterias, meeting halls, libraries, and conference centers. The job's work environment can also include outdoor facilities such as parks and campgrounds.

Profile

Working Conditions: Work Indoors
Physical Strength: Light Work
Education Needs: Junior/
   Technical/Community College,
   Bachelor's Degree
Licensure/Certification: Usually Not
   Required
Physical Abilities Not Required: No
   Heavy Labor
Opportunities For Experience:
   Volunteer Work, Part-Time Work
Holland Interest Score*: SEA

* See Appendix A

Occupation Interest

Any person interested in becoming a religious activities and education director should feel a strong allegiance to the spiritual denomination they wish to serve. A commitment to social services and education is equally important. Directors should possess administrative skills and enjoy working with others. Leadership skills are essential.

A Day in the Life—Duties and Responsibilities

The work of a religious activities and education director varies from day to day. A director's day often begins with a staff meeting to ensure that all projects and operations are running smoothly. These projects include religious-education classes, volunteer programs, and outreach missions. Some directors conduct various administrative duties related to their congregation, which can include updating community websites, sending e-mails, and making schedules for teachers, students, and clergy. Other directors manage charity initiatives such as fundraisers, meal programs for the homeless, and health clinics.

Some directors are responsible for oversight of family- or marriage-counseling services and substance-abuse programs. Activities and education directors also manage group programs such as summer camps and spiritual retreats for members of their community. They also recruit volunteers and conduct project-specific training seminars.

Duties and Responsibilities

- Assisting in worship services
- Sharing in decision-making of the church or community
- Teaching and counseling
- Visiting in homes or institutions
- Planning and working at medical, educational, agricultural and social activities
- Fund-raising for charitable activities

WORK ENVIRONMENT

Relevant Skills and Abilities

Interpersonal/Social Skills
- Cooperating with others
- Working as a member of a team

Organization & Management Skills
- Coordinating tasks
- Demonstrating leadership
- Managing people/groups

Physical Environment

Religious activities and education directors work at religious facilities or in general social-service settings, such as schools, hospitals, and charitable institutions. Some work may be done outdoors at parks and summer camps. Outreach work can take place in cities and towns of varying size.

Human Environment

Religious activities and education directors work in a community of people joined by a common religious faith. They work in groups of varying size and work one-on-one with clergy members, teachers, students, and volunteers. Directors work regularly with fellow worshippers and the business community.

Technological Environment

Contemporary office and communications technology is part of the job of a religious activities and education director. Basic computer skills are required, and knowledge of social media is important.

EDUCATION, TRAINING, AND ADVANCEMENT

High School/Secondary

Many religious denominations do not require any formal education of their religious activities and education directors. In this case, personal charisma, religious commitment, basic literacy, and dedication to the work are the only requirements. In other religious settings, a formal education or religious education is preferred or required.

High school students interested in a career as a religious activities and education director should take classes in the humanities, especially English, philosophy, and history. Classes in political science and psychology are also beneficial. Foreign languages can be useful, as well as classes in instrumental and vocal music, as music is often a part of spiritual activities.

In addition to secular studies, a person should study the religion of their choice or calling. This is done through attending religious teachings offered at churches, synagogues, mosques, madrassas, temples, shrines, or other religious facilities.

Suggested High School Subjects
- College Preparatory
- English
- Foreign Languages
- History

- Humanities
- Instrumental & Vocal Music
- Mathematics
- Philosophy
- Political Science
- Psychology
- Social Studies

Famous First

The first religious activities specialists in the military emerged during World War II, when it was recognized that, in addition to the spiritual activities performed by chaplains, work was needed in the area of supplying services such as musical direction, audio-visual aids, and clerical support.

College/Postsecondary

Some churches and religious denominations require that activities and education directors have some form of postsecondary education. Individuals interested in the profession can consider advanced degree programs in education, religious studies, or social work. In the United States, a degree in religious studies provides a solid basis for work for in many Christian denominations. Similarly, a degree in Jewish studies or Islamic studies can prepare individuals for work in these religions. A bachelor's degree in sociology provides a secular foundation on which those interested in religious work can build. A master's degree in any of the above subjects can prepare a person for an advanced career as a religious activities and education director. Other postsecondary education options include doctoral programs in education, religious studies, sociology, or social work.

Related College Majors
- Bible/Biblical Studies
- Pastoral Counseling & Specialized Ministries
- Religion/Religious Studies

- Religious Education
- Theology/Theological Studies

Adult Job Seekers

Adult job seekers interested in a career as a religious activities and education director should have a background in teaching, social work, or administrative work. Doing volunteer work at a religious institution is a good way to become qualified for an official position. Experience in community service is also a plus. Many religious denominations welcome adult job seekers who experience a calling to become active in religious work. In some cases, being of strong spiritual conviction is considered as important as formal education, training, or job experience.

Professional Certification and Licensure

The job of a religious activities and education director does not require any professional certification or licensure. However, if a director engages in accounting, social work, counseling, or teaching, some professional credentials may be required depending on state and national regulations.

Additional Requirements

As their work is dedicated to serving and reaching out to people, religious activities and education directors need strong interpersonal skills. They must be compassionate and have an interest in social services.

EARNINGS AND ADVANCEMENT

Earnings depend on the type and geographic location of the employer, the type of work performed and the individual's amount of responsibility, academic preparation and experience. Median annual earnings of religious activities and education directors were $38,160 in 2013.

Religious activities and education directors may receive paid vacations, holidays, and sick days; life and health insurance; and retirement benefits. These are usually paid by the employer. Some employers may also provide free housing, use of an automobile, allowances for travel, and educational reimbursements.

Metropolitan Areas with the Highest Employment Level in this Occupation

Metropolitan area	Employment[1]	Employment per thousand jobs	Hourly mean wage
New York-White Plains-Wayne, NY-NJ	1,120	0.21	$21.98
Portland-Vancouver-Hillsboro, OR-WA	1,040	1.01	$19.97
Chicago-Joliet-Naperville, IL	610	0.17	$21.24
Philadelphia, PA	610	0.33	$24.95
Nassau-Suffolk, NY	540	0.43	$21.25
Washington-Arlington-Alexandria, DC-VA-MD-WV	480	0.20	$31.52
Los Angeles-Long Beach-Glendale, CA	450	0.11	$31.08
Warren-Troy-Farmington Hills, MI	440	0.40	$15.39
San Diego-Carlsbad-San Marcos, CA	380	0.29	$31.62
Atlanta-Sandy Springs-Marietta, GA	340	0.15	$19.14

[1] Does not include self-employed. Source: Bureau of Labor Statistics

EMPLOYMENT AND OUTLOOK

Nationally, there were about 10,000 religious activities and education directors employed in 2012. Employment is expected to grow about as fast as the average for all occupations through the year 2022, which means employment is projected to increase 8 percent to 114 percent.

Employment Trend, Projected 2010–20

Community and Social Service Occupations: 17%

Religious Activities and Education Directors: 12%

Total, All Occupations: 11%

Note: "All Occupations" includes all occupations in the U.S. Economy. Source: U.S. Bureau of Labor Statistics, Employment Projections Program

Related Occupations
- Clergy
- Marriage & Family Therapist
- School Counselor
- Social & Human Service Assistant
- Social Worker
- Substance Abuse Counselor

Conversation With . . .
ADINA NEWMAN

Religious Activities and Educational Director
Religious School Director, Maryland Synagogue, 6 months
In the Education field, 15 years

1. **What was your individual career path in terms of education/training, entry-level job, or other significant opportunity?**

I started teaching 3 and 4 year olds in religious school before my bat mitzvah, on Saturday mornings at my local synagogue. I made a little money and kept up my skill set going into college, when I continued to teach and became a professional Torah reader to prepare students for their bar and bat mitzvahs. I majored in education at Boston University, got a master's in education policy & management policy at Harvard University, and another master's in elementary education at Brandeis University. I'm currently working toward a doctorate in educational administration and policy studies at George Washington University.

After I got my master's degrees, I was a curriculum designer for a publishing company. But I felt I needed the "street cred" — to be in the classroom — so I left to teach fifth grade for a couple of years in public schools.

I'm a person who tries things out. I tried curriculum and liked that; I taught, and liked that. Now, I oversee K-10 in a synagogue's religious school that meets Sundays and Wednesdays. We instill a sense of Jewish identity and community in students, and prepare for b'nai mitzvah. This job is part-time and works for my family because my husband and I have a baby. I also like the challenge of this job. I hire teachers, oversee the budget, order books, work with the Hebrew curriculum, and ride the wave of what's going on in the school. We also prepare for the High Holy Days in September and the programming that involves. This position is very front-loaded — just like any school — from August through the end of September. Overall, this job has been my goal for awhile, and it's a good fit.

2. **What are the most important skills and/or qualities for someone in your profession?**

All educators need to have flexibility because something is going to happen: a teacher may call in sick, you may need to sub, a kid might have a behavior issue. You need to be prepared for not being prepared. You need to understand language acquisition, for example, if you want your kids to learn Hebrew. You also need a knowledge of what's happening in your field in traditional schools and in religious schools in general. For example, in a traditional classroom it's understood there are different kinds of learners. A lot of religious schools still rely only on books. Here, your book is a supplement. We create stations and rotate to allow for instruction through multiple modalities so that kids might be doing things that are more tactile, or more visual, because we recognize what's working for different types of learners.

3. **What do you wish you had known going into this profession?**

In this position, you play therapist to students, teachers and parents. You are a sounding board for them. It's great to be that person people confide in to get the job done, but it's definitely something I did not expect.

4. **Are there many job opportunities in your profession? In what specific areas?**

There's always going to be some sort of director job somewhere in Jewish education. You need to know where to look, such as New York, Boston, or Florida. There's also Hillel, for higher education.

5. **How do you see your profession changing in the next five years, what role will technology play in those changes, and what skills will be required?**

Technology is of utmost importance. Right now, we are working on finding a way to get iPads. That's how the kids are learning in their traditional schools, and that's how you're going to get them through the door. Kids don't have to come here. In some cases, kids have been at their traditional school all day and they come here for two hours on a Wednesday night and we need to keep them engaged. Technology is the best way.

6. **What do you enjoy most about your job? What do you enjoy least about your job?**

I definitely like going down the hall, checking the classrooms and seeing the kids having a good time. That's wonderful. Unfortunately, we just don't have enough time to do what we want to do. In winter, for instance, we have snow days, and they hurt consistency and continuity.

7. **Can you suggest a valuable "try this" for students considering a career in your profession?**

A lot of synagogues have opportunities for leading. In classes, we have madrichim, which literally means "leaders," who are teaching assistants. Some synagogues even pay them. If you're in college already, go for it and apply for a position as a teacher. See how you feel about it.

SELECTED SCHOOLS

Many colleges and universities have bachelor's degree programs in counseling and rehabilitation therapy, often with a specialization in occupational therapy. The student may also gain an initial grounding in the field at a technical or community college. Consult with your school guidance counselor or research area post-secondary programs to find the right fit for you. Below are listed some of the more prominent schools in this field.

MORE INFORMATION

Buddhist Churches of America
1710 Octavia Street
San Francisco, CA 94109
415.776.5600
www.buddhistchurchesofamerica.org

Catholic Campus Ministry Association
1118 Pendleton Street, Suite 300
Cincinnati, OH 45202-8805
888.714.6631
www.ccmanet.org

National Association of Temple Educators
633 Third Avenue, 7th Floor
New York, NY 10017-6778
212.452.6510
www.natenet.org

National Council of Churches of Christ in the USA
475 Riverside Drive, Suite 880
New York, NY 10115
212.870.2227
www.ncccusa.org

R. C. Lutz/Editor

School Counselor

Snapshot

Career Cluster: Education & Training; Human Services

Interests: Helping others, working with students, solving problems, human behavior

Earnings (Yearly Average): $53,600

Employment & Outlook: Average Growth Expected

OVERVIEW

Sphere of Work

School counselors, also called guidance counselors or educational counselors, provide educational and career counseling to students from elementary school through the postsecondary level. They may also assist students with their social and personal development, particularly those students with unique abilities and challenges. Most school counselors work from an office located within a school setting, specializing in counseling a particular age range of students; some school counselors specialize in career counseling and work in or maintain offices off campus.

School counselors support students in their efforts to succeed academically and

develop realistic career goals, learn to resolve conflict and develop relationships with peers, and cope with family abuse, addiction, or other health issues. The overall goal of a school counselor is to help students (or other clients) attain the highest possible developmental skill level based on each student's needs and challenges. In the course of their work, the school counselor must also take care to protect each student's right to privacy, and must adhere to strict ethical and legal standards articulated by the American School Counselor Association (ASCA) and the Family Education Rights and Privacy Act (FERPA).

Work Environment

School counselors spend their workdays seeing students in school settings, college and university career counseling offices, job training and placement programs, and private counseling practices. Most school counselors work from a private office within a school or college, although vocational counselors may work independently. Given the diverse demands of school counseling, school counselors may need to work days, evenings, and weekends to meet student, client, or program needs, but in general they should expect to be at work during school hours.

Profile

Working Conditions: Work Indoors
Physical Strength: Light Work
Education Needs: Master's Degree
Licensure/Certification: Required
Physical Abilities Not Required: No Heavy Labor
Opportunities For Experience: Military Service, Volunteer Work
Holland Interest Score*: SAE

* See Appendix A

Occupation Interest

Individuals drawn to the school counseling profession tend to be intelligent and have the ability to quickly assess situations, find resources, and solve problems. Further, they should demonstrate caring and find satisfaction in helping others. Those most successful at the job of school counselor display traits such as time management, knowledge of human behavior, initiative, and concern for individuals and society; they should also be capable of inspiring students' trust, confidence, and respect. School counselors should also be comfortable working with a wide range of people, including those considered at-risk and those from diverse cultural, social, and educational backgrounds.

A Day in the Life—Duties and Responsibilities

The daily occupational duties and responsibilities of school counselors
will be determined by the individual's area of job specialization and
work environment. Specialties of educational counseling include
school counseling, vocational counseling, and college career planning
and placement counseling.

A school counselor's primary role is to provide academic, social, and
emotional support—both practical and empathetic—to students. Some
ways in which a school counselor can accomplish this goal include
using scientifically-researched intervention strategies with a student
in crisis, helping a student evaluate his or her talents and interests to
conceive realistic career goals, and serving as a mentor for students
while maintaining the professional distance advised by ASCA ethical
guidelines. School counselors, during the course of a day's work, may help
a student cope with family issues or problems that are interfering with
the student's educational or developmental goals, listen to and share
coping strategies with a student who is being bullied by a peer, monitor
a peer counseling group, and conduct routine interviews with high school
students regarding future college and career goals. Although high school
counselors do more career counseling than elementary-level school
counselors, both types of students benefit from conversations about which
particular careers best fit their emerging talents and abilities.

In addition to the range of responsibilities described above, all school
counselors are responsible for completing student and client records
and required documentation, such as referral forms, on a daily basis.

Duties and Responsibilities

- Appraising individual's interests, aptitudes, abilities and personality characteristics using records, tests, interviews and professional sources
- Assisting in understanding and overcoming individuals' social and emotional challenges
- Consulting with students, teachers, parents, social workers and other professionals
- Collecting educational, occupational and economic information
- Assisting in personal decisions and the planning and implementation of career decisions

OCCUPATION SPECIALTIES

School Counselors

School Counselors are primarily concerned with the personal and social development of students and with helping them plan and achieve their educational and vocational goals.

Employment Counselors

Employment Counselors are concerned with career planning, placement and adjustment to employment of youths and adults.

College Career Planning and Placement Counselors

College Career Planning and Placement Counselors assist college students in examining their own interests, values, abilities and goals in exploring career alternatives and in making career choices.

WORK ENVIRONMENT

Physical Environment

The immediate physical environment of school counselors varies based on their caseload and specialization. School counselors spend their workdays seeing students in elementary, junior high, and high schools, college and university career counseling offices, job training and placement programs, and private counseling practices.

Human Environment

School counselors work with a wide variety of people and should be comfortable working and talking with children of all ages, although most school counselors eventually focus on a specific age range of students. School counselors frequently interact with students, teachers, colleagues, supervisors, students' parents and other family members, unemployed people, and students living with mental, physical, developmental, or emotional disabilities. The ethical standards upheld by school counselors are strict and specific due to the nature of counseling students under the age of eighteen, and also the fact that some students may experience family abuse or face potential legal issues.

Relevant Skills and Abilities

Communication Skills
- Listening attentively
- Speaking effectively
- Writing concisely

Interpersonal/Social Skills
- Cooperating with others
- Providing support to others
- Working as a member of a team

Organization & Management Skills
- Coordinating tasks
- Demonstrating leadership
- Managing people/groups
- Performing duties that change frequently

Research & Planning Skills
- Analyzing information
- Developing evaluation strategies

Technological Environment

School counselors use a range of telecommunication tools to perform their job and should be comfortable using computers to access student and client records as well as job listings and forums. In addition, school counselors must learn how to maintain confidential records without compromising the privacy or future aspirations of juvenile clients. This may involve using a private recordkeeping system rather than storing information in a computer or database.

EDUCATION, TRAINING, AND ADVANCEMENT

High School/Secondary

High school students interested in pursuing a career as a school counselor should prepare themselves by developing good study habits. The study of foreign languages, public safety, sociology, psychology, and education will provide a strong foundation for work as a school counselor or college-level work in the field. Due to the range of school counseling job requirements, high school students interested in this career path will benefit from seeking internships, volunteer opportunities, or part-time work that expose the students to diverse educational programs and professions.

Suggested High School Subjects
- Child Growth & Development
- College Preparatory
- Composition
- English
- Literature
- Psychology
- Social Studies
- Sociology
- Speech

Famous First

The first person to develop a comprehensive school guidance program was Jesse B. Davis, principal of Grand Rapids Central High School, pictured, in Michigan in 1907. Davis instructed the school's English teachers to have students write weekly essays on topics related to career choice, their plans for the future, or what the model man or woman was like, in their view. In 1913 Davis was made director of vocational guidance for the Grand Rapids school district, and helped found the National Vocational Guidance Association (now the National Career Development Association).

College/Postsecondary

Postsecondary students interested in becoming school counselors should work towards a master's degree in counseling or a related field such as psychology or social work. Classes in education and foreign languages may also prove useful in their future work. Postsecondary students can gain work experience and potential advantage in their future job searches by securing internships or part-time employment in career placement or job training programs.

Related College Majors

- Counselor Education/Student Counseling & Guidance Services
- Psychology

Adult Job Seekers

Adults seeking employment as school counselors should have earned, at a minimum, a bachelor's degree in counseling or related field such as psychology or social work. Employers are increasingly requiring school counselors to have a master's of counseling, school guidance, rehabilitation counseling, or social work and related national certification. Adult job seekers should educate themselves about the educational and professional license requirements of their home states and the organizations where they seek employment. Professional counseling associations, such as the National Employment Counseling Association and the Commission on Rehabilitation Counselor Certification, generally offer career workshops and maintain lists and forums of available jobs.

Professional Certification and Licensure

School counselors should pursue the certification and licensure required of their job specialty. Certification options include school counseling certification, general counseling certification, school guidance certification, rehabilitation counseling certification, mental health counseling certification, or social work certification. School counselors working with students at the elementary, secondary, or college level, for example, may earn the National Certified School Counselor (NCSC) designation or certification awarded by the American School Counselor Association (ASCA). Those earning the NCSC certification will have successfully completed a master's degree in counseling or related field, two years of supervised counseling

experience, supervisor references, and the National Counselor
Examination for Licensure and Certification examination.

Specific requirements for counselor licensing, including additional
coursework, continuing education, and supervised hours, vary by
state.

Additional Requirements

Successful school counselors engage in ongoing
professional development to maintain their
certifications. High levels of integrity and personal and
professional ethics are required of school counselors,
as individuals in this role serve as a role model and mentor mainly
to juveniles and have access to personal information. Membership in
professional counseling associations is encouraged among all school
counselors as a means of building status within the professional
community and networking, and also of maintaining high ethical
standards and knowledge of best practices in the field.

Fun Fact

The Teacher of the Year has been recognized in a ceremony at the White House
every year since 1952, when President Harry S. Truman initiated the program.
But it wasn't until 2015 that the School Counselor of the Year was recognized
in a White House ceremony, after First Lady Michelle Obama made good on her
promise while working with school counselors on her Reach Higher Initiative.

Sources: https://www.whitehouse.gov/the-press-office/2015/01/30/remarks-first-lady-presentation-school-counselor-year-award

http://www.mea-mft.org/Articles/paul_andersen_is_national_teacher_of_the_year_finalist.aspx

EARNINGS AND ADVANCEMENT

Earnings depend on the type, size, geographic location, and union affiliation of the employer, and the individual's education, experience and specialty. School counselors had median annual earnings of $53,600 in 2013. The lowest ten percent earned less than $31,850, and the highest ten percent earned more than $86,870.

Many school counselors are compensated on the same pay scale as teachers. School counselors can earn additional income working summers in the school system or in other jobs.

School counselors may receive paid vacations, holidays, and sick days; life and health insurance; and retirement benefits. These are usually paid by the employer.

Metropolitan Areas with the Highest
Employment Level in this Occupation

Metropolitan area	Employment	Employment per thousand jobs	Hourly mean wage
New York-White Plains-Wayne, NY-NJ	10,650	2.03	$32.69
Los Angeles-Long Beach-Glendale, CA	9,700	2.44	$33.14
Chicago-Joliet-Naperville, IL	5,930	1.60	$31.51
Phoenix-Mesa-Glendale, AZ	4,650	2.61	$23.38
Washington-Arlington-Alexandria, DC-VA-MD-WV	4,630	1.95	$31.86
Houston-Sugar Land-Baytown, TX	4,460	1.62	$26.87
Philadelphia, PA	4,340	2.36	$26.78
Atlanta-Sandy Springs-Marietta, GA	3,530	1.53	$27.86
Dallas-Plano-Irving, TX	3,350	1.56	$27.95
Boston-Cambridge-Quincy, MA	3,270	1.87	$30.42

Source: Bureau of Labor Statistics

EMPLOYMENT AND OUTLOOK

School counselors held about 262,000 jobs nationally in 2013. Employment is expected to grow about as fast as the average for all occupations through the year 2022, which means employment is projected to increase 9 percent to 15 percent. Increasing elementary, middle school and secondary school enrollments and an expansion in the responsibilities of school counselors will all contribute to job growth in this field.

Employment Trend, Projected 2010–20

Community and Social Service Occupations: 17%

School Counselors: 12%

Total, All Occupations: 11%

Note: "All Occupations" includes all occupations in the U.S. Economy. Source: U.S. Bureau of Labor Statistics, Employment Projections Program

Related Occupations
- Clergy
- Employment Specialist
- Healthcare Social Worker
- Marriage & Family Therapist
- Parole & Probation Officer
- Psychologist
- Rehabilitation Counselor
- Religious Activities & Education Director
- Social & Human Service Assistant
- Social Worker
- Substance Abuse Counselor
- Vocational Rehabilitation Counselor

Related Military Occupations
- Personnel Specialist

Conversation With . . .
TAWNYA W. PRINGLE

School Counselor
Hoover High School, San Diego
School Counselor, 27 years

1. What was your individual career path in terms of education/training, entry-level job, or other significant opportunity?

My career path consisted of working with teenagers in a residential treatment facility right after I graduated with my bachelor's degree in psychology. I had also done some volunteer work at a crisis line near San Diego State University, where I went to school. While I was in graduate school, I had a part-time job as a guidance assistant in an elementary school, which also served as my internship for the field of school counseling. Now I work as a school counselor in The Academy of Literature, Media and Arts (ALMA) at Hoover High in San Diego. One hundred percent of students in the school qualify for free or reduced lunch.

2. What are the most important skills and/or qualities for someone in your profession?

To be an excellent school counselor, you must have a passion for helping youth; the ability to be an agent of change within a school; the ability to work with parents as well as school staff and administration; good presentation skills; and cultural sensitivity. It's a plus if you are bilingual.

3. What do you wish you had known going into this profession?

I wish I had more training in the areas of working with special needs students and how to collect data effectively. I took statistics, but when I went to graduate school, school data collection wasn't taught; it is now. The reason it's important is that it gives staff and parents a way to quantify and measure results.

4. Are there many job opportunities in your profession? In what specific areas?

There are school counseling positions in some states and, hopefully, with the new emphasis on school counseling, there will be more. In July 2014, First Lady Michelle

Obama spoke at the American School Counselor Association's annual conference and said, "School counseling is a necessity to ensure that all our young people get the education they need to succeed in today's economy."

Usually, there are more jobs at the middle and high school levels than at the elementary level. Elementary school counselors tend to play a preventive role.

5. How do you see your profession changing in the next five years? What role will technology play in those changes, and what skills will be required?

In the next five years, school counseling will continue to move forward in the area of gathering data for the purposes of improving student success and closing the achievement gap. In addition, there is now a strong emphasis on preparing students to be college- and career-ready with the skills necessary to compete in a global society. School counselors will need to have additional training in preparing students for the post-secondary-school world and in career exploration for all fields. Technology will be used to gather and analyze data that is relevant to student achievement. It also will continue to change and improve the efficiency of how we communicate with parents, students and other staff.

6. What do you enjoy most about your job? What do you enjoy least about your job?

I love my job as a school counselor. Every day I feel lucky that I get to be a student advocate for high school youth from all cultures. I love the fact that I can be a part of making their dreams come true. I love helping at-risk students refuse to give up and helping them to realize that education in empowering!

The one part of my job that I most dislike has to do with hand-counting credits when I am doing transcript reviews. Still today, there is no technology out there that will do this for you. It's exhausting and although you do it only a couple of times a school year, when your caseload is 450 students, it's hard not to make mistakes.

7. Can you suggest a valuable "try this" for students considering a career in your profession?

I would advise working in a school setting, shadowing a school counselor at every level (elementary, middle and high school) for a few days in a row, and also working in a culturally diverse area. Any type of customer service job is good because you get exposure to all kinds of people. Almost any type of experience you have working around students between the ages of 5 and 18 would be valuable.

SELECTED SCHOOLS

Many colleges and universities have bachelor's degree programs in education; some offer a specialization in school counseling. The student may also gain an initial grounding in the field at a technical or community college. Consult with your school guidance counselor or research post-secondary programs in your area. Below are listed some of the more prominent schools in this field.

Ohio State University
Columbus, OH 43210
614.292.6446
www.osu.edu

Penn State University
University Park
State College, PA 16801
814.865.4700
www.psu.edu

University of Central Florida
4000 Central Florida Boulevard
Orlando, FL 32816
407.823.2000
www.ucf.edu

University of Florida
Gainesville, FL 32611
352.392.3261
www.ufl.edu

University of Georgia
Athens, GA 30602
706.542.3000
www.uga.edu

University of Maryland
College Park, MD 20742
301.405.1000
www.umd.edu

University of Minnesota
Minneapolis, MN 55455
612.625.5000
www.umn.edu

University of Missouri
Columbia, MO 65211
573.882.2121
missouri.edu

University of North Carolina, Greensboro
1400 Spring Garden Street
Greensboro, NC 27412
336.334.5000
www.uncg.edu

University of Wisconsin
Madison, WI 53706
608.263.2400
www.wisc.edu

MORE INFORMATION

American Counseling Association
5999 Stevenson Avenue
Alexandria, VA 22304
800.347.6647
www.counseling.org

**American School Counselor
Association**
1101 King Street, Suite 625
Alexandria, VA 22314
800.306.4722
www.schoolcounselor.org

**International Vocational
Education and Training
Association**
186 Wedgewood Drive
Mahtomedi, MN 55115
www.iveta.org

**National Career Development
Association**
305 N. Beech Circle
Broken Arrow, OK 74012
918.663.7060
www.ncda.org

**National Organization for Human
Services**
1600 Sarno Road, Suite 16
Melbourne, FL 32935
www.nationalhumanservices.org

Simone Isadora Flynn/Editor

Social Worker

Snapshot

Career Cluster: Human Services

Interests: Social work, psychology, sociology, counseling, political science, mental health

Earnings (Yearly Average): $44,200

Employment & Outlook: Faster Than Average Growth Expected

OVERVIEW

Sphere of Work

Social workers are social service professionals committed to improving the social and behavioral lives of individuals, families, and communities. Social workers help at-risk or overwhelmed individuals to find resources, develop new coping strategies, resolve problems and conflicts, and secure opportunities. Social workers work with individual clients to lessen the impact, and in some cases resolve, unemployment, poverty, drug and alcohol dependency, homelessness, and domestic abuse. Social workers may work with individuals, families, or targeted populations such as prisoners and the elderly.

Work Environment

Social workers see clients in a wide variety of settings, including offices, residential facilities, homeless shelters, schools, prisons, hospitals, and substance abuse clinics. Social workers may have a fixed office where they receive and see clients; others might spend the majority of their work hours traveling to meet with clients. Given the diverse demands of the profession, social workers may need to work days, evenings, and weekends to meet client or caseload needs.

Profile

Working Conditions: Work Indoors
Physical Strength: Light Work
Education Needs: Master's Degree
Licensure/Certification: Required
Physical Abilities Not Required: No Heavy Labor
Opportunities For Experience: Internship, Military Service, Volunteer Work, Part-Time Work
Holland Interest Score*: ESA, SEA, SEC

* See Appendix A

Occupation Interest

Individuals drawn to the social work profession tend to be intelligent and socially conscious people who have the ability to quickly assess situations, find resources, demonstrate caring, and solve problems. Those who succeed in social work display traits such as leadership, knowledge of human behavior, initiative, project management, and interest in and concern for society. Social workers should enjoy spending time with a wide range of people, including those considered at-risk and those from diverse cultural, social, and educational backgrounds.

A Day in the Life—Duties and Responsibilities

The daily occupational duties and responsibilities of social workers are determined by their job specialization. Professional social work specializations include licensed clinical social worker, child and family social worker, school social worker, medical and public health social worker, mental health and substance abuse social worker, and administrative social worker. Licensed clinical social workers have state licensure and certification that allows them to provide psychotherapy and counseling services to individual clients, families, and community groups.

Child and family social workers help families and children to locate and access services and aid, as well as provide ongoing or targeted counseling to improve family dynamics. Child and family social workers provide workshops and individual counseling on topics such as adoption, foster care, domestic violence, sibling rivalry, and homelessness. They also serve as a voluntary or court-ordered connection between families and social service agencies.

School social workers help to improve the socio-emotional and academic experience of individual students and school groups. They provide workshops and individual counseling on topics such as conflict resolution, sexual education, school attendance, and drug addiction, as well as serve as a connection between students, teachers, and families.

Medical and public health social workers help at-risk clients and their families locate and access physical and psychological support services. Medical and public health social workers offer workshops and counseling on topics such as living with illness, care-giving, and end of life preparation. They may also coordinate health related transportation and housing needs.

Mental health and substance abuse social workers help people living with mental illnesses and substance abuse. They provide counseling and workshops on topics such as ending drug dependency and managing mental illness, and help their clients maintain family relationships and secure employment and housing.

Administrative social workers work outside of patient or client care; they conduct research, determine policy, and plan social service programs targeted at domestic abuse, unemployment, homelessness, substance abuse, and poverty.

Duties and Responsibilities

- Interviewing and counseling clients and families regarding their physical, social and psychological concerns
- Evaluating information to determine client problems
- Compiling records of client reaction and progress
- Assisting clients in improving their personal and social functioning by helping them secure needed services
- Determining clients' possible needs for future assistance
- Working with families that have serious conflicts, including those involving child or spousal abuse or divorce

OCCUPATION SPECIALTIES

Child Welfare Caseworkers

Child Welfare Caseworkers help parents with child-rearing problems and aid children and youths with difficulties in social adjustment.

School Social Workers

School Social Workers aid children having difficulty adapting to school life. They consult with parents, teachers, counselors and other school personnel.

Psychiatric Social Workers

Psychiatric Social Workers provide assistance to mentally or emotionally disturbed patients in hospitals, clinics and other medical centers. They are part of a psychiatric team that diagnoses and treats patients for their mental illness.

Family Caseworkers

Family Caseworkers aid families having problems concerning family relationships or other aspects of their social functioning and how it affects the family and the community.

Correctional-Treatment Specialists

Correctional-Treatment Specialists provide services for inmates of correctional institutions.

Alcohol-and-Drug Abuse Program Administrators

Alcohol-and-Drug Abuse Program Administrators coordinate government programs dealing with the prevention and treatment of alcohol and drug abuse problems affecting work performance of employees.

WORK ENVIRONMENT

Relevant Skills and Abilities

Communication Skills
- Expressing thoughts and ideas
- Speaking effectively
- Writing concisely

Interpersonal/Social Skills
- Cooperating with others
- Counseling others
- Providing support to others
- Working as a member of a team

Organization & Management Skills
- Coordinating tasks
- Demonstrating leadership
- Managing people/groups
- Research & Planning Skills
- Analyzing information
- Creating ideas
- Developing evaluation strategies

Physical Environment

A social worker's immediate physical environment varies based on their caseload and specialization. Social workers spend their workdays seeing clients in a wide variety of settings, including offices, outpatient facilities, nursing homes, residential facilities, homeless shelters, schools, prisons, hospitals, and substance abuse clinics.

Human Environment

Social workers work with a wide variety of people and should be comfortable meeting with colleagues, staff, children, people with mental illness, incarcerated people, the elderly, people with physical illnesses, homeless people, abusers and the abused, and families.

Technological Environment

Social workers use telecommunication tools to perform their job and must be comfortable using computers to access client records.

EDUCATION, TRAINING, AND ADVANCEMENT

High School/Secondary

High school students interested in pursuing a career in social work should prepare themselves by developing good study habits. High school-level study of foreign languages, sociology, psychology, political science, and education will provide a strong foundation for college-level work in social work. Due to the diversity of social work specialties, high school students interested in this career path will benefit from seeking internships or part-time work that expose the students to diverse groups of people and social needs.

Suggested High School Subjects
- Algebra
- Applied Communication
- Child Growth & Development
- College Preparatory
- Composition
- English
- Foreign Languages
- Keyboarding
- Political Science
- Psychology
- Social Studies
- Sociology

Famous First

The first institution in the United States designed to assist those in need was the almshouse established by William Penn, pictured, in Philadelphia in 1713. Initially, it was open only to Quakers, but a second house was open to all.

College/Postsecondary

Postsecondary students interested in becoming social workers should work towards a minimum of a bachelor's degree in social work; however, many positions require at least a master's degree. Coursework in education, psychology, political science, and foreign languages may also prove useful in their social work practice. Postsecondary students can gain work experience and potential advantage in their future job searches by securing internships or part-time employment in social service agencies or with at-risk populations such as the elderly or the homeless.

Related College Majors

- Community Health Services
- Housing Studies
- Psychology, General
- Social Work

Adult Job Seekers

Adults seeking employment as social workers should have earned, at a minimum, a bachelor's degree in social work or a related field such as psychology or sociology. Some social service organizations and specialties require a master's degree in social work and foreign language proficiency. Adult job seekers should educate themselves about the educational and professional license requirements of their home states (or the states in which they choose to practice) and the organizations where they seek employment. Adult job seekers will benefit from joining professional associations to help with networking and job searching. Professional social work associations, such as the Action Network for Social Work Education and Research (ANSWER) and the Center for Clinical Social Work, generally offer career workshops and maintain lists and forums of available jobs.

Professional Certification and Licensure

Professional certification and licensure is required of all practicing social workers. The social work licensure process varies by state and specialty. Licensed Social Work Associate (LSWA), Licensed Social Worker (LSW), Licensed Certified Social Worker (LCSW), and Licensed Independent Clinical Social Worker (LICSW) will need different amounts and types of education and supervised work experience. In general, social workers interested in clinical social work practice will need the highest amount of supervised hours (approximately 3,000 hours) to earn their clinical license. Consult credible professional associations within your field and follow professional debate as to the relevancy and value of any certification program.

Additional Requirements

Individuals who find satisfaction, success, and job security as social workers will be knowledgeable about the profession's requirements, responsibilities, and opportunities. Successful social workers engage in ongoing professional development. High levels of integrity and personal and professional ethics are required of social workers, as social workers interact with at-risk people and groups and have access to personal and confidential information. Membership in professional social work associations is encouraged among junior and senior social workers as a means of building one's status in the professional community and networking.

EARNINGS AND ADVANCEMENT

Earnings depend on the type, size and geographic location of the employer and the individual's education, experience and skill.

Median annual earnings of the various types of social workers in 2013 were: mental health and substance abuse social workers, $40,970; child, family and school social workers, $42,120; and healthcare social workers, $50,820.

Social workers may receive paid vacations, holidays, and sick days; life and health insurance; and retirement benefits. These are usually paid by the employer. Employers may provide automobiles for field work and reimbursement for travel expenses.

Metropolitan Areas with the Highest Employment Level in this Occupation

Metropolitan area	Employment[1]	Employment per thousand jobs	Hourly mean wage
New York-White Plains-Wayne, NY-NJ	4,420	0.84	$29.64
Los Angeles-Long Beach-Glendale, CA	3,720	0.94	$29.99
Chicago-Joliet-Naperville, IL	2,530	0.68	$29.33
Riverside-San Bernardino-Ontario, CA	1,400	1.16	$28.48
Oakland-Fremont-Hayward, CA	1,130	1.13	$38.32
Portland-Vancouver-Hillsboro, OR-WA	1,120	1.09	$23.75
Nassau-Suffolk, NY	1,090	0.88	$31.78
Visalia-Porterville, CA	1,030	7.74	$22.61
Atlanta-Sandy Springs-Marietta, GA	940	0.41	$25.25
Santa Ana-Anaheim-Irvine, CA	840	0.58	$28.82

[1] Does not include self-employed. Source: Bureau of Labor Statistics

EMPLOYMENT AND OUTLOOK

There were approximately 722,000 social workers employed nationally in 2012. Employment is expected to grow faster than the average for all occupations through the year 2022, which means employment is projected to increase 16 percent to 25 percent. Competition for jobs is stronger in cities, where demand for social services often is highest and training programs for social workers are common. However, job opportunities should also be good in rural areas, which often find it difficult to hire and keep qualified social workers. Job prospects may be best for social workers with a background in gerontology and substance abuse treatment.

Employment Trend, Projected 2010–20

Community and Social Service Specialists (All): 19%

Social Workers: 19%

Total, All Occupations: 11%

Note: "All Occupations" includes all occupations in the U.S. Economy. Source: U.S. Bureau of Labor Statistics, Employment Projections Program

Related Occupations
- Case Worker/Social Services Assistant
- Employment Specialist
- Marriage Counselor
- Medical Social Worker
- Parole and Probation Officer
- Psychologist
- Rehabilitation Counselor
- Religious Worker
- School Counselor
- Substance Abuse Counselor
- Vocational Rehabilitation Counselor

Related Military Occupations
- Caseworker & Counselor
- Social Worker

Conversation With . . .
MYRA HIDALGO, LCSW

Social Worker
Private Practice, New Orleans, LA, 13 years
Licensed Clinical Social Worker, 22 years

1. What was your individual career path in terms of education/training, entry-level job, or other significant opportunity?

I started as a psychology major because I wanted to understand more about people and why we do the things we do, and I also wanted to understand more about myself. I initially wanted to work in experimental psychology with animals. At that time, I was seeing a therapist who was a clinical social worker and through that experience realized I had been afraid to do clinical work. After I went into a doctoral program in animal behavior, I realized I had a lot more to offer, and felt I was not using my strengths and resources to their fullest. At that point, I left the doctoral program and went to a graduate program in social work.

I got my first job before I entered social work school, working as a residential counselor with homeless women and children at a shelter. Then, through social work school, I did a year-long internship working with children and their families in an outpatient psychiatric clinic. I learned a lot about child development and families' mental health. I went on to work for different non-profit mental health services agencies, including with children, adolescents and adults affected by HIV. Later, I worked as a clinical director for a non-profit agency where my duties included supervising and training students and new professionals who were working toward their licensure in social work, marriage and family therapy, and professional counseling. I also got into grant writing. Eventually, I opened a private practice, wrote a book, and began a doctoral program, which was disrupted by Hurricane Katrina. After I finished my coursework, I decided not to pursue a dissertation because I wanted to devote more time to my practice.

2. What are the most important skills and/or qualities for someone in your profession?

Self-awareness and humility. We make decisions constantly as we move through a client's therapy and treatment. Without self-awareness, a therapist's own issues can creep into the work and affect the decisions you make and the questions you ask and that may not be in the best interest of the client.

3. What do you wish you had known going into this profession?

That it's OK to have your own issues that you address in therapy before going into this field. What's important is how well you have resolved and understand your own issues.

4. Are there many job opportunities in your profession? In what specific areas?

The profession is changing. One of the good things about social work, as opposed to other helping professions, is that it's very diverse and the focus can be as broad as working with global populations or as focused as working with families and individuals. Social work started out being broadly focused on larger social issues, then from the 1970s to the '90s became more focused on working with individuals and families. Now the pendulum is swinging toward the middle, with many social workers doing individual counseling, and others working with larger groups for social change such as advocating for marginalized communities such as the poor or disadvantaged.

5. How do you see your profession changing in the next five years? What role will technology play in those changes, and what skills will be required?

One big issue is maintaining confidentiality in light of technology. With the use of technology in communication and the pervasiveness of social media, people are putting more and more of their private information into the public arena, including therapists as well as patients. Therapists have access to client information outside of therapy sessions. Licensing boards need to figure out how to change laws to maintain the ethical basis of the work we do and people's privacy.

6. What do you enjoy most about your job? What do you enjoy least about your job?

I feel privileged to be able to watch people on their journeys through very difficult times to a place of peacefulness or acceptance or well-being. And, as a therapist in private practice, I like being my own boss and setting my own schedule.

I least enjoy the challenge of balancing my own happiness and emotional needs with the emotional demands of the work. Also, one tough thing about being in private practice is that you don't have colleagues around you, so it can be lonely. I address that by getting together monthly with other clinical social workers in private practice in a peer consultation group.

7. Can you suggest a valuable "try this" for students considering a career in your profession?

Volunteer at a non-profit organization in your community, and see if you're motivated to help create meaningful changes in society and/or to help individuals who are suffering.

SELECTED SCHOOLS

Many colleges and universities have bachelor's degree programs in subjects related to social work. The student may also gain an initial grounding in the field at a technical or community college. Consult with your school guidance counselor or research post-secondary programs in your area. For more advanced positions, a master's degree is expected. Below are listed some of the more prominent schools in this field.

Boston College
Chestnut Hill, MA 02467
617.552.8000
www.bc.edu

Case Western Reserve University
10900 Euclid Avenue
Cleveland, OH 44106
216.368.2000
www.case.edu

Columbia University
116 St. and Broadway
New York, NY 10027
212.854.1754
www.columbia.edu

University of California, Berkeley
Berkeley, CA
510.642.6000
berkeley.edu

University of Chicago
5801 South Ellis Avenue
Chicago, IL 60637
773.702.1234
www.uchicago.edu

University of Michigan
500 South State Street
Ann Arbor, MI 48109
734.764.1817
www.umich.edu

University of North Carolina, Chapel Hill
Chapel Hill, NC
919.962.2211
www.unc.edu

University of Texas, Austin
Austin, TX 78712
512.471.3434
www.utexas.edu

University of Washington
Seattle, WA
206.543.2100
www.washington.edu

Washington University in St. Louis
1 Brookings Drive, South
St. Louis, MO 63130
314.935.5000
wustl.edu

MORE INFORMATION

American Board of Examiners in Clinical Social Work
241 Humphrey Street
Marblehead, MA 01945
800.694.5285
www.abecsw.org

American Case Management Association
11701 W. 36th Street
Little Rock, AR 72211
501.907.2262
www.acmaweb.org

Center for Clinical Social Work
27 Congress Street, #501
Salem, MA 01970
800.694.5285
www.centercsw.org

Council on Social Work Education
1701 Duke Street, Suite 200
Alexandria, VA 22314-3457
703.683.8080
www.cswe.org

National Association of Social Workers
750 First Street NE, Suite 700
Washington, DC 20002-4241
202.408.8600
www.naswdc.org

National Organization for Human Services
1600 Sarno Road, Suite 16
Melbourne, FL 32935
www.nationalhumanservices.org

Simone Isadora Flynn/Editor

Special Education Teacher

Snapshot

Career Cluster: Education & Training; Human Services

Interests: Teaching, education, preparing lessons, child development, student care, psychology

Earnings (Yearly Average): $56,920

Employment & Outlook: Slower Than Average Growth Expected

OVERVIEW

Sphere of Work

Special education teachers are teaching professionals that focus on the educational needs of students with physical, emotional, cognitive, or behavioral special needs. Special education teachers may be generalists with knowledge and talents in a wide range of subjects and special needs. Alternatively, they may have an academic specialization and training with speech impairment, hearing problems, language delays, mental retardation, seizures, orthopedic impairment, visual impairments, autism, traumatic brain

injuries, or learning disabilities. Special education teachers help to develop and provide the services of the individualized education plans (IEP) for every child in the public school system with documented special needs.

Work Environment

Special education teachers work in schools designed to meet to the social and educational needs of mainstream and special needs children. They work at all grade levels in both public and private school settings. Some special education teachers work in discrete special needs classrooms focusing on one age level or type of special need such as autism or physical disabilities. Others work in integrated special needs classrooms with students of many ages and special needs. Still others work in classrooms that have integrated mainstream and special needs students working alongside one another. Classrooms have different types and amounts of resources, such as art supplies, music lessons, and physical education facilities. The resources available depend on the financial resources of the school and district as well as the educational philosophy directing the curriculum.

Profile

Working Conditions: Work Indoors
Physical Strength: Light Work
Education Needs: Bachelor's Degree, Master's Degree
Licensure/Certification: Required
Physical Abilities Not Required: No Heavy Labor
Opportunities For Experience: Internship, Volunteer Work, Part-Time Work
Holland Interest Score*: SEC

* See Appendix A

Occupation Interest

Individuals drawn to special education tend to be intelligent, resourceful, creative, patient, and caring. Special education teachers, who instruct and nurture students with special needs, should find satisfaction in spending long hours interacting with and instructing children. They should be physically fit and able to move, lift, and carry students with physical disabilities as well as physically redirect students with behavioral or emotional problems. Successful special education teachers excel at communication and problem solving.

A Day in the Life—Duties and Responsibilities

A special education teacher's daily duties and responsibilities include planning, teaching, classroom preparation, student care, family outreach, school duties, and professional development.

Special education teachers prepare and teach lessons, modify the mainstream curriculum for students with special needs, and buy or secure donations for classroom or project supplies. They assign homework and projects, teach good study habits and life skills, grade student work, provide students with special needs accommodations (such as extra test time and homework modification), and maintain accurate academic and behavioral records for all students.

Classroom preparation and cleaning may include labeling materials, organizing desk and work areas, displaying student work on bulletin boards and display boards, and, depending on janitorial support, cleaning up and sanitizing at the end of the school day.

Special education teachers greet students as they arrive in the classroom, engage in student behavior modification and redirection, and promote a supportive learning environment. They also maintain student safety and health, provide appropriate levels of discipline in the classroom and school environment, build student cooperation and listening skills, and work to present lessons in multiple ways to accommodate diverse learning styles.

Some special education teachers may greet student families at school drop off and dismissal times and use a student school-family communication notebook. All teachers must communicate regularly with families about student health, experience, and performance.

Special education teachers attend staff meetings and meetings with family and social workers. They lead IEP development and review meetings and coordinate special education and mainstream classrooms. They also enforce school policies and participate in peer mentoring. Their professional development duties include attendance at professional meetings, continued training, and recertification as needed.

Special education teachers work daily to meet the needs of all students, families, fellow teachers, and school administrators. All special education teachers must adhere to the educational standards and rights described in the Individuals with Disabilities Education Act (IDEA).

Duties and Responsibilities

- Planning curricula and preparing lessons
- Arranging and adjusting tools, work aids and equipment used by students in classrooms
- Conferring with other staff members and professionals to develop programs to make the most of the students' potential
- Instructing students in subject areas
- Observing, evaluating and preparing reports on the progress of students
- Conferring with and reporting to parents pertaining to students' programs and adjustments

OCCUPATION SPECIALTIES

Teachers of Physically Impaired Students

Teachers of Physically Impaired Students instruct students in the elementary and secondary levels who are physically impaired. They evaluate students' abilities to determine the best training program for each individual.

Teachers of the Mentally Impaired

Teachers of the Mentally Impaired teach social skills and/or basic academic subjects in schools, hospitals and other institutions to mentally impaired students.

Teachers of the Hearing Impaired

Teachers of the Hearing Impaired teach elementary and secondary school subjects and special skills to deaf or hard-of-hearing students using lip reading, manual communication or total communication.

Teachers of the Visually Impaired

Teachers of the Visually Impaired teach elementary and secondary school subjects to visually-impaired and blind students using large-print materials and/or the Braille system.

Teachers of the Emotionally Impaired

Teachers of the Emotionally Impaired teach elementary and secondary school subjects including education on socially acceptable behavior to students with emotional impairments.

WORK ENVIRONMENT

Physical Environment

A special education teacher works primarily in the classroom. Special education teachers may have the autonomy and responsibility to modify the classroom layout and curriculum to meet the academic and social needs of students with special needs. They generally work forty-hour weeks and follow an annual academic schedule with ample winter, spring, and summer vacations. Summer teaching opportunities in summer school and camps are common.

Human Environment

Special education teachers are in constant contact with students with physical, cognitive, or emotional challenges as well as with families, social workers, therapists, school administrators, and fellow teachers. They must be comfortable working with people from a wide range of backgrounds and able to incorporate lessons on diversity and differences into their teaching.

Relevant Skills and Abilities

Communication Skills
- Expressing thoughts and ideas
- Speaking effectively
- Writing concisely

Interpersonal/Social Skills
- Being flexible
- Being sensitive to others
- Providing support to others

Organization & Management Skills
- Coordinating tasks
- Making decisions
- Managing people/groups

Research & Planning Skills
- Using logical reasoning

Technological Environment

Special education teachers use a wide variety of adaptive and instructional technologies, such as touch screens and communication devices. Special education teachers should be comfortable using Internet communication tools and teaching students to use educational software. They also often help students to use and care for adaptive technologies such as wheelchairs, orthotics, hearing and feeding aids, and dressing aids.

EDUCATION, TRAINING, AND ADVANCEMENT

High School/Secondary

High school students interested in becoming special education teachers should develop good study habits. Interested high school students should take a broad range of courses in education, anatomy, psychology, child development, science, math, history, language arts, physical education, and the arts. Those interested in the field of education may benefit from seeking internships or part-time work with special needs children at camps and afterschool programs.

Suggested High School Subjects
- Arts
- Audio-Visual
- Biology
- Child Growth & Development
- College Preparatory

- Composition
- Crafts
- English
- History
- Humanities
- Literature
- Mathematics
- Psychology
- Science
- Sociology
- Speech

Famous First

The first nationally mandated program to integrate students with special needs into regular school systems (rather than teach them in separate facilities) came with amendments to the Individuals with Disabilities Act of 1997. The act formally recognized the concept of "inclusion," or "inclusive education," reflecting an interest among educators and the public in "mainstreaming" students with disabilities.

College/Postsecondary

College students interested in special education should consider majoring in education and earning initial teaching certification as part of their undergraduate education program. Aspiring teachers should complete coursework in education, child development, and psychology. Prior to graduation, interested college students should gain teaching experience with special needs children, through internships or work. They should also research master's of education programs and state teaching certification requirements.

Related College Majors
- Education Administration & Supervision, General

- Education of the Blind & Visually Handicapped
- Education of the Deaf & Hearing Impaired
- Education of the Specific Learning Disabled
- Education of the Speech Impaired
- Elementary/Pre-Elementary/Kindergarten Teacher Education
- Secondary/Jr. High/Middle School Teacher Education
- Special Education, General

Adult Job Seekers

Adults seeking jobs as special education teachers should research the education and certification requirements of their home states as well of the schools where they might seek employment. Adult job seekers may benefit from employment workshops and job lists maintained by professional teaching associations, such as the American Federation of Teachers and the National Clearinghouse for Professions in Special Education.

Professional Certification and Licensure

All special education teachers must be licensed. Professional certification and licensure requirements for special education teachers vary between states and between schools. Special education teachers generally earn a master's in general education, with additional training in a special education area, such as learning or physical disabilities, and obtain a special education teaching license for kindergarten through high school. A small number of states require special education teachers to complete a master's of special education. State departments of education offer state teaching licenses and require continuing education and recertification on a regular basis. Successful job seekers will find out the requirements that apply to them and satisfy the requirements prior to seeking employment.

Additional Requirements

Individuals who find satisfaction, success, and job security as special education teachers will be knowledgeable about the profession's requirements, responsibilities, and opportunities. Successful special education teachers engage in ongoing professional development. Special education teachers must have high levels of integrity and ethics as they work with vulnerable minors and have access to the personal information of student families. Membership in professional teaching associations is encouraged among beginning and tenured special education teachers as a means of building status in a professional community and networking.

Fun Fact

The phrase "special education" entered our collective vocabulary in 1975, when the federal Individuals with Disabilities Education Act (IDEA) was enacted, requiring schools to provide "special education for children with qualifying disabilities." Eventually, the acronym "SPED" took on a derogatory quality.

Source: http://www.specialednews.com/the-history-of-special-education-in-the-united-states.htm

EARNINGS AND ADVANCEMENT

Earnings of special education teachers depend on the individual's education and experience and the type, size and geographic location of the employer. Median annual earnings of special education teachers were $56,920 in 2013. The lowest ten percent earned less than $38,550, and the highest ten percent earned more than $90,460.

The school calendar allows special education teachers to have national and state holidays off and receive winter and summer vacations. They may also receive life and health insurance and retirement benefits. These are usually paid by the employer.

Metropolitan Areas with the Highest Employment Level in this Occupation

Metropolitan area	Employment[1]	Employment per thousand jobs	Hourly mean wage
New York-White Plains-Wayne, NY-NJ	10,720	2.05	$75,690
Chicago-Joliet-Naperville, IL	3,910	1.06	$71,710
Los Angeles-Long Beach-Glendale, CA	3,630	0.91	$66,050
Philadelphia, PA	3,580	1.94	$68,320
Nassau-Suffolk, NY	2,900	2.35	$96,650
Minneapolis-St. Paul-Bloomington, MN-WI	2,450	1.37	$68,560
Washington-Arlington-Alexandria, DC-VA-MD-WV	1,730	0.73	$76,220
Atlanta-Sandy Springs-Marietta, GA	1,720	0.75	$54,180
Houston-Sugar Land-Baytown, TX	1,680	0.61	$52,120
Boston-Cambridge-Quincy, MA	1,650	0.94	$69,040

[1] Does not include self-employed. Source: Bureau of Labor Statistics

EMPLOYMENT AND OUTLOOK

There were about 443,000 special education teachers employed nationally in 2012. Nearly all were employed in public and private elementary, middle, and secondary schools. Employment is expected to grow slower than the average for all occupations through the year 2022, which means employment is projected to increase 3 percent to 10 percent. Job openings will mostly be created by continued growth in the number of special education students needing services. The need to replace special education teachers who switch to general education, change careers or retire will lead to additional job openings. At the same time, many school districts report shortages of qualified special education teachers. The most job opportunities will be available in inner city and rural schools. However, job growth could be limited by state and local government budget deficits.

Employment Trend, Projected 2010–20

Total, All Occupations: 11%

Education, Training, and Library Occupations: 11%

Special Education Teachers: 6%

Note: "All Occupations" includes all occupations in the U.S. Economy. Source: U.S. Bureau of Labor Statistics, Employment Projections Program

Related Occupations
- Audiologist
- Career/Technology Education Teacher
- Elementary School Teacher
- Secondary School Teacher
- Speech-Language Pathologist
- Vocational Rehabilitation Counselor

Conversation With . . .
SUSAN CAMPBELL

Special Education Teacher
Lexington Public Schools, Lexington, MA
Special Education teacher, 35 years

1. What was your individual career path in terms of education/training, entry-level job, or other significant opportunity?

I received a BA in psychology from Smith College, but I wasn't sure what I wanted to do with my degree. I ended up working as a childcare worker at a residential school for children with special needs. I connected with the students and was quickly promoted, first to lead a group of teachers, then into administrative positions. While working there, I was fortunate that the school made a master's degree in special education available at a very reasonable price. I became certified in Intensive Special Education, which I did for eight years. My next job, of 12 years, was as an administrator at a private day school for young children with special needs. After having a child of my own, I realized that working long hours twelve months of the year didn't leave me much time with my son. I also realized that I truly missed working directly with students. I left the private sector and was delighted to find a job in Lexington, MA, at a public elementary school. For the past 15 years, I have worked to include students with special needs in general education classes. I also teach a graduate course on inclusion at Simmons College in Boston.

2. What are the most important skills and/or qualities for someone in your profession?

I believe there are many important qualities a special education teacher must possess to be truly effective. First, you must have a willingness to be a lifelong learner. The field is always changing and it is vital to change with it. Secondly, you must be a good communicator. As a special education teacher, I interface with a wide variety of people: general educators, parents, specialists, paraprofessionals and administrators. In order to do my job effectively, I have to be able to listen carefully, express myself clearly and be willing to compromise when necessary.

3. What do you wish you had known going into this profession?

I wish I had known that many of the skills you need as a special educator aren't necessarily tied directly to teaching. As mentioned above, communication skills and continuing your own learning are keys to this profession. Had I known this, perhaps I would have taken different electives in order to prepare myself better. My advice is to look for courses, perhaps in the business department, on leadership, effective communication, and building strong teams.

4. Are there many job opportunities in your profession? In what specific areas?

School districts across the country have a mandate to provide services in the least restrictive environment possible; therefore, more and more districts are adding special educators. In addition, the number of students with special needs is increasing significantly in some areas. When I started teaching, the rate of autism was 1 in 10,000; currently it is 1 in 68. Teachers who can work effectively with these students, as well as with those with behavioral and emotional challenges, are in high demand at elementary, middle and high school levels.

5. How do you see your profession changing in the next five years? What role will technology play in those changes, and what skills will be required?

I believe the field of special education will continue to evolve as it seeks to provide the best possible services to the widest range of learners. Technology is key in capturing the attention of many learners and in providing other learners with access to the curriculum. Teachers need to keep abreast of the newest technology in regards to smart boards, apps, data collection software, and other e-resources.

6. What do you enjoy most about your job? What do you enjoy least about your job?

The things I enjoy most are the progress I see my students make and working with colleagues. There's no better feeling than seeing a student succeed where they didn't before, or watching them take a risk in their learning. It's also a wonderful feeling to collaborate with a fellow teacher on the design of a lesson that successfully reaches a wide range of learners. It feels terrific to see students excited about their learning. Paperwork and meetings, while a necessary part of the job, are my least favorite!

7. Can you suggest a valuable "try this" for students considering a career in your profession?

I suggest setting up an observation at a local school with the age group you see yourself working with. Take notes on what you see. Do you get excited? Can you think of ways you could make the lesson better? Or improve the classroom layout? Are there students you feel drawn to because they might be struggling? In the graduate course that I teach, one of the assignments is a site visit. Students often tell me how eye opening this task is!

SELECTED SCHOOLS

Many colleges and universities have bachelor's degree programs in education; some offer a specialization in special education. The student may also gain an initial grounding in the field at a technical or community college. Consult with your school guidance counselor or research post-secondary programs in your area. Below are listed some of the more prominent schools in this field.

University of Florida
Gainesville, FL 32611
352.392.3261
www.ufl.edu

University of Illinois at Urbana, Champaign
Champaign, IL
217.333.1000
illinois.edu

University of Kansas
1450 Jayhawk Boulevard
Lawrence, KS 66045
785.864.2700
www.ku.edu

University of Minnesota
Minneapolis, MN 55455
612.625.5000
www.umn.edu

University of Oregon
1585 East 13th Avenue
Eugene, OR 97403
541.346.1000
uoregon.edu

University of Texas, Austin
Austin, TX 78712
512.471.3434
www.utexas.edu

University of Virginia
Charlottesville, VA
934.924.0311
www.virginia.edu

University of Washington
Seattle, Washington
206.543.2100
www.washington.edu

University of Wisconsin
Madison, WI 53706
608.263.2400
www.wisc.edu

Vanderbilt University
2201 West End Avenue
Nashville, TN 37235
615.322.7311
www.vanderbilt.edu

MORE INFORMATION

**Alexander Graham Bell
Association for the Deaf & Hard
of Hearing**
3417 Volta Place, NW
Washington, DC 20007
202.337.5220
www.agbell.org

**American Association for
Employment in Education**
3040 Riverside Drive, Suite 125
Columbus, OH 43221
614.485.1111
www.aaee.org

**American Association of Colleges
for Teacher Education**
1307 New York Avenue, NW
Suite 300
Washington, DC 20005-4701
202.293.2450
www.aacte.org

American Federation of Teachers
Public Affairs Department
555 New Jersey Avenue, NW
Washington, DC 20001
202.879.4400
www.aft.org

**Association for Education and
Rehabilitation**
of the Blind and Visually Impaired
1703 N. Beauregard St., Suite 440
Alexandria, VA 22311
703.671.4500
www.aerbvi.org

Council for Exceptional Children
2900 Crystal Drive, Suite 1000
Arlington, VA 22202-3557
888.232.7733
www.cec.sped.org

**Learning Disabilities Association
of America**
4156 Library Road
Pittsburgh, PA 15234-1349
412.341.1515
www.ldanatl.org

**National Association of State
Directors of Special Education**
1800 Diagonal Road, Suite 320
Alexandria, VA 22314
703.519.3800
www.nasdse.org

National Education Association
1201 16th Street, NW
Washington, DC 20036-3290
202.833.4000
www.nea.org

Simone Isadora Flynn/Editor

Speech-Language Pathologist

Snapshot

Career Cluster: Education & Training; Health Care; Human Services

Interests: Anatomy, physiology, speech pathology, patient assessment, creating treatment plans, speech and audiology research

Earnings (Yearly Average): $70,810

Employment & Outlook: Faster Than Average Growth Expected

OVERVIEW

Sphere of Work

Speech-language pathologists, more commonly referred to as speech therapists, are trained to assess and treat disorders of expressive and receptive speech, voice, swallowing, and language. Speech-language pathologists treat clients with a wide range of speech-related problems, including swallowing issues, inability to make speech sounds, stutters, receptive language disorders (i.e.,

language processing and comprehension), and voice disorders. Speech-language pathology skills tend to be well compensated and in demand in a variety of work settings.

Work Environment

Speech-language pathologists work in therapeutic settings, such as medical clinics or hospitals, and in schools. In medical environments, speech-language pathologists generally partner with medical and social service professionals, such as doctors and social workers, to treat communication and swallowing problems caused by medical events, such as strokes or premature birth. In school settings, speech-language pathologists partner with educational professionals, such as teachers and special education coordinators, to address a student's speech-related deficiency or issue. Speech therapy, provided by a speech-language pathologist, is a common component of a special-needs child's individualized education plan (IEP).

Profile

Working Conditions: Work Indoors
Physical Strength: Light Work
Education Needs: Bachelor's Degree, Master's Degree
Licensure/Certification: Required
Physical Abilities Not Required: No Heavy Labor
Opportunities For Experience: Internship, Military Service, Volunteer Work, Part-Time Work
Holland Interest Score*: SAI

* See Appendix A

Occupation Interest

Individuals attracted to the speech-language pathology profession tend to be active people who enjoy hands-on work and close interaction with others. Individuals who excel as speech therapists exhibit traits such as intellectual curiosity, problem solving, a desire to help, and a social conscience. Speech-language pathologists must understand and respect science and scientific inquiry and be able to work as part of a team to meet patient needs.

A Day in the Life—Duties and Responsibilities

A speech-language pathologist's daily duties and responsibilities include full days of hands-on patient interaction and treatment, as well as administrative duties. Patients seen by speech-language pathologists include those experiencing developmental delays, structural deformities, learning disabilities, cleft palate, cerebral palsy, stroke complications, trauma complications, mental retardation, or hearing loss.

As a medical or therapeutic professional, speech-language pathologists interact with patients or clients on a daily basis. Daily work includes quantitative and qualitative assessment of patient speech problems using standardized tests and interviewing techniques; creating patient treatment plans; advising patients on the use of hearing communication devices. Speech-language pathologists also teach sign language to hearing impaired individuals and their families; meet with patient treatment teams or patient families; and provide eating and swallowing therapy to patients.

A speech-language pathologist's daily administrative responsibilities include the record keeping involved with patient evaluation and treatment. Speech-language pathologists must draft treatment plans, record notes following patient treatment sessions, provide written updates to patient treatment teams, and provide insurance companies with patient records and progress notes as required. Independent speech-language pathologists, who work outside of a school or medical clinic, may also be responsible for patient appointment scheduling and billing.

Academic speech-language pathologists may work in a research capacity rather than patient or clinical capacity. Academic speech-language pathologists have daily teaching, research, and publication responsibilities.

Duties and Responsibilities

- Planning or conducting therapy for impairments such as aphasia, stuttering and articulation problems
- Guiding and counseling patients and their families
- Consulting others concerned with the patient's welfare, such as doctors, physical therapists, social workers and teachers
- Conducting research related to speech and audiology
- Determining the range, nature and degree of impairment
- Coordinating test results with other information such as educational, medical and behavioral data
- Differentiating between organic and nonorganic causative factors

WORK ENVIRONMENT

Physical Environment

Speech-language pathologists work in classroom settings, hospitals, and medical or therapeutic offices. Classroom settings are arranged for students with desks, chairs, and floor seating. Medical settings are usually sparse and sterile. Therapeutic office settings used by speech-language pathologists may be shared with other therapeutic professionals, such as occupational, physical, or recreational therapists.'

Relevant Skills and Abilities

Analytical Skills
- Analyzing data

Communication Skills
- Expressing thoughts and ideas clearly

Interpersonal/Social Skills
- Being patient
- Cooperating with others
- Working as a member of a team

Organization & Management Skills
- Managing conflict

Research & Planning Skills
- Developing evaluation strategies

Technical Skills
- Performing scientific, mathematical and technical work

Human Environment

Speech-language pathologists usually work as part of a patient treatment team, including patient families, teachers, doctors, and additional therapists. As a member of a treatment team, speech-language pathologists participate in frequent team meetings and are responsible for communicating patient progress to fellow team members.

Technological Environment

Speech-language pathologists use a wide variety of technology in their work. Computers and Internet communication tools are a ubiquitous part of speech-language pathology work. In addition, speech-language pathologists generally learn how to use and teach sign language and assistive technological devices, such as hearing aids and computer touch screens.

EDUCATION, TRAINING, AND ADVANCEMENT

High School/Secondary

High school students interested in pursuing the profession of speech-language pathology in the future should develop good study habits. High school level coursework in biology, psychology, anatomy, sociology, and mathematics will prepare students for college- and masters-level studies. Students interested in the speech-language pathology field will benefit from seeking internships or part-time work with speech pathologists or people who have speech-related problems.

Suggested High School Subjects
- Biology
- Chemistry
- Child Growth & Development
- College Preparatory
- English
- Literature
- Physiology
- Science
- Speech

Famous First

The first television series to depict someone stuttering was the 1976 series I, Claudius, about the Roman Emperor Claudius. To avoid the stigma surrounding stuttering, Claudius's family kept him out of the public eye until his coronation, at the age of 49, in 41 AD. The first major motion picture to deal with the same subject was *The King's Speech* in 2010, which focused on the British regent George VI. In both cases the main subjects learn how to stop stuttering and communicate normally.

CLAUDIUS DISCOVERED BY THE PRÆTORIAN GUARD AND HAILED AS EMPEROR.

College/Postsecondary

Postsecondary students interested in pursuing training in speech-language pathology should complete coursework in speech studies, if offered by their school, as well as courses on biology, psychology, anatomy, sociology, and mathematics. Postsecondary students interested in attending graduate school in speech-language pathology will benefit from seeking internships or work with speech pathologists or people who have speech-related problems. Membership in the National Student Speech Language Hearing Association (NSSLHA) may provide networking opportunities and connections. Prior to graduating, college students interested in joining the speech-language pathology profession should apply to graduate school in speech-pathology or secure related work, such as speech-therapy assistant or speech-research assistant.

Related College Majors
- Audiology/Hearing Sciences
- Communication Disorders, General
- Education of the Speech Impaired
- Speech & Rhetorical Studies
- Speech Pathology & Audiology
- Speech-Language Pathology

Adult Job Seekers

Adult job seekers in the field of speech-language pathology have generally completed master's- or doctoral-level training in speech pathology from an accredited university, as well as earned necessary professional certification and licensure. Speech-language pathologists seeking employment will benefit from the networking opportunities, job workshops, and job lists offered by professional speech pathology associations such as American Speech-Language-Hearing Association (ASHA).

Professional Certification and Licensure

Speech-language pathologists are required to have earned a professional certification prior to beginning professional practice. The leading speech-language pathology certification is the Certificate of Clinical Competence (CCC) awarded by the American Speech-Language-Hearing Association. The CCC is awarded in speech-language pathology (CCC-SLP) and audiology (CCC-A). The CCC application process involves the passing of an examination as well as the submission of official transcript and clinical fellowship evaluation. Consult credible professional associations within your field and follow professional debate as to the relevancy and value of any certification program.

Additional Requirements

Individuals who find satisfaction, success, and job-security as speech-language pathologists will be knowledgeable about the profession's requirements, responsibilities, and opportunities. Successful speech-language pathologists engage in ongoing professional development. Speech-language pathologists must have high levels of integrity and ethics, as they work with confidential and personal patient information. Membership in professional speech-language pathology associations is encouraged among junior and senior speech-language pathologists as a means of building status within a professional community and networking.

Fun Fact

The Centers for Disease Control estimate the lifetime costs for all people with hearing loss born in the year 2000 will total $2.1 billion, resulting mostly from lost wages due to inability or limited ability to work.

Source: CDC and The American Speech-Language-Hearing Association

EARNINGS AND ADVANCEMENT

Earnings depend on the type and geographic location of the employer and the individual's ability, experience and education. Median annual earnings of speech-language pathologists were $70,810 in 2013. The lowest ten percent earned less than $44,860, and the highest ten percent earned more than $109,800.

Speech-language pathologists usually receive paid vacations, holidays, and sick days; life and health insurance; and retirement benefits. These are usually paid by the employer.

Metropolitan Areas with the Highest Employment Level in this Occupation

Metropolitan area	Employment[1]	Employment per thousand jobs	Hourly mean wage
Chicago-Joliet-Naperville, IL	4,900	1.32	$37.93
New York-White Plains-Wayne, NY-NJ	4,780	0.91	$42.71
Houston-Sugar Land-Baytown, TX	2,670	0.97	$34.98
Dallas-Plano-Irving, TX	2,490	1.16	$34.40
Los Angeles-Long Beach-Glendale, CA	2,140	0.54	$39.95
Nassau-Suffolk, NY	2,100	1.70	$42.52
Boston-Cambridge-Quincy, MA	1,780	1.02	$37.81
Minneapolis-St. Paul-Bloomington, MN-WI	1,710	0.95	$35.61
St. Louis, MO-IL	1,660	1.28	$34.50
Edison-New Brunswick, NJ	1,500	1.53	$42.13

[1] Does not include self-employed. Source: Bureau of Labor Statistics

EMPLOYMENT AND OUTLOOK

There were approximately 134,000 speech-language pathologists employed nationally in 2012. About one-half were employed in preschools, elementary and secondary schools or colleges and universities. Others were in hospitals; physicians' offices; speech, language and hearing centers; home health agencies; child day care services and other facilities.

Employment of speech-language pathologists is expected to grow faster than the average for all occupations through the year 2022, which means employment is projected to increase 15 percent to 24 percent. This is due in part to growth in the population of middle age and older persons, when the possibility of speech, language, swallowing and hearing problems increases. Medical advances are also improving the survival rate of premature infants and trauma and stroke victims, who then need treatment. In addition, many states now require that all newborns be screened for hearing loss and receive appropriate early treatment.

Employment Trend, Projected 2010–20

Health Diagnosing and Treating Practitioners: 20%

Speech-Language Pathologists: 19%

Total, All Occupations: 11%

Note: "All Occupations" includes all occupations in the U.S. Economy. Source: U.S. Bureau of Labor Statistics, Employment Projections Program

Related Occupations
- Audiologist
- Special Education Teacher

Related Military Occupations
- Speech Therapist

Conversation With . . .
ANDREA RODRIGUEZ

Speech Language Pathology Researcher, Tallahassee, FL
Speech Pathologist, 8 years

1. What was your individual career path in terms of education/training, entry-level job, or other significant opportunity?

I first learned about speech-language pathology in a sociology course in my sophomore year of college. The professor was out sick, so her daughter, a speech-language pathologist (SLP), filled in for her. She told us that she helps kids improve their speech, language and social skills and that SLPs were in high demand. I was interested in finding a profession where I could make a difference and help kids with disabilities succeed, so I asked to shadow her for a day. After observing her work with children at an outpatient clinic, I was sure this was the field for me. She was helping kids learn skills such as using speech to communicate their wants and needs, and understand language in order to follow directions at home and school.

I got a bachelor's degree in communication disorders, which allowed me to work as a speech-language pathology assistant, but to be a licensed speech-language pathologist you need a master's degree. When I was getting my master's, I received specialized training in working with children from high poverty communities. I did internships in an elementary school, a private speech therapy clinic, a memory disorders clinic, and working with young children in an early intervention program. Then I worked for an early intervention agency serving infants and toddlers with communication delays and disorders. In early intervention, therapy is provided in a child's natural environment, so I spent most of my day conducting assessments and providing services either in people's homes or at preschools, working with the children, parents and teachers.

I decided to enroll in a doctoral program to learn more about research. I now have a doctorate in speech language pathology and work as a researcher at a university. My research focuses on how to use technology to improve speech and language outcomes for young children with communication disorders. I hope to eventually work as a college professor in speech-language pathology.

2. What are the most important skills and/or qualities for someone in your profession?

It's essential to have an authentic desire to help others. Excellent written and verbal communication skills are a big part of the job because SLPs frequently share information with clients, family members, doctors, teachers, reading specialists, and physical and occupational therapists. You have to have a love of learning – to do this job, you have to keep up with research on evidence-based practices as well as complete required continuing education. Efficient time management is another critical skill.

3. What do you wish you had known going into this profession?

I wish I had known how many ways there are to specialize. Most of us wear many hats and serve clients with a variety of disorders: expressive and receptive language, speech articulation, stuttering, autism, dyslexia, word finding difficulties, or motor-speech disorders. Some SLPS specialize in one of these areas, which can make them more marketable. I also wish I had known how important it is for SLPs to work as a team with other professionals, especially for clients with complex medical needs or significant impairments.

4. Are there many job opportunities in your profession? In what specific areas?

Speech-language pathologists are in high demand! The American Speech-Language Hearing Association cites several reasons for this, including an increase in older populations, increased rates of survival for premature babies and trauma/stroke victims, and an increase in students eligible for special education services (http://www.asha.org/Careers/Market-Trends/). Many school districts report a shortage of SLPs.

5. How do you see your profession changing in the next five years, what role will technology play in those changes, and what skills will be required?

Technology can play a huge role in speech and language assessment and intervention. Video/audio recording, in particular, has made documentation and feedback easier and more accessible. Many settings have moved to a 'paperless' system of record keeping. We're using mobile devices and apps to track clients' progress toward their communication goals. Telepractice, which uses technology to provide therapeutic services remotely—for instance, video conferencing in rural areas where the SLP isn't able to travel between schools—is on the rise. Using mobile device apps to support intervention service delivery is becoming more popular as well. For example, an individual with limited verbal ability can use an iPad to make requests via a picture board or to participate in conversations via text-to-speech applications.

6. What do you enjoy most about your job? What do you enjoy least about your job?

Every day, I feel like I'm making a difference by helping young children with communication disorders participate more fully in their typical activities. I also love that each day is different!

As with many professions, paperwork is a necessary part of the job, but it's a lot less fun than the rest of my workday!

7. Can you suggest a valuable "try this" for students considering a career in your profession?

See if you can shadow an SLP for a day. The American Speech-Language-Hearing Association website (http://www.asha.org/) is a great resource. The Careers section has good information about planning your education, salary data, etc. Look for speech-language pathology blogs. Many are geared toward parents and professionals.

SELECTED SCHOOLS

Many colleges and universities have bachelor's degree programs related to, or focusing on, speech-language pathology. The student may also gain an initial grounding at a technical or community college. Consult with your school guidance counselor or research post-secondary programs in your area. Below are listed some of the more prominent schools in this field.

Northwestern University
633 Clark Street
Evanston, IL 60208
847.491.3741
www.northwestern.edu

Purdue University
610 Purdue Mall
West Lafayette, IN 47907
765.494.4600
www.purdue.edu

University of Arizona
Tucson, AZ 85721
520.621.2211
www.arizona.edu

University of Kansas
1450 Jayhawk Boulevard
Lawrence, KS 66045
785.864.2700
www.ku.edu

University of Iowa
Iowa City, IA 52242
319.335.3500
www.uiowa.edu

University of Pittsburgh
4200 Fifth Avenue
Pittsburgh, PA 15260
412.624.4141
www.pitt.**edu**

University of Texas, Austin
Austin, TX 78712
512.471.3434
www.utexas.edu

University of Washington
Seattle, Washington
206.543.2100
www.washington.edu

University of Wisconsin
Madison, WI 53706
608.263.2400
www.wisc.edu

Vanderbilt University
2201 West End Avenue
Nashville, TN 37235
615.322.7311
www.vanderbilt.edu

MORE INFORMATION

American Cleft Palate-Craniofacial Association
1504 E. Franklin Street, Suite 102
Chapel Hill, NC 27514
919.933.9044
www.cleftline.org

American Speech-Language-Hearing Association
2200 Research Boulevard
Rockville, MD 20850-3289
800.638.8255
www.asha.org

National Student Speech Language Hearing Association
2200 Research Boulevard, #322
Rockville, MD 20850
www.nsslha.org

Simone Isadora Flynn/Editor

Substance Abuse Counselor

Snapshot

Career Cluster: Human Services

Interests: Counseling, psychology, sociology, crisis intervention, leading workshops

Earnings (Yearly Average): $38,620

Employment & Outlook: Faster Than Average Growth Expected

OVERVIEW

Sphere of Work

Substance abuse counselors treat people with drug and alcohol addictions. Operating within a subfield of the social work profession, substance abuse counselors are often identified under the broader heading of "addiction professionals," and as such, they may also deal with issues like gambling problems and eating disorders. Substance abuse counselors help addicts and at-risk individuals to find substance abuse treatment and rehabilitation resources, develop new coping strategies, and resolve

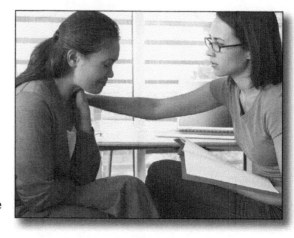

personal and interpersonal problems and conflicts. They work with individual clients to lessen the impact, and in some cases resolve, their dependency and its consequences, such as unemployment, disease, homelessness, abuse, and broken families. Substance abuse counselors also engage in advocacy, education, and outreach efforts to individuals, families, and communities affected by substance abuse and addiction.

Work Environment

Substance abuse counselors spend their workdays seeing clients in a variety of settings, including offices, mental health agencies, residential facilities, homeless shelters, prisons, hospitals, detoxification facilities, and substance abuse clinics. Substance abuse counselors may have a fixed office where they see clients, or they may spend a good deal of time on the road, traveling to meet with clients and their families. Given the diverse demands of the substance abuse or addiction profession, substance abuse counselors may need to work days, evenings, weekends, or on-call hours to meet client or caseload needs.

Profile

Working Conditions: Work Indoors
Physical Strength: Light Work
Education Needs: Bachelor's Degree
Licensure/Certification: Required
Physical Abilities Not Required: No Heavy Labor
Opportunities For Experience: Internship, Apprenticeship, Military Service, Volunteer Work, Part-Time Work
Holland Interest Score*: SEC

* See Appendix A

Occupation Interest

Individuals drawn to the substance abuse counseling profession tend to be intelligent and socially conscious people who are able to quickly assess clients' situations and help them find resources for solving their personal problems. Individuals who train as substance abuse counselors also receive related training in behavioral disorder counseling. Those who succeed in substance abuse counseling display traits such as leadership, understanding of human behavior, initiative, project management, and concern for individuals and society. Substance abuse counselors should be comfortable interacting with the wide range of people who suffer from addiction and substance abuse, including those from diverse cultural, social, and educational backgrounds.

A Day in the Life—Duties and Responsibilities

The daily occupational duties and responsibilities of substance abuse counselors vary by job specialization and employer. Areas of specialization include drug and alcohol dependency, eating disorders, gambling disorders, family counseling, adolescent counseling and treatment, assessment and evaluation, education and outreach, and legal advocacy. Potential daily duties and responsibilities include the following: completing client intake interviews for drug rehabilitation or residential facilities; conducting background interviews with clients to record information on client health, family, education, work history, drug history, and personal goals; working with a treatment team to develop personalized treatment plans for clients; and providing counseling and workshops on topics such as ending addiction, healthy body image, and alternative coping methods.

Substance abuse counselors may also offer clients crisis counseling, assistance maintaining or rebuilding family relationships, help with welfare, childcare, and employment applications, and basic instruction in practical life skills such as cooking, cleaning, and shopping. They may help clients arrange transportation and housing and refer them to community services or agencies. Counselors also participate in client team meetings and provide client updates to supervisors and families. Other duties include leading workshops for clients in residential facilities; visiting housebound clients; providing student workshops on drug and alcohol addiction; performing court-ordered in-home visits to record information on client home size, cleanliness, and number of inhabitants.

In addition to the range of responsibilities described above, all substance abuse counselors are responsible for completing patient charts and required documentation on a daily basis.

Duties and Responsibilities

- Interviewing prospective clients
- Greeting new clients and establishing a person-to-person relationship
- Conducting individual and group counseling sessions
- Providing individual guidance and encouragement
- Presenting a variety of educational material to clients
- Assisting clients in seeking and obtaining employment
- Doing follow-up work on discharged clients to determine the effectiveness of the treatment
- Counseling and conducting educational classes for families
- Conducting daily client counts as scheduled
- Reading the notes made by other clinical staff members

WORK ENVIRONMENT

Relevant Skills and Abilities

Communication Skills
- Persuading others
- Speaking effectively
- Writing concisely

Interpersonal/Social Skills
- Cooperating with others
- Providing support to others
- Teaching
- Working as a member of a team

Organization & Management Skills
- Coordinating tasks
- Making decisions
- Managing people/groups
- Paying attention to and handling details

Physical Environment

A substance abuse counselor's immediate physical environment varies based on their caseload and specialization. Social workers spend their workdays seeing clients in a wide variety of settings including offices, mental health agencies, residential facilities, homeless shelters, prisons, hospitals, detoxification facilities, and substance abuse clinics.

Human Environment

Substance abuse counselors work with a wide variety of people and should be comfortable meeting

- Performing duties that change frequently

Research & Planning Skills
- Analyzing information
- Solving problems

Technical Skills
- Working with data or numbers

with colleagues, staff, people suffering the extreme physical effects of end-stage addiction, teenagers, incarcerated people, homeless people, and families.

Technological Environment

Substance abuse counselors use computers, cell-phones, and Internet communication tools to perform their job. For instance, substance abuse counselors must be comfortable using computers to access client records, cars to drive to client homes and facilities, and cell phones to ensure availability during on-call hours.

EDUCATION, TRAINING, AND ADVANCEMENT

High School/Secondary

High school students interested in pursuing a career in substance abuse counseling should prepare themselves by developing good study habits. High school-level study of sociology, psychology, biology, education, and foreign languages will provide a strong foundation for college-level work in counseling and social work. Due to the diversity of substance abuse specialties (including drug addiction, gambling addiction, and eating disorders), high school students interested in this career path will benefit from seeking internships or part-time work that will expose them to diverse groups of people with a variety of social needs.

Suggested High School Subjects
- Audio-Visual
- Biology
- Chemistry
- College Preparatory
- English

- Foreign Languages
- Government
- Health Science Technology
- Psychology
- Social Studies
- Sociology
- Speech

Famous First

The first Twelve-Step rehabilitation program was created by Alcoholics Anonymous in New York City in 1935. The organization was founded by William "Bill W." Wilson and Dr. Robert H. Smith. It seeks to help alcoholics control their addiction through guided group discussion, reliance on a "higher power," and a step-by-step return to sobriety.

College/Postsecondary

Postsecondary students interested in becoming substance abuse counselors should pursue a bachelor's degree in counseling or social work. Coursework in counseling, crisis intervention, ethics, management, psychology, sociology, and foreign languages may also prove useful in their counseling practice. Postsecondary students can gain work experience and potential advantage in their future job searches by securing internships or part-time employment in public health agencies or with addiction treatment programs.

Related College Majors
- Alcohol/Drug Abuse Counseling
- Community Health Services

Adult Job Seekers

Adults seeking employment as substance abuse counselors should have a bachelor's degree. Many public health agencies and social service organizations require that counselors have bachelor's degrees (or higher), a second language proficiency, and substance abuse counselor certification. Adult job seekers should educate themselves about the educational and professional license requirements of their home states and the organizations where they seek employment. Adult job seekers will benefit from joining professional associations to help with networking and job searching. Professional counseling associations, such as the Association for Addiction Professionals, generally offer job-finding workshops and maintain lists and forums of available jobs.

Professional Certification and Licensure

Professional certification and licensure of substance abuse counselors is voluntary but recommended. The leading options for substance abuse counselor certification include the Licensed Clinical Alcohol and Drug Counselor (LCADC) or Certified Alcohol and Drug Counselor (CADC). These state-based certifications are offered through state certification boards for addiction professionals. Additionally, many states offer their own levels of voluntary certification. Consult credible professional associations within your field and follow professional debate as to the relevancy and value of any certification program.

Additional Requirements

High levels of integrity and personal and professional ethics are required of substance abuse counselors, as they must interact with addicts and at-risk people and have access to client personal information. Membership in professional associations is encouraged among junior and senior substance abuse counselors as a means of building status within the professional community and networking. Successful substance abuse counselors engage in ongoing professional development.

Fun Fact

In the late 1800s, Sigmund Freud and some American doctors believed they had found a good way to treat alcoholism and morphine addiction: prescribe cocaine. There were also a number of bottled home cures available at the time, most of which contained alcohol, opium, morphine, cannabis or cocaine.

Source: www.aa-semi.org/archive/45/The-Evolution-of-the-Dark-World-of-Alcoholism

EARNINGS AND ADVANCEMENT

Earnings of substance abuse counselors depend on the employer and the individual's education, experience, length of employment and job responsibilities. Median annual earnings of substance abuse counselors were $38,620 in 2013. The lowest ten percent earned less than $25,200, and the highest ten percent earned more than $60,160.

Substance abuse counselors may receive paid vacations, holidays, and sick days; life and health insurance; and retirement benefits. These are usually paid by the employer.

Metropolitan Areas with the Highest Employment Level in this Occupation

Metropolitan area	Employment[1]	Employment per thousand jobs	Hourly mean wage
New York-White Plains-Wayne, NY-NJ	4,620	0.88	$22.72
Philadelphia, PA	3,200	1.74	$19.13
Los Angeles-Long Beach-Glendale, CA	2,500	0.63	$16.33
Pittsburgh, PA	1,720	1.52	$17.80
Chicago-Joliet-Naperville, IL	1,410	0.38	$18.45
Phoenix-Mesa-Glendale, AZ	1,320	0.74	$19.83
Baltimore-Towson, MD	1,250	0.97	$19.76
Boston-Cambridge-Quincy, MA	1,160	0.66	$21.46
Washington-Arlington-Alexandria, DC-VA-MD-WV	1,050	0.44	$25.22
Riverside-San Bernardino-Ontario, CA	1,030	0.86	$18.43

[1] Does not include self-employed. Source: Bureau of Labor Statistics

EMPLOYMENT AND OUTLOOK

Substance abuse counselors held about 90,000 jobs nationally in 2012. Employment is expected to grow much faster than the average for all occupations through the year 2022, which means employment is projected to increase 30 percent or more. This is due in part to employers who are offering assistance programs that provide drug and alcohol abuse counseling for their employees. In addition, drug offenders are increasingly being sent to treatment programs rather than to jail. These jobs are not attractive to everyone due to the emotionally draining work and relatively low pay, so qualified applicants should not have difficulty finding work.

Employment Trend, Projected 2010–20

Substance Abuse Counselors: 31%

Community and Social Service Occupations: 17%

Total, All Occupations: 11%

Note: "All Occupations" includes all occupations in the U.S. Economy. Source: U.S. Bureau of Labor Statistics, Employment Projections Program

Related Occupations
- Case Worker/Social Services Assistant
- Marriage Counselor
- Psychologist
- Religious Worker
- School Counselor
- Social Worker
- Vocational Rehabilitation Counselor

Related Military Occupations
- Caseworker & Counselor

Conversation With . . .
SARAH FOWLER

Substance Abuse Counselor
Private Practice, Scarborough, Maine
Licensed Clinical Professional Counselor (LCPC)
2 years

1. What was your individual career path in terms of education/training, entry-level job, or other significant opportunity?

I have my bachelor's degree in human resources management. After I graduated, I did recruitment at rehabilitation hospitals, mainly recruiting physical therapists, occupational therapists and physicians. Then I stayed home for many, many years raising my five children. One day, I was having coffee with a friend who was a licensed psychologist. It was like a role reversal: he was pouring his heart out to me. He said, "You are such a good listener. You should think about counseling." I started dabbling in graduate courses in clinical mental health and substance abuse. I got a master's degree in clinical mental health counseling and a Certificate for Alcohol & Drug Counseling (CADC) just because I knew there was going to be such a need for it with people I saw in my practice. The co-occurring stuff is just everywhere. Plus, I have personal experience with addiction and recovery within my family. I'm in private practice, and I also work part-time at a residential treatment facility for men who are very late-stage addicts.

2. What are the most important skills and/or qualities for someone in your profession?

It takes someone who is compassionate, someone who is really non-judgmental and a good listener. You have to be very open to what you're going to come across.

You have to understand the behaviors that come with addiction: the manipulation and lying and controlling. The longer you're in the profession, the better your BS detector is. But you have to see beyond that and understand that the behavior doesn't define who they are. There's so much shame around what they have done. Compassion, understand-ing and empathy are the big things.

I don't believe that personal experience with addiction is necessary, but that can be a really big sticking point for people getting treatment. Many people in the profession are in recovery themselves. You typically don't even have to have a college degree to get your addiction counseling certificate.

3. **What do you wish you had known going into this profession?**

This is such a petty thing, but the insurance issue is so enormous. I really had no clue there were so many stipulations as to what could and could not be covered in terms of my services.

4. **Are there many job opportunities in your profession? In what specific areas?**

There are job opportunities for people who have alcohol and drug counseling experience, but I would not say they're abundant. Pretty much everybody that I know is in pri-vate practice, because of the flexibility and pay. Pay is not great in facilities and agen-cies.

5. **How do you see your profession changing in the next five years? What role will technology play in those changes, and what skills will be required?**

I see the profession growing because the prescription drug addiction problem is growing, as is the heroin epidemic. As far as technology goes, people are utilizing it for things such as online counseling and webinars and group therapy.

I see less drug maintenance programs, such as methadone, in the future. Insurance regulations are changing and no longer covering it. It's also a question of treatment philosophy. There's a large group in favor of it, but there's an equally large, if not larger, group that thinks it's outdated and that there are less addictive drugs someone could go on. Suboxone is gaining in popularity. You can wean off it a lot faster than methadone.

The general public is getting to be a little more understanding toward addicts, but people are judged harshly for being drug addicts and alcoholics. It is really stigmatized, unfortunately. But it's getting better and the modalities for treatment are getting more effective.

6. **What do you enjoy most about your job? What do you enjoy least about your job?**

What I enjoy most is working with people who are struggling every day, and seeing the changes in them. Week after week they physically look better and feel emotionally better. Their heads start getting clearer. It's a learning process for them of a whole new world beyond their substance. It's really a transformation. For me, it's a gift to see some-one want something so badly and work so hard for it.

Then there are the very, very sad cases, where clients die either by their own hand or an overdose. Seeing someone leave treatment and you know they're in a bad place and a week later they're no longer on this earth; seeing the hopelessness of someone prior to that happening—that's hard to take.

7. **Can you suggest a valuable "try this" for students considering a career in your profession?**

Go to any open Al Anon, Alcoholics Anonymous (AA) or Narcotics Anonymous (NA) meeting. You don't have to say anything, you don't have to do anything. Just listen. That's a wonderful learning experience.

SELECTED SCHOOLS

Many colleges and universities have bachelor's degree programs in subjects related to counseling and social work. The student may also gain an initial grounding at a technical or community college. Consult with your school guidance counselor or research area post-secondary programs to find the right fit for you. For a list of top schools in the field of social work, see the entry "Social Worker" in the present volume. For a list of top schools in the field of rehabilitation counseling, see the entry "Rehabilitation Counselor" in this volume.

MORE INFORMATION

Addiction Technology Transfer Center Network
www.addictioncareers.org

American Academy of Health Care Providers in the Addictive Disorders
314 W. Superior Street, Suite 508
Duluth, MN 55802
218.727.3940
www.americanacademy.org

American Counseling Association
5999 Stevenson Avenue
Alexandria, VA 22304
800.347.6647
www.counseling.org

American Group Psychotherapy Association
25 E. 21st Street, 6th Floor
New York, NY 10010
877.668.2472
www.agpa.org

Association for Addiction Professionals
1001 N. Fairfax Street, Suite 201
Alexandria, VA 22314
800.548.0497
www.naadac.org

National Board for Certified Counselors
3 Terrace Way, Suite D
Greensboro, NC 27403-3660
336.547.0607
www.nbcc.org

Simone Isadora Flynn/Editor

Vocational Rehabilitation Counselor

Snapshot

Career Cluster: Human Services
Interests: Social work, advocacy for people with disabilities, counseling
Earnings (Yearly Average): $32,230
Employment & Outlook: Faster Than Average Growth Expected

OVERVIEW

Sphere of Work

Vocational rehabilitation counselors, also called rehabilitation or employment specialists, provide job training and job placement support services to individuals with disabilities. In general, vocational rehabilitation counselors work to help their clients become more independent, employable, and productive. Vocational rehabilitation counselors support clients living with disabilities

present since birth or impairments resulting from illness, disease, addiction, accident, or injury. For instance, individuals experiencing joblessness or employment challenges related to HIV/AIDS, schizophrenia, or intellectual disability may be eligible for vocational rehabilitation counseling as required under the Rehabilitation Act of 1973 and the Americans with Disabilities Act (ADA). Veterans are eligible for vocational rehabilitation counseling through the Vocational Rehabilitation and Employment (VR&E) VetSuccess Program. Vocational rehabilitation counselors offer a range of counseling services, which includes overseeing job training and vocational counseling programs and creating rehabilitation plans for clients.

Work Environment

Vocational rehabilitation counselors spend their workdays seeing clients in a wide variety of settings, including public or private rehabilitation facilities, mental health facilities, schools and universities, insurance companies, job training and placement programs, prisons and hospitals, and private counseling practices. Vocational rehabilitation counselors may have an office or may travel to see clients. Given the diverse demands of rehabilitative counseling, vocational rehabilitation counselors may need to work days, evenings, weekends, and on-call hours to meet client or caseload needs.

Profile

Working Conditions: Work Indoors
Physical Strength: Light Work
Education Needs: Bachelor's Degree, Master's Degree
Licensure/Certification: Required
Physical Abilities Not Required: No Heavy Labor
Opportunities For Experience: Internship, Volunteer Work, Part-Time Work
Holland Interest Score*: SEC

* See Appendix A

Occupation Interest

Individuals drawn to the vocational rehabilitation counseling profession tend to be intelligent and socially conscious and able to quickly assess situations, find resources, demonstrate caring, and solve problems. Successful vocational rehabilitation counselors display traits such as time management, knowledge of human behavior, initiative, and concern for individuals and society. Vocational rehabilitation counselors should find satisfaction in spending time with a wide range of people, including those considered at-risk and those from diverse cultural, social, and educational backgrounds.

A Day in the Life—Duties and Responsibilities

A vocational rehabilitation counselor's daily duties and responsibilities are determined by the individual's job specifications and work environment.

A vocational rehabilitation counselor works closely with clients to assess needs and provide assistance. He or she first must undertake client evaluations to assess mental, academic, and vocational aptitude, work history, and job readiness. The vocational rehabilitation counselor then works with clients to develop counseling goals and objectives into individualized plans. The counselor recommends jobs, professions, and training programs to clients, oversees client job search efforts, and assists clients with employment applications. Vocational rehabilitation counselors and clients also collaborate to resolve work-related problems such as transportation difficulties or scheduling conflicts.

Vocational rehabilitation counselors may provide additional services depending on client needs. These can include helping clients attain assistive devices, such as wheelchairs, that enable independence and employment, organizing on-site job training for clients, leading workshops for clients in residential facilities, and helping clients arrange transportation to and from work.

A vocational rehabilitation counselor acts a liaison between clients, community agencies, and employers. Vocational rehabilitation counselors must participate in client team meetings and provide client updates to supervisors and client families. They also develop connections and familiarity with local employment agencies, and refer clients to community services or agencies as needed. They may also negotiate job modifications for their clients.

All vocational rehabilitation counselors ensure that rehabilitation programs meet the requirements of the Rehabilitation Act and the Americans with Disabilities Act. In addition, all vocational rehabilitation counselors are responsible for completing client records and required documentation, such as referral forms and insurance forms, on a daily basis.

Duties and Responsibilities

- Determining the eligibility of persons who apply for vocational rehabilitation services
- Interviewing clients regarding their abilities, interests and the nature and extent of their disability
- Reviewing clients' work histories
- Arranging for personality, vocational and medical evaluations
- Evaluating test results and conferring with clients on a plan of action for employment
- Arranging for medical treatment, training and other services
- Meeting with medical and other personnel to discuss progress and problems of clients
- Collecting educational and occupational information
- Assisting clients in job search, placement and adjustment

WORK ENVIRONMENT

Physical Environment

The immediate physical environment of vocational rehabilitation counselors vary based on their caseload and specialization. Vocational rehabilitation counselors spend their workdays seeing clients in a wide variety of settings, including public or private rehabilitation facilities, mental health facilities, schools and universities, insurance companies, job training and placement programs, prisons and hospitals, and private counseling practices.

Human Environment

Vocational rehabilitation counselors interact with many people and should be comfortable meeting with colleagues, staff, client families, incarcerated people, and people living with mental, physical, and emotional disabilities.

Relevant Skills and Abilities

Communication Skills

- Expressing thoughts and ideas
- Speaking effectively
- Writing concisely

Interpersonal/Social Skills

- Being able to remain calm
- Cooperating with others
- Working as a member of a team

Organization & Management Skills

- Coordinating tasks
- Handling challenging situations
- Making decisions
- Managing people/groups

Research & Planning Skills

- Using logical reasoning

Technological Environment

Vocational rehabilitation counselors use computers and telecommunication tools to perform their job. Vocational rehabilitation counselors must be comfortable using computers to access client records. They may drive cars to client homes and facilities and use cell phones to ensure availability during on-call hours.

EDUCATION, TRAINING, AND ADVANCEMENT

High School/Secondary

High school students interested in pursuing a career as a vocational rehabilitation counselor should prepare themselves by developing good study habits. Coursework in foreign languages, public safety, sociology, psychology, and education can provide a strong foundation for college-level work in the vocational rehabilitation counseling field. Due to the range of vocational rehabilitation counseling job requirements, high school students interested in this career path may benefit from seeking internships or part-time work that expose the students to diverse groups of people and social needs.

Suggested High School Subjects
- Arts
- College Preparatory
- English
- Health Science Technology
- Psychology
- Social Studies
- Sociology
- Speech

Famous First

The first vocational guidance chair at a college was established at Indiana University, Bloomington, pictured, in 1914. The first professor was Robert Josselyn Leonard, who served from June 1914 to April 1918. Today, one can still study vocational rehabilitation at IU's School of Social Work.

College/Postsecondary

Postsecondary students interested in becoming vocational rehabilitation counselors should work towards an undergraduate degree in counseling or a related field such as psychology or social work. Coursework in education, public safety, and foreign languages may also prove useful in their future work. Postsecondary students can gain work experience and potential advantage in their future job searches by securing internships or part-time employment in job training programs or with individuals or groups living with physical, mental, or emotional disabilities. Interested college students should consider applying to master's degree programs in the field.

Related College Majors
- Community Health Services
- Counselor Education/Student Counseling & Guidance Services
- Psychology, General

Adult Job Seekers

Adults seeking employment as vocational rehabilitation counselors should have earned, at a minimum, an undergraduate degree in counseling or similar subject such as psychology or social work. Employers are increasingly requiring vocational rehabilitation counselors to hold a master's degree in rehabilitation counseling or a similar field and obtain national certification. Adult job seekers should educate themselves about the educational and professional license requirements of their home states and the organizations where they seek employment.

Adult job seekers may benefit from joining professional associations to help with networking and job searching. Professional rehabilitation counseling associations, such as the National Employment Counseling Association (NECA) and the Commission on Rehabilitation Counselor Certification (CRCC), generally offer career workshops and maintain lists and forums of available jobs.

Professional Certification and Licensure

Vocational rehabilitation counselors seeking professional certification, as a condition of employment or professional development, may choose to pursue the Certified Rehabilitation Counselor (CRC) designation. The CRC designation is awarded through the CRCC. Candidates must have a master's of rehabilitation counseling or related field, demonstrate work experience, and complete a written national examination. Certified rehabilitation counselors are eligible to apply for state mental health counselor licenses. Specific licensure requirements, including additional coursework, continuing professional education, and supervision, vary by state.

Additional Requirements

Individuals who find satisfaction, success, and job security as vocational rehabilitation counselors will be knowledgeable about the profession's requirements, responsibilities, and opportunities. Successful vocational rehabilitation counselors engage in ongoing professional development. Vocational rehabilitation counselors must have high levels of integrity and ethics as they interact with vulnerable people and have access to personal information. Membership in professional counseling associations is encouraged among all vocational rehabilitation counselors as a means of building status in a professional community and networking.

EARNINGS AND ADVANCEMENT

Earnings of vocational rehabilitation counselors vary among private and public agencies and depend on the geographic location of the employer and the individual's level of education and experience. Median annual earnings of vocational rehabilitation counselors were $32,230 in 2013. The lowest ten percent earned less than $21,170, and the highest ten percent earned more than $60,020.

Vocational rehabilitation counselors may receive paid vacations, holidays, and sick days; life and health insurance; and retirement benefits. These are usually paid by the employer.

Metropolitan Areas with the Highest
Employment Level in this Occupation

Metropolitan area	Employment[1]	Employment per thousand jobs	Hourly mean wage
New York-White Plains-Wayne, NY-NJ	4,940	0.94	$19.25
Los Angeles-Long Beach-Glendale, CA	3,140	0.79	$16.43
Seattle-Bellevue-Everett, WA	2,620	1.81	$22.15
Philadelphia, PA	2,440	1.33	$19.24
Boston-Cambridge-Quincy, MA	2,190	1.25	$20.35
Minneapolis-St. Paul-Bloomington, MN-WI	1,810	1.01	$20.16
Chicago-Joliet-Naperville, IL	1,760	0.48	$18.49
Riverside-San Bernardino-Ontario, CA	1,600	1.33	$15.41
Washington-Arlington-Alexandria, DC-VA-MD-WV	1,590	0.67	$20.62
Tacoma, WA	1,370	5.24	$16.93

[1] Does not include self-employed. Source: Bureau of Labor Statistics

EMPLOYMENT AND OUTLOOK

Nationally, there were approximately 120,000 vocational rehabilitation counselors employed in 2012. Employment is expected to grow faster than the average for all occupations through the year 2022, which means employment is projected to increase up to 20 percent. The number of people who need vocational rehabilitation counseling will rise as advances in medical technology continue to save lives that only a few years ago would have been lost.

Employment Trend, Projected 2010–20

Rehabilitation Counselors: 20%

Community and Social Service Occupations: 17%

Total, All Occupations: 11%

Note: "All Occupations" includes all occupations in the U.S. Economy. Source: U.S. Bureau of Labor Statistics, Employment Projections Program

Related Occupations
- Career/Technology Education Teacher
- Employment Specialist
- Marriage Counselor
- Rehabilitation Counselor
- School Counselor
- Social Worker
- Special Education Teacher
- Substance Abuse Counselor

Conversation With . . .
MARYLEE LOSARDO

Vocational Rehabilitation & Employment Specialist
Edith Nourse Rogers VA Medical Center, Bedford, MA
Vocational Rehabilitation Counselor, 7 years

1. What was your individual career path in terms of education/training, entry-level job, or other significant opportunity?

I got a bachelor's degree in psychology in 1994 and was hired by one of my professors to be project manager on a National Institute on Drug Abuse research project. Then I went to work doing research at the Veterans Health Administration Mental Illness Research, Education, and Clinical Center. After you do research for a while and you work with clinicians, you start to see that if you were a clinician, you could move a client forward and take more of an active role. You can't do that with research. So while working full time I went to school part time for my master's degree in Rehabilitation Counseling from the University of Massachusetts/Boston in 2009. I took the Certified Rehabilitation Counselor (CRC) exam and became licensed. Some public sector programs don't require a master's degree or CRC licensing, but they pay less and likely offer less autonomy and less diversity of tasks.

2. What are the most important skills and/or qualities for someone in your pro-fession?

One of the most important skills is something called "Reflective Listening"—

a counseling technique that summarizes to the client the stories they report, to help them gain insight. You will need fluency in one or more counseling methods geared to move clients along in a short amount of time, such as Motivational Interviewing or Cognitive Behavioral Therapy. Writing is important. You have to write Individualized Treatment Plans with realistic and measurable goals; clear, concise assessment reports and progress notes; and resumes and cover letters for clients. Organizational skills and computer literacy are a must.

3. What do you wish you had known going into this profession?

When I decided to do this, I considered the counseling and working with clients. I didn't think about the paperwork. I can only speak for the public sector, but there is an enormous amount required: assessments, treatment plans, reports measuring outcomes, correspondence for clients, etc. Because administrative tasks are so great, you often have to decide which clients' needs will be your priority. It can be frustrating.

I was familiar with the profession because of my previous work. However, some students – especially those coming to the master's program directly from undergraduate school– didn't understand that Rehabilitation Counseling involves vocational counseling and assisting clients so they can obtain employment. Their incorrect understanding was that rehabilitation counseling focused on occupational therapy, which rehabilitates clients who've experienced medical or mental health problems with living skills such as re-learning how to use eating utensils or go food shopping.

4. Are there many job opportunities in your profession? In what specific areas?

Rehabilitation counseling has a bright future. Federal and state governments continue to invest in vocational rehabilitation and employment services. Typical jobs in the public sector and within non-profit organizations are vocational rehabilitation counselors; assessment center staff who perform vocational testing; vocational case managers; and job developers who educate and form partnerships with employers.

In the private sector, most insurance companies employ a staff of Certified Rehabilitation Counselors to assess employees collecting Workers' Compensation or short-term disability insurance; to refer employees injured on the job to training programs; to investigate employees who are on leave for on-the-job injuries and are suspected of fraud in collecting Workers' Comp or other disability insurance; and to provide court testimony against employees accused of fraud.

5. How do you see your profession changing in the next five years? What role will technology play in those changes, and what skills will be required?

Public sector programs for people with disabilities will grow, and, unfortunately, programs for veterans will, too, because of continued military conflicts. Vocational counseling is a relatively new field, with much research now underway. People with disabilities need better self-esteem and confidence, because they tend to internalize their limitations. The field is really coming up with methods to help them see their strengths and to find the job they want and not just any job.

Technology will continue to provide accommodations that help people with disabilities improve their job skills, thus increasing their marketability.

6. What do you enjoy most about your job? What do you enjoy least?

Because a person's identity is often tied to having a job, helping someone find and keep a job is enormously rewarding. The journey to this outcome is also rewarding, as you help the client identify strengths and relate more to those strengths than to his or her limitations. What I least enjoy is the paperwork, though it is necessary for funding and clinical accountability.

7. **Can you suggest a valuable "try this" for students considering a career in your profession?**

Career centers are located in major municipalities in every state and are open to the public. You can drop in and utilize any of the services: vocational testing, meetings with a rehabilitation counselor, or workshops.

SELECTED SCHOOLS

Many colleges and universities have bachelor's degree programs in subjects related to vocational rehabilitation counseling. The student may also gain an initial grounding at a technical or community college. Consult with your school guidance counselor or research area post-secondary programs to find the right fit for you. For a list of top schools related to this field, see the entries "Occupational Therapist," "Rehabilitation Counselor," "Social Worker," and "Special Education Teacher" in the present volume.

MORE INFORMATION

American Rehabilitation Counseling Association
www.arcaweb.org

American Counseling Association
5999 Stevenson Avenue
Alexandria, VA 22304
800.347.6647
www.counseling.org

Commission on Rehabilitation Counselor Certification
1699 E. Woodfield Road, Suite 300
Schaumburg, IL 60173
847.944.1325
www.crccertification.com

National Board for Certified Counselors
3 Terrace Way, Suite D
Greensboro, NC 27403-3660
336.547.0607
www.nbcc.org

National Organization for Human Services
1600 Sarno Road, Suite 16
Melbourne, FL 32935
www.nationalhumanservices.org

Simone Isadora Flynn/Editor

What Are Your Career Interests?

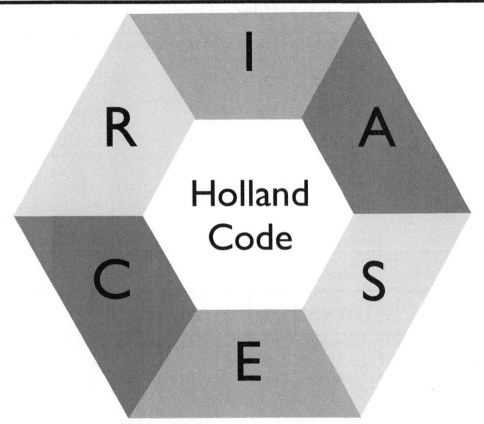

This is based on Dr. John Holland's theory that people and work environments can be loosely classified into six different groups. Each of the letters above corresponds to one of the six groups described in the following pages.

Different people's personalities may find different environments more to their liking. While you may have some interests in and similarities to several of the six groups, you may be attracted primarily to two or three of the areas. These two or three letters are your "Holland Code." For example, with a code of "RES" you would most resemble the Realistic type, somewhat less resemble the Enterprising type, and resemble the Social type even less. The types that are not in your code are the types you resemble least of all.

Most people, and most jobs, are best represented by some combination of two or three of the Holland interest areas. In addition, most people are most satisfied if there is some degree of fit between their personality and their work environment.

The rest of the pages in this booklet further explain each type and provide some examples of career possibilities, areas of study at MU, and co-curricular activities for each code. To take a more in-depth look at your Holland Code, take a self-assessment such as the SDS, Discover, or a card sort at the MU Career Center with a Career Specialist.

Realistic *(Doers)*

People who have athletic ability, prefer to work with objects, machines, tools, plants or animals, or to be outdoors.

Are you?
practical
straightforward/frank
mechanically inclined
stable
concrete
reserved
self-controlled

independent
ambitious
systematic

Can you?
fix electrical things
solve electrical problems
pitch a tent
play a sport
read a blueprint
plant a garden
operate tools and machine

Like to?
tinker with machines/vehicles
work outdoors
be physically active
use your hands
build things
tend/train animals
work on electronic equipment

Career Possibilities
(Holland Code):

Air Traffic Controller (SER)
Archaeologist (IRE)
Athletic Trainer (SRE)
Cartographer (IRE)
Commercial Airline Pilot (RIE)
Commercial Drafter (IRE)
Corrections Officer (SER)

Dental Technician (REI)
Farm Manager (ESR)
Fish and Game Warden (RES)
Floral Designer (RAE)
Forester (RIS)
Geodetic Surveyor (IRE)
Industrial Arts Teacher (IER)

Laboratory Technician (RIE)
Landscape Architect (AIR)
Mechanical Engineer (RIS)
Optician (REI)
Petroleum Geologist (RIE)
Police Officer (SER)
Practical Nurse (SER)

Property Manager (ESR)
Recreation Manager (SER)
Service Manager (ERS)
Software Technician (RCI)
Ultrasound Technologist (RSI)
Vocational Rehabilitation
    Consultant (ESR)

Investigative *(Thinkers)*

People who like to observe, learn, investigate, analyze, evaluate, or solve problems.

Are you?
inquisitive
analytical
scientific
observant/precise
scholarly
cautious

intellectually self-confident
Independent
logical
complex
Curious

Can you?
think abstractly
solve math problems
understand scientific theories
do complex calculations
use a microscope or computer
interpret formulas

Like to?
explore a variety of ideas
work independently
perform lab experiments
deal with abstractions
do research
be challenged

Career Possibilities
(Holland Code):

Actuary (ISE)
Agronomist (IRS)
Anesthesiologist (IRS)
Anthropologist (IRE)
Archaeologist (IRE)
Biochemist (IRS)
Biologist (ISR)

Chemical Engineer (IRE)
Chemist (IRE)
Computer Systems Analyst (IER)
Dentist (ISR)
Ecologist (IRE)
Economist (IAS)
Electrical Engineer (IRE)

Geologist (IRE)
Horticulturist (IRS)
Mathematician (IER)
Medical Technologist (ISA)
Meteorologist (IRS)
Nurse Practitioner (ISA)
Pharmacist (IES)

Physician, General Practice (ISE)
Psychologist (IES)
Research Analyst (IRC)
Statistician (IRE)
Surgeon (IRA)
Technical Writer (IRS)
Veterinarian (IRS)

Artistic *(Creators)*

People who have artistic, innovating, or intuitional abilities and like to work in unstructured situations using their imagination and creativity.

Are you?		Can you?	Like to?
creative	original	sketch, draw, paint	attend concerts, theatre, art
imaginative	introspective	play a musical instrument	exhibits
innovative	impulsive	write stories, poetry, music	read fiction, plays, and poetry
unconventional	sensitive	sing, act, dance	work on crafts
emotional	courageous	design fashions or interiors	take photography
independent	complicated		express yourself creatively
Expressive	idealistic		deal with ambiguous ideas
	nonconforming		

Career Possibilities
(Holland Code):

Actor (AES)	Copy Writer (ASI)	Interior Designer (AES)	Medical Illustrator (AIE)
Advertising Art Director (AES)	Dance Instructor (AER)	Intelligence Research Specialist	Museum Curator (AES)
Advertising Manager (ASE)	Drama Coach (ASE)	(AEI)	Music Teacher (ASI)
Architect (AIR)	English Teacher (ASE)	Journalist/Reporter (ASE)	Photographer (AES)
Art Teacher (ASE)	Entertainer/Performer (AES)	Landscape Architect (AIR)	Writer (ASI)
Artist (ASI)	Fashion Illustrator (ASR)	Librarian (SAI)	Graphic Designer (AES)

Social *(Helpers)*

People who like to work with people to enlighten, inform, help, train, or cure them, or are skilled with words.

Are you?		Can you?	Like to?
friendly	cooperative	teach/train others	work in groups
helpful	generous	express yourself clearly	help people with problems
idealistic	responsible	lead a group discussion	do volunteer work
insightful	forgiving	mediate disputes	work with young people
outgoing	patient	plan and supervise an activity	serve others
understanding	kind	cooperate well with others	

Career Possibilities
(Holland Code):

City Manager (SEC)	Historian (SEI)	Park Naturalist (SEI)	Teacher (SAE)
Clinical Dietitian (SIE)	Hospital Administrator (SER)	Physical Therapist (SIE)	Social Worker (SEA)
College/University Faculty (SEI)	Psychologist (SEI)	Police Officer (SER)	Speech Pathologist (SAI)
Community Org. Director	Insurance Claims Examiner	Probation and Parole Officer	Vocational-Rehab. Counselor
(SEA)	(SIE)	(SEC)	(SEC)
Consumer Affairs Director	Librarian (SAI)	Real Estate Appraiser (SCE)	Volunteer Services Director
(SER)Counselor/Therapist	Medical Assistant (SCR)	Recreation Director (SER)	(SEC)
(SAE)	Minister/Priest/Rabbi (SAI)	Registered Nurse (SIA)	
	Paralegal (SCE)		

Enterprising *(Persuaders)*

People who like to work with people, influencing, persuading, leading or managing for organizational goals or economic gain.

Are you?		Can you?	Like to?
self-confident	ambitious	initiate projects	make decisions
assertive	agreeable	convince people to do things	be elected to office
persuasive	talkative	your way	start your own business
energetic	extroverted	sell things	campaign politically
adventurous	spontaneous	give talks or speeches	meet important people
popular	optimistic	organize activities	have power or status
		lead a group	
		persuade others	

**Career Possibilities
(Holland Code):**

Advertising Executive (ESA)	Credit Analyst (EAS)	Foreign Service Officer (ESA)	Politician (ESA)
Advertising Sales Rep (ESR)	Customer Service Manager	Funeral Director (ESR)	Public Relations Rep (EAS)
Banker/Financial Planner (ESR)	(ESA)	Insurance Manager (ESC)	Retail Store Manager (ESR)
Branch Manager (ESA)	Education & Training Manager	Interpreter (ESA)	Sales Manager (ESA)
Business Manager (ESC)	(EIS)	Lawyer/Attorney (ESA)	Sales Representative (ERS)
Buyer (ESA)	Emergency Medical Technician	Lobbyist (ESA)	Social Service Director (ESA)
Chamber of Commerce Exec	(ESI)	Office Manager (ESR)	Stockbroker (ESI)
(ESA)	Entrepreneur (ESA)	Personnel Recruiter (ESR)	Tax Accountant (ECS)

Conventional *(Organizers)*

People who like to work with data, have clerical or numerical ability, carry out tasks in detail, or follow through on others' instructions.

Are you?		Can you?	Like to?
well-organized	practical	work well within a system	follow clearly defined
accurate	thrifty	do a lot of paper work in a short	procedures
numerically inclined	systematic	time	use data processing equipment
methodical	structured	keep accurate records	work with numbers
conscientious	polite	use a computer terminal	type or take shorthand
efficient	ambitious	write effective business letters	be responsible for details
conforming	obedient		collect or organize things
	persistent		

**Career Possibilities
(Holland Code):**

Abstractor (CSI)	Claims Adjuster (SEC)	Elementary School Teacher	Medical Records Technician
Accountant (CSE)	Computer Operator (CSR)	(SEC)	(CSE)
Administrative Assistant (ESC)	Congressional-District Aide (CES)	Financial Analyst (CSI)	Museum Registrar (CSE)
Budget Analyst (CER)	Cost Accountant (CES)	Insurance Manager (ESC)	Paralegal (SCE)
Business Manager (ESC)	Court Reporter (CSE)	Insurance Underwriter (CSE)	Safety Inspector (RCS)
Business Programmer (CRI)	Credit Manager (ESC)	Internal Auditor (ICR)	Tax Accountant (ECS)
Business Teacher (CSE)	Customs Inspector (CEI)	Kindergarten Teacher (ESC)	Tax Consultant (CES)
Catalog Librarian (CSE)	Editorial Assistant (CSI)		Travel Agent (ECS)

BIBLIOGRAPHY

General

Bauman, Sheri. *Essential Topics for the Helping Professional.* Boston: Pearson, 2007.

Burger, William R. *Human Services in Contemporary America.* Belmont, CA: Brooks/Cole, 2014.

Corey, Marianne Schneider. *Becoming a Helper.* Belmont, CA: Brooks/Cole, 2009.

Emener, William G., et al. *A Guidebook to Human Service Professions: Helping College Students Explore Opportunities in the Human Services Field.* Springfield, IL: Charles C. Thomas Publishing, 2009.

Moffat, Colleen Teixeira. *Helping Those in Need: Human Services Workers.* Washington, DC: Bureau of Labor Statistics, 2011.

Watkins, Marie. *Service Learning: From Classroom to Community to Career.* St. Paul, MN: Jist Publishing, 2005.

Woodside, Marianne R., and Tricia McClam. *An Introduction to Human Service.* Belmont, CA: Brooks/Cole, 2011.

Counseling, Advising & Therapy

Capuzzi, David, and Mark D. Stauffer. *Career Counseling: Foundations, Perspectives, Applications.* New York: Routledge, 2011.

Davis, William B. *An Introduction to Music Therapy.* Silver Spring, MD: American Music Therapy Association, 2008.

Edmunds, Vesta. *Playlady: Tales of a Recreational Therapist.* Parker, CO: Outskirts Press, 2011.

Hodges, Shannon. *101 Careers in Counseling.* New York: Springer Publishing, 2012.

Hughey, Kenneth F. *A Handbook of Career Advising.* San Francisco: Jossey-Bass, 2011.

Junge, Maxine Borowsky. *The Modern History of Art Therapy in the United States.* Springfield, IL: Charles C. Thomas Publishing, 2010.

Knox, David, and Caroline Schacht. *Choices in Relationships: An Introduction to Marriage and the Family.* Boston: Cengage Learning, 2015.

Koscinski, Cara. *The Pocket Occupational Therapist for Families of Children with Special Needs.* London: Jessica Kingsley, 2012.

Kottler, Jeffrey A. *Introduction to Counseling: Voices from the Field.* Belmont, CA: Brooks/Cole, 2010.

Kuther, Tara L., and Roberto D. Morgan. *Careers in Psychology: Opportunities in a Changing World.* Belmont, CA: Wadsworth Cengage, 2013.

Levine, Adele. *Run, Don't Walk: The Curious and Chaotic Life of a Physical Therapist inside Walter Reed Army Medical Center.* New York: Penguin, 2014.

Lusted, Marcia Amidon. *Jump-Starting a Career in Physical Therapy and Rehabilitation.* New York: Rosen Publishingm, 2014.

Parker, Randall, and Jeanne Boland Patterson. *Rehabilitation Counseling: Basics and Beyond.* Austin, TX: ProEd, 2012.

Patterson, JoEllen, et al. *Essential Skills in Family Therapy.* New York: Guilford Press, 2009.

Social Work, Community Service & Education

Bransford, Cassandra L. *Becoming a Caseworker.* New York: Learning Express, 2008.

Cramer, Susan. *Confessions of a Special Ed Teacher.* Victoria, BC, Canada: Trafford Publishing, 2006.

Davis, Tamara E. *Exploring School Counseling.* Stamford, CT: Cengage, 2015.

Djiegielewski, Sophia. *The Changing Face of Health Care Social Work: Opportunities and Challenges.* New York: Springer Publishing, 2013.

Doelling, Carol Nesslein. *Social Work Career Development: A Handbook for Job Hunting and Career Planning.* Washington, DC: National Association of Social Workers, 2005.

Gordon, Howard R.D. *The History and Growth of Career and Technical Education in America.* Long Grove, IL: Waveland Press, 2014.

Grobman, Linda May. *Days in the Lives of Social Workers: 58 Professionals Tell Real-Live Stories from Social Work Practice.* Harrisburg, PA: White Hat Communications, 2011.

Guilford, Arthur M., et al. *The Speech-Language Pathologist: From Novice to Expert.* Boston: Pearson, 2006.

Moore, Barbara J., and Judy J. Montgomery. *Making a Difference for America's Children: Speech-Language Pathologists in Public Schools.* Austin, TX: ProEd, 2008.

Ritter, Jessica A. *101 Careers in Social Work.* New York: Springer Publishing, 2014.

Turnbull, Ann, et al. *Exceptional Lives: Special Education in Today's Schools.* Upper Saddle River, NJ: Pearson Educational, 2010.

INDEX